# COMING OF AGE

## Volume 3, The Best of ACLD

D1621784

# COMING

Co-edited b

an

# OF AGE

elected Papers from the 18th International Conference of the
ssociation for Children and Adults with Learning Disabilities

## VILLIAM M. CRUICKSHANK, Ph.D.

*chool of Public Health*
*niversity of Michigan*

## ANET W. LERNER, Ph.D.

*chool of Education*
*ortheastern Illinois University*

SYRACUSE UNIVERSITY PRESS     1982

Copyright © 1982 by SYRACUSE UUNIVERSITY PRESS
Syracuse, New York 13210

All Rights Reserved

*First Edition*

**Library of Congress Cataloging in Publication Data**
Main entry under title:

Coming of age.

    (The Best of ACLD; v. 3)
    Includes bibliographies.
    1. Learning disabilities—Congresses. I. Cruick-
shank, William M. II. Lerner, Janet W. III. Associa-
tion for Children and Adults with Learning Disabilities.
IV. Series.
LC4704.C64     371.9          81-21404
ISBN 0-8156-2258-9 (pbk.)      AACR2

*Manufactured in the United States of America*

# CONTENTS

PREFACE                                                                    ix

PRESSING CURRENT ISSUES                                                     1

1 IEPs—Gateway for Legal Entanglement                                      3
  *Eugene T. Connors and Richard S. Vacca*

2 Growing Up Creatively Gifted with Learning Disabilities                  24
  *E. Paul Torrance*

3 Specific Preschool Medical Findings which Predict Specific
  Learning Outcomes                                                        36
  *Lawrence C. Hartlage and Cathy F. Telzrow*

FAMILY AND SOCIAL SYSTEMS

4 Making Practice Perfect: Pointers for Parents                            47
  *Theresa E. Laurie and George E. Maitland*

5 Effectiveness of Paraprofessional Counselors in a Structured
  Self-Concept Enhancement Program for Children with
  Learning Problems                                                        61
  *Mervyn Skuy and Michael Marcus*

6 A Structural Family Therapy Approach to the Treatment of
  Learning Disabilities                                                    72
  *Ann M. Varna Garis and Laura Green*

DEVELOPMENT OF MENTAL PROCESSING
  ABILITIES

7 Serial Order Behavior: To Understand It a Scientific
  Challenge, an Educational Necessity                                      87
  *William H. Gaddes*

8 Visual Selective Attention and the Learning Disabled Child:
  Implications for Word Recognition Abilities                              108
  *Ronald W. Schworm*

9 The Development of Memory Skills in Children: Portraying
  Learning Disabilities in Terms of Strategy and Knowledge
  Deficiencies                                                             127
  *John W. Hagen and Craig R. Barclay*

10 Social Perceptual Processing Problems: Psychological and
   Educational Considerations                                    142
   *Paul J. Gerber*

NEW STRATEGIES FOR TEACHING READING

11 Phonemic Analysis in the Teaching of Reading                  155
   *Lise Wallach and Michael A. Wallach*

12 Error Monitoring: A Learning Strategy for Improving Adoles-
   cent Academic Performance                                     170
   *Jean B. Schumaker, Donald D. Deshler, Gordon R. Alley,
   Michael M. Warner, Frances L. Clark, Sue Nolan*

13 Improving Reading Skills through Auricular
   Reading Techniques                                            184
   *Joseph A. Bukovec*

14 Teaching and Assessing Disabled Readers:
   A Strategies Approach                                         192
   *N. Dworkin, Y. Dworkin, R. Huhn*

WRITTEN LANGUAGE PROBLEMS

15 Written Language Disorders in Learning Disabled Students: A
   Preliminary Report                                            211
   *Susan A. Vogel and Mary Ross Moran*

16 Write Right or Left: A Practical Approach to Handwriting      226
   *Rosa A. Hagin and Archie A. Silver*

# CONTRIBUTORS

Gordon R. Alley, Ph.D., University of Kansas Institute for Research in Learning Disabilities, Lawrence, Kansas

Craig R. Barclay, Ph.D., University of Michigan, Ann Arbor, Michigan

Joseph A. Bukovec, Ed.D., The Communications Workshop, Teaneck, New Jersey

Frances L. Clark, Ph.D., University of Kansas Institute for Research in Learning Disabilities, Lawrence, Kansas

Eugene T. Connors, Ph.D., James Madison University, Harrisonburg, Virginia

Donald D. Deshler, Ph.D., University of Kansas Institute for Research in Learning Disabilities, Lawrence, Kansas

Nancy Dworkin, Ph.D., Center for Unique Learners, Rockville, Maryland

Y. Dworkin, Ph.D., Center for Unique Learners, Rockville, Maryland

William H. Gaddes, Ph.D., University of Victoria, British Columbia, Canada

Ann M. Varna Garis, Ph.D., Delta Consultants, Inc., and University of Rhode Island, Providence, Rhode Island

Paul J. Gerber, Ph.D., University of New Orleans, New Orleans, Louisiana

Laura A. Green, University of Rhode Island, Providence, Rhode Island

John W. Hagen, Ph.D., University of Michigan, Ann Arbor, Michigan

Rosa A. Hagin, Ph.D., New York University Medical Center, New York, New York

Lawrence C. Hartlage, Ph.D., Medical College of Georgia, Augusta, Georgia

Ralph H. Huhn, Ph.D., McNeese State University, Lake Charles, Louisiana

Theresa E. Laurie, Ed.D., University of Pittsburgh, Pittsburgh, Pennsylvania

George E. Maitland, Ed.D., University of Pittsburgh, Pittsburgh, Pennsylvania

Michael Marcus, University of the Witwatersrand, Johannesburg, Republic of South Africa

Mary Ross Moran, Ph.D., University of Kansas Institute for Research in Learning Disabilities, Lawrence, Kansas

Sue Nolan, University of Kansas Institute for Research in Learning Disabilities, Lawrence, Kansas

Jean B. Schumaker, Ph.D., University of Kansas Institute for Research in Learning Disabilities, Lawrence, Kansas

Ronald W. Schworm, Ph.D., University of Rochester Medical Center, Rochester, New York

Archie A. Silver, M.D., Medical School, University of South Florida, Tampa, Florida

Mervyn Skuy, Ph.D., University of the Witwatersrand, Johannesburg, Republic of South Africa

Cathy F. Telzrow, Cuyahoga Special Education Service Center, Cleveland, Ohio

E. Paul Torrance, Ph.D., University of Georgia, Athens, Georgia

Richard S. Vacca, Ph.D., Virginia Commonwealth University, Richmond, Virginia

Susan A. Vogel, Ph.D., Barat College, Lake Forest, Illinois

Lise Wallach, Ph.D., Duke University, Durham, North Carolina

Michael A. Wallach, Ph.D., Duke University, Durham, North Carolina

# PREFACE

$C$ OMING OF AGE is the theme of the third volume of the series *The Best of ACLD*. The papers in this volume were selected from presentations made at the eighteenth annual conference of ACLD, the Association for Children and Adults with Learning Disabilities, held in Atlanta in 1981. The title, *Coming of Age*, is a recognition that the field of learning disabilities, after eighteen years of conferences sponsored by ACLD, has reached the age of maturity. Having passed through its years of creation and formation, the field of learning disabilities is now emerging as an established and recognized field of study. During the eighteen years of ACLD conferences, the field of learning disabilities evolved through years of creation, years of rapid growth, years of uncertainty and testing, years of new and widening relationships, and finally, in 1981, the field reached the stage of an established and proven discipline.

From the hundreds of presentations at the Atlanta conference and the 87 written papers submitted to the ACLD Editorial Committee, sixteen papers were selected by the Committee for inclusion in this volume. Each written submission was read and judged by four members of the Editorial Board. The objective of the editors was to capture the best of the 1981 ACLD conference in a permanent written document. The papers represent the multidisciplinary nature of the field of learning disabilities and include the fields of education, medicine, psychology, parenting, law, and counseling. They represent new areas of interest and research, and they represent continuing areas of interest and concern.

The book is organized into five sections. Part I, *Pressing Current Issues,* contains three papers on subjects under current debate and discussion. These include an analysis of the legal implications of the IEP, a subject which affects every teacher, child, and parent (Connors and Vacca); a discussion of the segment of the learning disabled population who are gifted (Torrance); and a study of the medical factors in pre-schoolers that predict later learning achievement (Hartlage and Telzrow).

Part II, *Family and Social Systems,* contains three papers that focus on the child's primary social milieu. These include suggestions for

ix

parents (Laurie and Maitland); paraprofessional counseling (Skuy and Marcus); and family therapy treatment (Garis and Green).

The subject of Part III, *Development of Mental Processing Abilities,* is one that has been hotly debated and of increasing interest throughout the past eighteen years. Updated research on the subject includes serial order behavior (Gaddes); visual selective attention (Schworm); the development of memory skills (Hagen and Barclay); and social perceptual processing problems (Gerber).

The most prevalent academic problem noted in students with learning disabilities is difficulties in reading. Part IV, *New Strategies for Teaching Reading,* includes five papers on new methods for teaching reading. They include a comprehensive paper on phonemic analysis (Wallach and Wallach); error monitoring (Deschler et al.); auricular reading techniques (Bukovec); and strategies approach for teaching and assessing disabled readers (Dworkn, Dworkin, Huhn).

Part V consists of two papers on *Written Language Problems,* a much neglected area of academic difficulty. These include a report on written language disorders in college students (Vogel and Moran), and a study of handwriting (Hagin and Silver).

The ACLD Editorial Board for the 1981 ACLD conference welcomes you to this collection. We hope this volume plays its part in helping the field of learning disabilities "come of age."

For the Editorial Committee
for Selected Papers
Janet W. Lerner, Ph.D.

Archie A. Silver, M.D.
University of South Florida
  College of Medicine
Tampa, Florida

Sara G. Tarver, Ph.D.
University of Wisconsin
Madison, Wisconsin

Eli Tash
Co-Chairman
St. Francis Children's Activity
  and Achievement Center
Milwaukee, Wisconsin

Joseph Torgesen, Ph.D.
Florida State University
Tallahassee, Florida

Joseph Wepman, Ph.D.
Palm Springs, California

Elisabeth H. Wiig, Ph.D.
Boston University
Boston, Massachusetts

Beatrice Wong, Ph.D.
Simon Fraser University
Burnaby, British Columbia

COMING OF AGE

Volume 3, The Best of ACLD

# PRESSING CURRENT ISSUES

# IEPs—Gateway for Legal Entanglement

*Eugene T. Connors and Richard S. Vacca*

S o FAR, the federal courts have been unwilling to hold that the *Education for All Handicapped Children Act* (PL 94-142) itself creates (either directly or by implication) a private remedy for damages. In a recent federal district court case from Connecticut involving a learning disabled child, monetary damages were sought for alleged negligence of a public school board "in failing to implement an appropriate educational program earlier in the plaintiff's school career." [1] The case, *Laughran v. Flanders,* offers an excellent example of a dominant judicial attitude that sees issues of teaching methodology and educational priorities (upon which a claim for damages in educational negligence hinges) as not appropriate for resolution by courts of law.

In granting defendant school board's motion to dismiss the damage claim, Chief Judge Clarie offered the following rationale:

> The thrust of federal legislation in the field of special education has been to provide financial assistance to the states, in their effort to provide each one of their handicapped children with an appropriate education. Recognition of a private remedy for damages, as alleged in this instance, would compel these programs to shift their focus. Insulation of school officials from liability would take precedence over the implementation of innovative educational reforms. Recognition of the plaintiff's claim would cause special education programs to suffer, since administrators would balk at implementing new curricula and techniques for fear of exposing themselves to liability should these innovations fail. [2]

Unlike the consistent judicial attitude expressed in litigation involving PL 94-142, some cases concerning Section 504 of the Rehabilitation Act of 1973 [3] have received a different judicial review and interpretation. *Hairston v. Drosick* offers an excellent example. [4]

A case from West Virginia involving a spina bifida child, *Hairston* firmly established precedent that Section 504 creates a private cause of action, enforceable through federal court action. The decision offers a precedent to apply in future, similar situations involving Section 504 and possibly where provisions of PL 94-142 are, at the same time, also before the court. The United States Supreme Court's recent decision (April 29, 1981) in *Camenish v. University of Texas,* 616 F(2d) 127 (Fifth Circuit, 1980; cert. granted November 3, 1980) may serve to clarify some issues on point.[5]

It is our opinion that the individualized educational program mandate (IEP) represents the one facet of PL 94-142 most conducive to legal challenge for remedy in the form of money damages. To put it another way, the IEP offers judges some manageable factors to analyze as they attempt to fix blame and seek out fault, if in fact they exist.

## PL 94-142

The passage of PL 94-142 (The Education for All Handicapped Children Act)[6] in 1975 ushered in an era of educational rights for handicapped pupils. In spite of this Act's complexity and vastness, most handicapped pupils with learning disabilities and their parents or guardians are primarily concerned with five particular sections: The section dealing with free access to education (1219.4), the section describing what types of conditions constitutes a handicap (121a.5), the section detailing "appropriate education" as a function of an Individualized Education Program (IEP) (121a.340), the section regarding placing students in the Least Restrictive Environment (121a.550), and the section detailing "appropriate education" as a function of an Individualized Education Program (IEP) (121a.340), the section regarding placing students in the Least Restrictive Environment (121a.550), and the section outlining the pupils' and parents' due process rights (121a.568) all constitute the body of the substantive issues found in PL 94-142.

As expected, PL 94-142 has fostered numerous law suits throughout the country. In examining this litigation, it quickly becomes clear that some of these suits concern the development, implementation, and evaluation of the IEP. Indeed, the IEP is the heart of PL 94-142 because it controls not only the goals of the educational program, but also the educational setting (Least Restrictive Environment), the length of the school year, instructional methodology, future evaluations, determination of acceptable progress, and matters concerning discipline and extra-curricular activities. The IEP is, essentially, the hub of the special education wheel. All aspects of the special education program are derived from this written document.

### The Individualized Education Program (IEP)

The particulars of the Individualized Education Program are detailed in sections 121a.340–121a.360 of PL 94-142. The section begins with a short description of what an IEP is: "As used in this part, the term "individualized education program" means a written statement for a handicapped child that is developed and implemented in accordance with §121a.341–121a.349."[7] The act states that each local school division is responsible for initiating and conducting "meetings for the purpose of developing, reviewing, and revising a handicapped child's individualized education program."[8] These meetings are of extremely great importance in the IEP process. At these meetings, evaluation data are reviewed and an appropriate educational program is created for each handicapped child. Section 121a.344 even lists those individuals who are *required* to attend *each* IEP meeting.

(a) General. The public agency shall insure that each meeting includes the following participants:
   (1) A representative of the public agency, other than the child's teacher, who is qualified to provide, or supervise the provision of, special education.
   (2) The child's teacher.
   (3) One or both of the child's parents, subject to §121a.345.
   (4) The child, where appropriate.
   (5) Other individuals at the discretion of the parent or agency.
(b) Evaluation personnel. For a handicapped child who has been evaluated for the first time, the public agency shall insure:
   (1) That a member of the evaluation team participates in the meeting; or
   (2) That the representative of the public agency, the child's teacher, or some other person is present at the meeting, who is knowledgeable about the evaluation procedures used with the child and is familiar with the results of the evaluation.[9]

It is both interesting and important to note that Part 2 of 121a.344 requires the child's teacher (or teachers) to attend the IEP meetings. Frequently a classroom teacher is told that a handicapped child will be in her regular classroom and she must accept him. This situation, while failing to meet the letter of the law as required in 121a.344(2), is also creating a grave educational disservice. How can the classroom teacher hope to make progress toward the IEP goals if she is not an active participant in the development of these goals? Also, the child with a learning disability might be arbitrarily placed (by an administrator or special education supervisor) in a classroom which will be too restrictive or not restrictive enough. Such children frequently require much specialized instruction requiring close (if not constant) supervision and instruction by the teacher. How can a handicapped child receive this attention in a class with 30 other pupils? PL 94-142 requires an appropriate educational program leading towards progress in as normal a setting as possible (least restrictive environment). However, the key is educational progress—not the setting. The entire purpose of PL 94-142 is to provide the needed educational benefits to handicapped children not to sacrifice educational quality for the administrative advantages of mainstreaming. If the classroom teacher is actively involved in the development of the IEP, she may be able to provide the needed input regarding whether or not her classroom situation is appropriate for various handicapping conditions. This involvement of each of the child's perspective teachers helps inappropriate mainstreaming from taking place. An improperly mainstreamed child will make little educational progress himself and may detract from the education of others.

### Content of the IEP

What kinds of things should an IEP contain? Again, the law specifically states the content of IEPs:

The individualized education program for each child must include:
(a) A statement of the child's present levels of educational performance;
(b) A statement of annual goals, including short term instructional objectives;
(c) A statement of the specific education and related services to be provided to the child, and the extent to which the child will be able to participate in regular educational programs;
(d) The projected dates for initiation of services and the anticipated duration of the services; and
(e) Appropriate objective criteria and evaluation procedures and schedules for determining, on at least an annual basis, whether the short term instructional objectives are being achieved.[10]

The IEP should be a written document signed by all the child's prospective teachers, the parents of the child, and any educational specialists and administrators involved in the development process.

The child's progress (or lack of) should be reviewed at least annually and adjustments made to the IEP to provide for increased or furtherance of the educational goals.

## Court Cases Concerning the IEP

There have been several interesting court cases relating to IEP content. A recent case from Pennsylvania addresses the issue of the 180 day school year in relationship to the child's need for year long education. *Battle v. Commonwealth of Pennsylvania* (629 F.2d 269, Third Circuit Court of Appeals, 1980) concerns an administrative policy that "sets a limit of 180 days of instruction per year for all children, handicapped or not."[11] Patricia Sue Battle and four other handicapped children challenged that administrative policy as being in violation of PL 94-142. The federal court immediately identified the critical issue, stating: "At the center of the controversy in this case is the definition of 'free appropriate public education.' ... The individualized educational program (IEP) provides the vehicle for giving content to be required 'free appropriate public education.'"[12]

While the Third Circuit Court recognized the difficulties involved in appropriating funds beyond the 180 day period, the court chose to let the states solve their own policy and fiscal problems. "Moreover, the decision to establish certain educational objectives for handicapped children profoundly impacts on the allocation of scarce educational resources. ... We believe that these hard decisions of resource allocation, like the determinations of educational policy are best left to the states."[13]

The court then overturned the lower District Court's decision upholding the 180-day policy: "We therefore conclude that inflexible application of a 180 day maximum prevents the proper formulation of appropriate educational goals for individual members of the plaintiff class."[14] Therefore, the United States Third Circuit Court of Appeals ruled that if educational need requires more than the standard 180 day education, the public schools must meet that need regardless of local or state policies concerning a 180-day limit.

A 1979 decision by the Second Circuit Court of Appeals upheld the right of certain mentally handicapped children to be mainstreamed into the regular classroom in spite of the fact that such children were carriers of Serum Hepatitis B.[15] The court found that while this stream of hepatitis could be transmitted by "blood to blood" routes (needle injections, transfusions, et cetera), there was no conclusive evidence that the disease is transmitted orally through saliva. Therefore, the court upheld a lower court's decision requiring the mainstreaming of these children. However, the Second Circuit Court did provide a means for the school board to reopen the case if medical evidence becomes more supportive of their position at some future date. "In short, the strength of the appellees' evidence and the weakness of the Board's evidence abundantly support the conclusions reached by the District Court. We wish to make clear, however, that the Board is not barred from returning to court at some point in the future when it has evidence to support any plan appropriate to a significant health risk."[16]

Another New York case addressed the concern of providing a sign language interpreter for a deaf student in her regular classroom. *Rowley v. Board of Education of the Hendrick Hudson Central School District, Westchester County* was decided by a United States District Court in New York in 1980.[17] Amy Rowley sued the school district alleging that their failure to provide her with a sign language interpreter was in violation of PL 94-142.

This case is significant because the school division attempted to rebut the student's allegations by presenting evidence that Amy was achieving (academically) at a higher rate than her normal peers without the sign language interpreter. The school district claimed that Amy's education was, therefore, completely adequate. However, the district court found the school district's claims erroneous:

> While this evidence firmly establishes that Amy is receiving an "adequate" education, since she performs better than the average child in her class and is advancing easily from grade to grade, it establishes little more. I find that the defendants' emphasis on her academic performance and the suggestion that only academic deficiencies would induce them to provide Amy with an interpreter are based on an erroneous understanding of the law; they ignore the importance of comparing her performance to that of nonhandicapped students of similar intellectual calibre and comparable energy and initiative.[18]

Indeed, the court pondered what attainment Amy might achieve if her energies were totally diverted to academics and not split between academics and the translating process.

> Moreover, Amy's IQ does not represent the full measure of her potential. The defendants' own witnesses have established by their testimony Amy's energy, her intellectual assertiveness, her rapport with her teachers and her interest in learning. These are significant elements of her potential which are not reflected in her IQ but which are undoubtedly reflected in the results of her achievement and other academic tests. It seems likely that much of Amy's energy and eagerness goes into compensating for her handicap; if the need for some of that compensation were eliminated, her energy could be channeled into greater excellence in classroom performance. It is unfair and contrary to law to penalize her for her own efforts and those of her parents, by which she has remained slightly above the median of her class.[19]

Consequently, the district court ruled that the school division must provide a sign language interpreter in Amy's classes. The school division appealed this decision to the Second Circuit Court of Appeals. That court upheld the decision of the district court. However, the appellate court did seek to restrict the applicability of its decision. "Finally, we wish to emphasize the narrow scope of our holding. This is not a class action in which the needs of all deaf school children are being determined. The evidence upon which our decision rests is concerned with a particular child, her atypical family, her upbringing and training since birth, and her classroom experience. In short, our decision is limited to the unique facts of this case and is not intended as authority beyond this case."[20]

### Student Discipline

The IEP is even involved to a certain degree in the discipline of students. A 1979 case from Indiana addresses the issue of whether or not suspending a pupil for misbehaving violates PL 94-142.[21]

Dennis Doe was attending a school for the mildly mentally handicapped. In October, 1978, the principal of the school suspended Dennis for disciplinary reasons and recommended expulsion. A hearing was held and Dennis was subsequently expelled. Dennis' mother brought suit against the school division alleging violation of PL 94-142.

The United States District Court Judge for the Northern District Indiana ruled that PL 94-142 prohibits the expelling (long-term suspension) of a pupil if the disruption arises from the pupil's handicapping conditions. "A school which accepts Handicapped Act funds is prohibited from expelling students whose handicaps cause them to be disruptive. The school is allowed only to transfer the disruptive student to an appropriate, more restrictive, environment."[22] However, the court did uphold the right of the school to suspend or expel pupils whose disruptive behavior is totally unrelated to their handicap. "But the Handicapped Act does not prohibit all expulsions of disruptive handicapped children. It only prohibits the expulsion of handicapped children who are disruptive because of their handicap. Whether a handicapped child may be expelled because of his disruptive behavior depends on the reason for the disruptive behavior. If the reason is the handicap, the child cannot be expelled. If the reason is not the handicap, the child can be expelled."[23] Pupils whose handicap contributes to their misbehavior may not be suspended or expelled. However, such pupils may be placed in a more restrictive setting. This disciplinary process should be included in each child's IEP so that all parties concerned understand the appropriate disciplinary procedures. The court in *Doe v. Koger* also stated that if a more restrictive environment was not possible, then suspension or expulsion may be allowed. "A disruptive handicapped student may be suspended only if the school is unable to immediately place the student in an appropriate, more restrictive, environment."[24]

Another case which dealt with the same issue is *Stuart v. Nappi*.[25] In this case, Kathy Stuart, a high school pupil, was gradually being mainstreamed into regular classes. As this process took place, her misbehavior increased. Finally, after Kathy partook in a school-wide disturbance, she was suspended for ten days and recommended for expulsion for the balance of the school year.

The pupil sued in federal district court to keep the school board from conducting an expulsion hearing. The court ruled that Kathy could not be expelled for its educational deprivement could cause irreparable injury. "The expulsion of handicapped children not only jeopardizes their right to an education in the least restrictive environment, but is inconsistent with the procedures established by the Handicapped Act for changing the placement of disruptive children. The Handicapped Act prescribes a procedure whereby disruptive children are transferred to more restrictive placements when their behavior significantly impairs the education of other children."[26] The court did, however, state that handicapped pupils are not immune from disciplinary measures and suggested some guidelines in dealing with them.

> It is important that the parameters of this decision are clear. This Court is cognizant of the need for school officials to be vested with ample authority and discretion. It is, therefore, with great reluctance that the Court has intervened in the disciplinary process of Danbury High School. However, this intervention is of a limited nature. Handicapped children are either immune from a school's disciplinary process nor are they entitled to participate in programs when their behavior impairs the education of other children in the program. First, school authorities can take swift disciplinary measures, such as suspension, against disruptive handicapped children. Secondly, a PPT (Planning and Placement Team) can request a change in the placement of handicapped children who have demonstrated that their present placement is inappropriate by disrupting the education of other children. The Handicapped Act thereby affords schools with both short-term and long-term methods of dealing with handicapped children who are behavioral problems.[27]

Therefore, in at least two cases dealing with the issue of discipline, the handicapped child's right to an education has been affirmed. Schools are prohibited from taking disciplinary measures against a handicapped pupil if the misbehavior is a result of the handicapping condition. However, schools do have the right to place the misbehaving pupil in a more restrictive setting. Of course, other disciplinary alternatives can be worked out between the educators and the parents during the IEP process.

### Extracurricular Activities

Do handicapped pupils have the right to participate in extracurricular activities? This question has been adjudicated by several courts in the United States recently. A typical result of such cases can be illustrated by *Doe v. Marshall*.[28] In this case, a handicap (severe psychiatric difficulties) caused John Doe to live with his grandparents rather than with his parents. Consequently, he transferred schools to the division in which his grandparents lived. In spite of the recommendation of John Doe's therapists that his participation in varsity football to be highly therapeutic in nature, the school refused to allow him to play football citing a Texas restriction regarding John Doe's legal residence. The pupil was qualified in all other respects to play varsity football.

John's parents filed suit against the school division asking the court to enjoin the school from blocking his participation. The U.S. District Court in Galveston ruled that making John ineligible to play football was in violation of PL 94-142.

> In treatment of emotionally disturbed adolescents, it is frequently necessary to have them removed from the home and placed in foster care in order to relieve acute symptoms of emotional illness. The policy allows no exceptions for this valid need as it relates to emotionally handicapped students. Frequently, this removal is done on an informal basis. Here, the family has moved carefully and deliberately and in accordance with the Texas Family Code to secure thier son's full legal rights.

> In addition, the transfer of (John) was done for therapeutic reasons, with full documentation of (John's) handicap and prescribed treatment. To make (John) ineligible because of his transfer is to make him ineligible because of his treatment for a handicap in violation of 29 U.S.C. 794 (the Handicap Act).[29]

Therefore, John was allowed to play football. Other similar cases establish handicapped pupils' rights to participate in extracurricular activities if they are qaulified to do so.[30] Under no circumstances can a pupil be discriminated against solely because of his or her handicap.[31]

## THE IEP AND ACCOUNTABILITY

The issue of accountability regarding the content of the IEP is a hotly contested one at the present time. Pl 94-142 addresses this issue in 121a.349:

> Each public agency must provide special education and related services to a handicapped child in accordance with an individualized education program. However, Part B of the Act does not require that any agency, teacher, or other person be held accountable if a child does not achieve the growth projected in the annual goals and objectives.
>
> (20 U.S.C. 1412(2)(B); 1414(a) (5), (6); Cong. Rec. at H 7152 (daily ed., July 21, 1975).)
>
> *Comment.* This section is intended to relieve concerns that the individualized education program constitutes a guarantee by the public agency and the teacher that a child will progress at a specified rate. However, this action does not relieve agencies and teachers from making good faith efforts to assist the child in achieving the objectives and goals listed in the individualized education program. Further, the section does not limit a parent's right to complain and ask for revisions of the child's program, or to invoke due process procedures, if the parent feels that these efforts are not being made.[32]

There are several very important statements in the above quote. Note that 121a.349 states "Part B of the Act *does not require* that any agency, teacher, or other person be held accountable if... "[33] The Act *does not state* that an agency or teacher *is not accountable*. It merely suggests that such agencies and personnel do not necessarily have to be accountable.

The ultimate status of the IEP has not been determined. However, several courts are viewing this written document as a legal contract as provided under state law. Remember, Section 121a.349 does not forbid the IEP from being viewed as a contract; it merely states that federal law does not require such an interpretation. A later section of this paper will address the issue of the contractual status of the IEP.

Generally, the recorded *causes of complaints* regarding individualized educational programs fall into seven distinct categories. These categories are generally stated as (1) improper committee composition, (2) improper development procedures followed, (3) timelines for development not observed, (4) required portions omitted, (5) included services not provided, (6) implementation delayed, and (7) included services not provided free.

Since the enactment of PL 94-142, the *sine qua non* role of the IEP has been consistently emphasized by courts of law. Recently, for example, the United States Court of Appeals for the Third Circuit rendered its decision in the *Battle* case (mentioned previously) which involved a class action challenge to a Pennsylvania statute which set as a limit 180 days of instruction per year for all children, handicapped or not.[34] In finding that statute incompatible with the federal act, the court depicted the IEP as the "heart" of the federal mandate to meet each child's *unique needs.* Said the Third Circuit Court:

> The IEP is the statutory vehicle for formulating the educational objectives and the educational program for each child. We consider it most persuasive that at this fundamental point in the educational decision making process, the statute requires consideration of each individual child. ... Moreover, as difficult as it is to define the scope of the "unique needs" which must be met by special education ... , there can be little doubt that by requiring attention to "unique needs," the Act demands that special education be tailored to the individual.[35]

Hayes and Higgins remind us that not only is the IEP the "cornerstone" of the law and the "management tool" for resources and goals, it is also "one way to document assurance of an appropriate education."[36] Moreover, these authors clearly state that the requirements of PL 94-142 (and the key element of the IEP) make "teachers responsible and accountable for assuring that each handicapped child receive the required special education and related services set forth in the IEP."[37]

Writing two years ago, Hayes and Higgins saw the accountability of teachers as resting on the *delivery* of education and related services to handicapped children placed in their classrooms. It is our opinion, however, that the standard has changed and thus an *eighth* cause of complaint category has been established and added to the previously mentioned seven causes. Accountability in the 1980's will be expressed and measured in terms of "student progress and achievement." The burden will fall squarely on the shoulders of classroom teachers, responsible for implementing IEPs, to show (demonstrate) that children are better for what has been done to, with, and for them.

### Educational Negligence: An Expanding Concept

According to Woods, writing in a recent edition of the *Tulsa Law Journal:* "In recent years, increasing public dissatisfaction with this nation's educational systems has stimulated a move to find redress in the courtroom. Frustrated plaintiffs who believe the schools have failed in their duty to educate children have become increasingly aware of the possibility of a legal remedy for their grievances."[38]

Note Woods' language in the preceding quotation. She is *not saying* that plaintiffs are challenging whether or not school systems have failed to carry out their duty to educate; rather, she suggests that plaintiffs are claiming that school systems "failed in carrying out their duty to educate children."[39] To put it another way, professionals may have carried out their duty to provide an educational opportunity, but have erred in carrying out that duty with detrimental results in student progress or the lack thereof.

In 1974, Vacca composed an article entitled "Educational Malpractice." Published in the *University of Richmond Law Review,*[40] the purpose of the piece was to demonstrate the legal vulnerability of professionals in public schools to suits for damages in situations where students had suffered actual physical injury. At the time (six years ago), the case law on point clearly showed that liability for student injury was generally limited to the negligent tort, and to matters resulting in physical injury occurring in certain *high risk* settings (e.g., science laboratories, vocational education laboratories, gymnasia, and playgrounds).

The current liability arena is gradually expanding to include situations other than physical injury. According to Klein, writing in the *Suffolk Law Review:*

> ...Plaintiffs with skill deficiencies due to negligent instruction are seeking to expand that liability to cover their injuries. They are charging educators with educational malpractice — the failure to demonstrate the skill and knowledge of a reasonable educator under similar circumstances. An educational malpractice claim is intended to redress the injuries suffered by serious students — those who have made bona fide efforts to meet the demands of course work and the expectations of school officials, who have been led by annual promotions and graduation to believe that they have, in fact, performed in a satisfactory manner, and who have then discerned that they are grossly undereducated according to the demands of contemporary society.[41]

So far, where this new wave of malpractice litigation has gone forward, states Klein, responsible government bodies (boards of education) and responsible school officials (board members, superintendents and principals) have been named as defendants, and not individual practitioners. In these suits the real issue involves "the cumulative effect of the conduct of educators who fail to assess the needs of students regardless of their performance."[42]

## Grounds for Taking Malpractice Actions: Implications for IEPs

Upon what basis or grounds will plaintiffs (in educational malpractice actions) take their complaint? According to Woods, there are *four* possible grounds: (1) negligence, (2) intentional or negligent misrepresentation, (3) breach of contract, and (4) a claim under 42 USC 1983 (constitutional tort).[43]

Negligence is never presumed by a court. Negligence must be proved by the preponderance of evidence presented. For a viable cause of action to exist, a plaintiff must bring negligence "home to the defendant." Emerging from the malpractice litigation of the late 1970s[44] is a *prevailing practice* standard for examining matters of alleged educational misfeasance (improper performance of a lawful act). In future court cases, when attempting to determine the possible presence of any professional blame for a child's lack of educational progress, a judge will most likely ask the following question: "Given all the data regarding this student and his or her deficiencies, abilities, problems, and home environment (most often referred to as "cultural diversity"), what should a reasonable and prudent practitioner, with similar training and experience, have done?" A corollary question will then be asked. "Did the practitioner fail to act properly or omit doing something that should have been done?" The answers to these questions will determine the success of plaintiff parent's allegations of professional malpractice.

It is important to note, however, that educational malpractice suits may contain a "more" legitimate cause of action if the suit is brought by more than one injured pupil. As Connors correctly points out in *Educational Tort Liability and Malpractice,* the *Donohue* case (on which the more famous *Hoffman* decision was based) does not totally preclude educational malpractice actions in the future.[45] Indeed, the New York Supreme Court, Appellate Division stated:

> This determination does not mean that educators are not ethically and legally responsible for providing a meaningful public education for the youth of our State. Quite the contrary, all teachers and other officials of our schools bear an important public trust and may be held to answer for the failure to faithfully perform their duties. It does mean, however, that they may not be sued for damages by an individual student for an alleged failure to reach certain educational objectives.[46]

The best protection for public school systems and their staffs against potential educational malpractice suits grounded in claims of negligence will come from taking preventive steps.

Intentional or negligent misrepresentation states Jorgensen (writing in the *Albany Law Review*[47]) represents potential causes of action in education. "Misrepresentations of student progress on report cards, in interviews with parents, or in the award of a diploma would evidence a school's wrongdoing."[48]

As Woods has concluded based upon her review of the case law on point: "A student who has been repeatedly promoted and has been reported to be working at or near grade level in basic academic skills should be able to charge the schools with misrepresentation when he discovers after graduation that he is a "functional illiterate." The schools have a responsibility to keep the parents and students accurately informed of the student's progress. Conversely, parents and students have a right to know if they are not meeting standards set by the schools.[49] What are the typical "indicators of student progress," that parents and kids look to for their perceptions? Grades, test scores, and diplomas function as the formal and acceptable indicators of student "levels of functioning" in schools. And, "A school ... which inaccurately represents a student's competence and educational progress," states Woods, "should be held responsible for any damage to the student resulting from reliance on that misrepresentation."[50]

Breach of contract is another possible claim for bringing suit against a school division. In a cause of action grounded in breach of contract, some plaintiffs will most likely rely on compulsory attendance statutes and state regulations describing standards to be met in fulfilling minimal state requirements. Several states now require minimal student achievement on such requirements as a prerequisite for graduation. Others, however, will resort to different arguments to make their case.

Most states have at least five requirements for contractual status.[51] These are: (1) Offer and Acceptance, (2) Consideration, (3) Legal Subject Matter, (4) Legal Standing of the Parties, (5) Proper Legal Form. Offer and acceptance means that an offer was made by one party and accepted by the other. In the case of the IEP, the school division makes an offer and the parent or guardian accepts this offer by signing or agreeing to the IEP. Consideration is when there is an exchange of goods, services, or money. The school division is providing an educational program which the public (parents) pay for through taxes. The concerns of legal subject matter, legal standings of the signers, and proper legal form present no special problems in contract law.

Therefore, the IEP will meet all the requirements of a legal contract under most state laws. And since Section 121a.349 does not forbid its interpretation as a contract, some states courts might find it to be a legal contract under state law. This situation could present high levels of accountability for educators.

How can educators protect themselves if the IEP is ruled to be a bona fide, legal contract? First, express the child's projected attainment in *broad* goals and objectives. Second, have a disclaimer following these goals and objectives stating something like, "The aforementioned goals and objectives are broad attainment guidelines and targets. Neither this school division nor its personnel can guarantee that the pupil will necessarily reach these goals within the prescribed period of time." And third, never promise that the pupil will achieve specific educational objectives. No educator can guarantee that a pupil will be reading on the fifth grade level by the end of the academic year (for example). Educators can guarantee what they will do to help the child reach that objective, but they cannot guarantee the child's performance of reaching the objective.

A decision last year from a New York court might offer a hint of things to come regarding the IEP. In *Pietro v. St. Joseph's School,* a private school matter, the New York Supreme Court, Suffolk County, heard the complaint of parents who charged that their son was a victim of educational malpractice.[52] The complaint alleged that the boy attended St. Joseph's School from 1970 to 1978 and that the school authorities "failed to ascertain whether the child was capable of learning, failed to evaluate him, failed to provide him with special educational facilities, failed to hire proper personnel, and failed to teach in a manner the child could understand."[53]

Deciding against the parents and their attempt to recover tuition costs, the New York Court said, however, that it could conceive of a future successful malpractice suit by parents, "if an express agreement had been entered between a parent and a school in which the school contracted that the student would reach a certain proficiency after pursuing certain studies."[54]

It should be kept in mind that a simple definition of *contract,* states Corbin, is " ... a promise enforceable at law directly or indirectly."[55] And, states Gee and Sperry, "enforceable promises" may be interpreted to include "the professional services of teachers."[56]

As previously mentioned, the reader should be aware that the USOE final regulations (Section 121a.349) do provide the following comment: "This section is intended to relieve concerns that the individualized educational program constitutes a guarantee by the public agency and the teacher that a child will progress at a specified rate."[57] This same comment continues, however, that "this section does not relieve agencies and teachers from making good faith efforts to assist the child in achieving the objectives and goals listed in the individualized education program."[58] It is our belief that this last statement represents a crack in the legal armor.

Breach of warranty may offer a new vehicle for bringing suits in education. Some lawyers are beginning to suggest that breach of warranty, and not breach of contract or breach of civil rights guarantees, will be the claim of plaintiffs in future educational malpractice cases. In breach of warranty actions damages are recoverable for the breach.

Unlike negligence, liability (liability in tort), "'warranty liability' is generally associated with contract liability."[59] In both, however, the standard of performance will be used to judge the matter.

Technically, a warranty is defined as a promise (obligation imposed by law) made by one party (expressed or implied) upon which another party may rely.[60] A warranty "implies a contractual relation between the party making the warranty and the beneficiary of the warranty."[61] The promise is based upon factual information and makes certain guarantees regarding the quality and character of the services to be performed.

Thus, questions can be raised concerning inferences drawn by parents from what is implied by those writing and discussing IEP's. Is the notion of warranty contained in the IEP process? We believe that it is.

Constitutional tort action, taken under 42 USC 1983 (the codification of the Civil Rights Act of 1871) represents an alternative action to the ones just reviewed. Lawyers call this a constitutional or civil rights tort action wherein plaintiffs seek either equitable remedy or remedy in the form of money damages (legal relief) for having been deprived of their constitutional guarantees (Fourteenth Amendment guarantees of both property and liberty) or for being deprived of guarantees and benefits of a federal statute.

The Civil Rights Act of 1871, Section 1983, reads: "Every person who, under color of any statute, ordinance, regulation, custom, or usage, of any State or Territory, subjects, or causes to be subjected, any citizen of the United States or other person with the jurisdiction thereof to the deprivation of any rights, privileges, or immunities secured by the Constitution and laws, shall be liable to the party injured in an action at law, suit in equity, or other proper proceeding for redress."[62] It should be noted that Section 1983 supercedes any and all sovereign (governmental) immunity which state and local officials may possess.

In our opinion, 42 USC 1983 cannot be taken casually. It may have the most potential for taking public school boards and administrators into court. As Tom Shannon pointed out in 1976: "Section 1983 is an expanding funnel through which a whole variety of litigation may be brought against public school people. . . . In a very real sense, Section 1983 can be considered the most significant "malpractice" law for public school people in our nation. As the "malpractice" concept develops further, Section 1983 actions against public school people should proliferate."[63]

A highly probable legal implication of the current "student competency testing" movement, for example, concerns the inevitable consequences of testing all children (exceptional and nonexceptional) using the same tests and evaluative criteria. Also, there are other more serious questions to be asked about testing mainstreamed exceptional children in mathematics and reading. And, what about exceptional children the severity of whose handicap requires the delivery of educational services in a "special setting?"

In the 1980's public school systems cannot refuse to give a student a high school diploma "solely because of a handicap." Nor can they award a handicapped pupil a "piece of paper that creates a stigma." The legal ramifications of federal legislation dealing with the handicapped (1973 Rehabilitation Act §504 and PL 94-142 in particular), plus recent court decisions that speak to the concept of "dead end education" are multiple and far reaching.

In *Goss v. Lopez*, the United States Supreme Court stated emphatically that knowledge and skills to be gained from the education guaranteed by the state are property entitlements of all children of school age.[64] Thus, as evidenced through the decisions of subsequent courts, any infringement on that right, no matter how slight, must be accompanied by the basic elements of due process of law. As Draba has observed, "It is difficult to imagine a school system that would make graduation conditional upon reading ability without providing careful measures to ensure accuracy and fairness."[65]

Other recent court decisions, especially those concerning the issue of education for handicapped children, have insisted that a child's right to education means more than mere entry to the school. According to McCarthy and Thomas, "Mere school attendance does not assure that educational benefits are accruing to the child."[66] The hard decision that is now faced by educators and judges alike, involves a determination of "the benefits that should accrue to each child in return for mandated attendance."[67]

The most litigious element in today's special education situations is the matter of "substantial progress." To put it another way, advocates for disabled children are saying: "You have identified the handicap and you have placed the child in an educational program. The big question now becomes one of progress being made by that child, because of what you have done for him or her."

A recent report (April 16, 1980) of a coalition of advocates for education of the handicapped reported, among other things (based upon a six-month's study in eleven states), that many children are denied "related" services essential to enable them "to benefit from" their special education program.[68] Note the emphasis placed on "benefit from their program."

In addition, the coalition cited the following "injustices":
1. Thousands of children remain on waiting lists for evaluation and placement.
2. Institutionalized children are routinely excluded from any kind of schooling or are denied appropriate services.
3. Handicapped children are unnecessarily segregated in special schools.
4. Black children are misclassified as "educable mentally retarded" three times more often than are white children.
5. Handicapped children are illegally suspended or expelled from school.
6. Many students in special education classes lack the required individual evaluations and program plans or have "canned" plans.[69]

## CONCLUDING STATEMENT

The Individualized Education Program (IEP) is the heart of the special educational program particularly in cases of learning disability. The IEP regulates a variety of educational considerations such as the classroom environment of the program, the educational content of the program, the methodology of instruction, the length of the school year, disciplinary matters, and participation in extracurricular activities.

There has already been some litigation concerning the IEP. The exact legal status of the IEP, however, has not been decided in most states, since Section 121a.349 neither forbids the interpretation of the IEP as a legal and binding contract by state courts nor requires such an interpretation either.

Most cases which have dealt with PL 94-142, thus far, were more concerned with specific aspects of the IEP rather than the overall issue of educational malpractice. There is more than ample legal groundwork to bring an educational malpractice suit against a school division. We believe that the IEP represents a very real possibility of evolving into an instrument for bringing legal challenges of educational malpractice.

## REFERENCES

1. 470 F. Supp. 110 (D.C. Conn., 1979).

2. *Supra* note 1 at 115.

3. 20 U.S.C. 794 (1973).

4. 423 F. Supp. 180 (S.D. W.Va., 1976).

5. 49 USLW 4468 (April 29, 1981).

6. Public Law 94-142, 20 U.S.C. §1401–1461.

7. *Supra* note 6 at §121a.340.

8. *Id.* note 6 at §121a.343.

9. *Id.* note 6 at §121a.344.

10. *Id.* note 6 at §121a.346.

11. *Battle v. Commonwealth of Pennsylvania,* 629 F. 2d 269 (1980), also see *Armstrong v. Klein,* 376 F. Supp. 583 (D.C. Pa., 1979).

12. *Supra* note 11.

13. *Id.* note 11.

14. *Id.* note 11.

15. *New York State Association for Retarded Children v. Carey,* 612 F. 2d 644 (1979).

16. *Supra* note 15.

17. *Rowley v. Board of Education of the Hendrick Hudson Central School District, Westchester County,* 483 F. Supp. 528 (S.D. New York, 1980).

18. *Supra* note 17.

19. *Id.* note 17.

20. *Id.* note 17, affirmed 632 F. 2d 945 (1980), also see *Hairston v. Dresick,* 423 F. Supp. 180 (S.D. W.Va., 1976), *Tatro v. State,* 625 F. 2d 557 (Fifth Circuit, 1980), and *Camenish v. University of Texas,* 616 F. 2d 127 (Fifth Circuit, 1980).

21. *Doe v. Koger,* 480 F. Supp. 225 (N.D. Ind., 1979).

22. *Supra* note 21.

23. *Id.* note 21.

24. *Id.* note 21.

25. *Stuart v. Nappi,* 443 F. Supp. 1235 (D.C. Conn., 1978), also see *Howard v. Friendship Independent School District,* 454 F. Supp. 634 (S.D., Texas, 1978), and *Southeast Warren Community School District v. Department of Public Instruction,* 285 N.W. 2d 173 (Iowa, 1979).

26. *Supra* note 25.

27. *Id.* note 25.

28. *Doe v. Marshall,* 459 F. Supp. 1190 (S.D. Texas, 1978).

29. *Supra* note 28.

30. *Kampmeier v. Harris,* 411 N.Y.S. 2d 744 (1978).

31. Since the U.S. Supreme Court decision in *Southeastern Community College v. Davis*, 99 S.Ct. 2361 (1979), the phrase "No otherwise qualified handicapped individual" (Section 504 of the 1973 *Rehabilitation Act*) has been interpreted as: "the person is qualified for the activity despite his or her handicap."

32. *Supra* note 6 at s121a.349.

33. *Id.* note 6 at 121a.349.

34. *Supra* note 11.

35. *Id.* note 11.

36. J. Hayes and S. T. Higgins, "Issues Regarding the IEP: Teachers on the Front Line," *Exceptional Children* (January 1978) at 267.

37. *Supra* note 36 at 267.

38. Nancy L. Woods, "Educational Malfeasance: A New Cause of Action for Failure to Educate," 14 *Tulsa Law Journal* 383 (1978).

39. *Supra* note 38.

40. R. S. Vacca, "Teacher Malpractice," 8 *University of Richmond Law Review* 447 (Spring 1974).

41. A. J. Klein, "Educational Malpractice: Can the Judiciary Remedy the Growing Problem of Functional Illiteracy?" 13 *Suffolk Law Review* 27 (Winter 1979).

42. *Supra* note 41.

43. *Supra* note 38.

44. *Peter W. v. San Francisco Unified School District*, 60 C.A. 3d 184, 131 Cal. Rptr. 854 (1976), *Donahue v. Copiaque Union Free School District*, 407 N.Y.S. 874, 64 A.D. 2d 69 (1978), and *Hoffman v. Board of Education of City of New York*, 410 N.Y.S. 2d 99, 64 A.D. 2d 369 (1978).

45. Eugene T. Connors, *Educational Tort Liability and Malpractice* (Bloomington, Ind.: Phi Delta Kappa, 1981).

46. *Donohue v. Copiaque Union Free School District*, 407 N.Y.S. 874, 64 A.D. 2d 69 (1978).

47. C. A. Jorgenson, "Donohue v. Copiaque Union Free School District: New York Chooses Not to Recognize 'Educational Malpractice,'" 43 *Albany Law Review* 339 (Winter 1979).

48. *Supra* note 47.

49. *Supra* note 38.

50. *Id.* note 38.

51. S. Kern Alexander, *Public School Law* (St. Paul, Minn.: West Publishing, 1980), at 578.

52. *Pietro v. St. Joseph's School*, 48 U.S.L.W. 2229 (N.Y. Supreme Court, 1979).

53. *Supra* note 52.

54. *Id*. note 52.

55. *Corbin on Contracts* (1952) in E. G. Gee and D. J. Speery, *Education, Law and the Public Schools: A Compendium* (Boston, Mass.: Allyn and Bacon, 1978) at C26.

56. *Supra* note 55 at 626.

57. *Supra* note 32.

58. *Id*. note 32.

59. *Words and Phrases,* 1980 Cum. Ann. Pock. Part, at 41.

60. *Supra* note 59 at 40.

61. *Id*. note 59 at 40.

62. 42 U.S.C. §1983.

63. T. A. Shannon, "The U.S. Civil Rights Act: A New Dimension in the Liability of Public School People," *Current Legal Issues in Education* (Topeka, Kan.: NOLPE, 1976) at 105.

64. *Goss v. Lopez,* 419 U.S. 565 (1975).

65. R. E. Draba, "Reading Ability as a Graduation Requirement" in Harper and Kilan (eds.) *Reading and the Law* (Newark, Del.: I.R.A., 1978) at 30.

66. M. M. McCarthey and S. B. Thomas, "The Right to an Education: New Trends from Special Education Litigation," 7 *NOLPE School Law Journal* 80 (1977).

67. *Supra* note 66.

68. 1 *Department of Education Weekly* (April 23, 1980) at 3.

69. *Supra* note 68.

# 2

# Growing Up Creatively Gifted with Learning Disabilities

*E. Paul Torrance*

I HESITATE to address this International Conference of the Association for Adults and Children with Learning Disabilities because I am no expert on the problems of learning disabilities. Yet I feel that I belong to this association. I have spent more than 65 years being a child and an adult with learning disabilities. In my research on the creatively gifted, I have encountered many children and adults with learning disabilities. As an "outsider" who feels like he belongs "inside," perhaps I can challenge you to look at your field from a different perspective. Just as I have for more than twenty years challenged the field of gifted education to broaden its concept of giftedness, I would like to challenge you to broaden your concept of learning disabled.

## A PERSONAL EXAMPLE

First, let me describe a personal example and something of my own experience as a creatively gifted person with learning disabilities. I grew up on a tenant farm in middle Georgia and attended a small rural school. By the time I was six years old, my parents had become aware at least of certain aspects of my giftedness and my learning disabilities. I had learned to walk and talk at a precocious age and I was a fast runner, but I was not very strong and there were many tasks for which I showed no aptitude whatsoever. As a result, I was not sent to school until I was seven years old, because my parents did not think that I was capable of walking the six-mile round trip to school and defend myself from the attacks of older and stronger children. The shame of my learning abilities did not become really intense, however, until it became clear that I could not learn how to plow a straight row, try as I might. In the environment in which I grew up, the shame and disgrace of not being able to plow a straight row was much greater than that of not being able to read, write, and do arithmetic.

When I was about thirteen years old, a very important thing happened (Torrance 1969). My father freed me of the expectation that I would have to succeed as a farmer, including plowing straight rows. It happened one evening as we were eating supper. Daddy stopped eating, looked at me, and stated seriously and calmly his conclusion, "It's plain now that you'll never be able to earn a living on the farm. You'll have to go to town and you'll have to get an education. It's time you learned to eat peas with a fork!"

There was no further discussion of the matter. There was no need for it. The facts my father had stated were indisputable. Though getting even a high school education seemed an impossible dream, I was committed to "getting an education" and it was all right with my family. This moment had put an end to years of desperate but unsuccessful straining to master the more skilled farm tasks. It signified to me that my father was accepting me as I was and that it was up to me to work out my own way of life. He really meant it. He proved it in every big decision after that time. I think he realized then that it would mean my alienation from the family but that it was necessary.

Just as I could not learn to plow a straight row in a field, I later learned that I could not pilot an automobile on a straight path on a highway. It was not until recently that I began to understand the nature of these learning disabilities. I think the moment of dawning insight came one day when I was trying to align my arms at 180 degree angles in one of the crystals that Derald Langham (1977) was using to present his GENESA theories. I simply could not master this skill. It then became clear that this had so long been a key in my learning disabilities that had brought me so much pain and shame and still constitutes a great deal of difficulty for me. I have been able to succeed in some other areas and those who are close to me generally accept my disabilities and we develop wonderful interdependent relationships. However, there are still occasional stubborn souls who want to teach me to drive an automobile.

In school, I was never classified as "learning disabled." In general, I learned easily the things that the school expected me to learn—at least the things that were expected of me in the classroom. In the second grade, I did have a penmanship problem, especially when writing on the blackboard. I wrote too small and could not keep my line straight. When my report card showed a failing grade in penmanship, my mother wrote sentences for me to copy in a ruled tablet. I practiced these at every spare moment and I still have a rather beautiful handwriting quite similar to my mother's and to that of the penmanship copy books. My strength, however, was in learning the things that the school expected me to learn. The excellence I attained in this way has in a sense freed me "to play my own game in my own way." I wish now that I had done this more fully.

It has only been in recent months that I have developed this insight, as I have worked with the followup data from my twenty-two-year longitudinal study of elementary school children I began studying in 1958. I have set forth some of these insights in a recent paper entitled "Growing Up Creatively Gifted" (1980) and in an interview published in the December 15, 1980, issue of the *U. S. News and World Report*. As a result of these two communications, I have been asked by many creatively gifted people with learning disabilities how they might function more effectively and achieve more success and satisfaction in life. I have offered them the following three sets of suggestions, which are actually some of the conclusions from my twenty-two-year longitudinal study of creative behavior.

1. Know your strengths. Understand them deeply. Take pride in them. Practice, develop, use, and exploit them.
2. Learn to free yourself from the expectations of others and walk away from the games that others insist that you play, even though you have no interest or aptitude for such games. Free yourself to play your own games in your own way in such a manner as to make the best possible use of your strengths, your potentialities.
3. Do not waste a lot of expensive, unproductive energy in trying to be well-rounded. Master the skills of interdependence, giving freely of your strength. What you give in this way is far more valuable than all you could give with mediocre performances of achievements for which you have no aptitude or will. People are generally highest motivated for the things that they do best.

## EXPANDED CONCEPTS OF GIFTEDNESS

Already, I am sure that this kind of advice causes many of you some difficulty. It calls for an expanded concept of giftedness beyond what commonly prevails today. During the past twenty years there has been in the field of gifted education an enormous expansion of the concept of "who is gifted." In 1972, our United States Office for the Gifted and

Talented expanded its concept of giftedness to include six different categories of gifted children: (1) the academically gifted, (2) the special aptitude academically gifted, (3) the creative, productive thinker, (4) giftedness in the visual and performing arts, (5) leadership, and (6) the psychomotor gifted (later deleted). However, even now, some states still have laws which recognize only that type of giftedness that is identified through the use of intelligence tests.

I believe we need still further expansion of our concept of "who is gifted." Who indeed is gifted? This is an important question in education. It makes an enormous difference in the way we treat children, the ways we teach them, how a community organizes its school system, and how children learn, grow, and achieve. Let me try to explain through a series of examples of children about which the question has been asked —"Are they gifted?"

Wally Vogel (Silver 1976) was eleven years old, deaf, and assigned to a class for mentally retarded children. His powerful drawing, "Shout in Silence," attracted the attention of Rawley Silver, an art teacher. She thought his art abilities and products were truly promising. She also discovered that his ability to solve problems in space were equally outstanding, betraying a level of intelligence never shown on tests of intelligence. His scores on the *Torrance Tests of Creative Thinking (Figural Form A)* (Torrance 1974) would place him in the upper .01 of one percent of his peers. Rawley Silver thought that he was gifted but the school system thought that he was mentally retarded. Rehabilitation officials did not think that he could profit from art training because his IQ was so low. Was Wally Vogel gifted? If Wally had been defined as gifted in art and problem solving and provided appropriate opportunities to use and develop these strengths, what might have been the consequences? If he is defined as mentally retarded (and deaf) and provided educational opportunities appropriate only to this definition, what would be the consequences? Which would be better for Wally Vogel? Which would best serve the needs of society?

John Torres was a strong, muscular, energetic, imaginative, twelve-year-old sixth grader who had never learned to read (Torrance & Myers 1970). He was known as the school's vandal, although no one had ever been able to prove that he and the boys he led made a shambles of the school each weekend. He had been a problem for teachers almost from the first day of his schooling. No one thought he could learn. His sixth grade teacher thought he was gifted. He was a veritable mechanical genius and could repair almost anything mechanical. He was a genius in leadership. He could attract other boys, organize them, and lead them in doing almost anything. His art work was also superior. His sixth grade teacher started by getting the student council to appoint John as head of the lunchroom committee to help arrange the cafeteria and keep things functioning. He recruited other boys to help and this was the beginning of many other leadership activities for John in improving the school. The vandalism in the school ceased. John learned to read as well as the average sixth grader and loved to go to school. Was John Torres gifted? Would it be better to treat John as gifted in the psychomotor, leadership, and visual art areas or as a retarded non-reader or as a behavior disorder case? Which is in John's best interest? Which is in society's best interest?

Bob Sanderson (Torrance 1962) was quite different from John Torres. He was not a troublemaker. He sat through classes sadly and quietly. He was withdrawn and rarely spoke to anyone. He used to be a brilliant basketball player but in the ninth grade he no longer played at all. He could not read, but his art teacher thought he was gifted as an artist and had an intelligence not betrayed by his scores on reading and intelligence tests. She was also his English teacher. She could not get him to respond even orally to her tests in literature. In desperation, she asked Bob to illustrate the poems and stories the class had read while the others took their tests. The depth of understanding and keen insights displayed through his drawings amazed the teacher and his classmates. Through Bob's drawings, they became aware of deeper meanings and insights into the literature they had read. Their appreciation and admiration of the thinking and feeling communicated through Bob's art made a difference in the way Bob felt about himself. He learned to read, started excelling in basketball again, and "rejoined society." Was Bob gifted? Would it be better to define Bob as gifted in art and basketball or as retarded in reading and emotionally disturbed? Which served Bob's interest better? Which served society's interest better?

Susan Longman had a really difficult time in school throughout her elementary school career. Her teachers and classmates regarded her as "stupid" and she displayed a number of rather serious learning disabilities. In dance, creative movement, and dramatics, she showed sheer genius. It was not until she was in high school that she learned how to use her genius for learning in the kinesthetic mode to achieve academic success. When she had to memorize the periodic tables in chemistry, she turned it into a song and danced it as she practiced her recitation of the periodic table. When the test came, her performance was perfect and she has never forgotten the periodic tables. Her style of learning and thinking and processing information is what we recognize now as specialized in the right cerebral hemisphere functions. It was through her own inventiveness that she was able to achieve well enough in high school to rank in the upper ten percent of a large graduating class. She is now a very successful mimist and teacher in this field. Again, I ask, is it better to define Susan as mentally retarded or as an excellent learner highly specialized in the right hemisphere cerebral functions?

We could continue almost endlessly with descriptions of people like Wally Vogel, John Torres, Bob Sanderson, and Susan Longman. Rarely would you find any of them in state-approved programs for gifted and talented students. In fact, I doubt that they would gain very much in such programs as we know them today. Yet no one can deny that they are gifted and talented nor that society needs desperately the kinds of giftedness and talent that they display.

## CREATIVELY GIFTED CHILDREN

Since about 1958, I have been something of an advocate for creatively gifted children. Many of these children do have learning disabilities (Torrance 1962) and as a group creativity seems to be one of their major strengths (Kandil & Torrance 1978). Unfortunately, school and societal pressures cause many of them to abandon this important strength. I could see this happening in the very beginnings of my research in 1958 and 1959. It has become much clearer now that we are completing our followup studies twenty-two years later. To show you something of the range of problems, let me describe briefly some of these cases.

### Frances Sundal: Early Death of Creativity

First, let me tell the story of Frances Sundal, now twenty-nine years old and still a postdoctoral student in a hard science. Her average IQ during the elementary school years was 141, and her scores on tests of creativity were consistently about a standard deviation below the mean. A large percentage of the study participants commented on the followup questionnaire about their enjoyment in taking the creativity tests. Frances is the only one who commented negatively. She wrote: "When I saw your name on the envelope, I remembered who you were and guessed that this would be a followup questionnaire. I guess those frustrating tests twenty years ago made an impression on me."

Frances was a highly intelligent, high achieving child and was highly successful on most school tasks. Since she could not perform well on the creativity tests, it is natural for her to have experienced them as frustrating. This was not her "game." She has been graduated from prestigious universities and has succeeded in traditional but not creative ways. She summarized her feelings and perceptions about her creativity as follows: "I consider myself very uncreative. I enjoy music and drama but only as an observer. . . . Scientifically, I feel successful but uncreative. My mentor's major criticism of my abilities was that I didn't have or didn't pursue good ideas."

Despite her excellent academic credentials (a Ph.D. from one of the country's most highly rated universities and two postdoctoral fellowships), she wrote, "I am insecure about my professional future. Can I find a job I like and can do?"

In Frances' collection of creativity tests, creative writing samples, autobiographical inventory, and the like, we find several clues that possibly shed some light upon her short-lived struggle to maintain her creativity and the capitulation which resulted in a learning disability in creative ways of thinking. In the fourth grade, she wrote an imaginative story about "The Woman Who Can But Won't Talk," chosen from a list of ten suggested titles about people and animals with unusual characteristics. Her story was as follows:

> Once there was a woman who would not talk. She could but she wouldn't talk.
>
> It had all started when she was 5 years old. Her friend told her what she bought Karen for her birthday. Her friend told her she wasn't supposed to tell but she did. She told everyone she knew.
>
> Of course, when she went to Karen's party everyone knew what the friend was giving Karen.
>
> From that day on the woman never talked because she was afraid she would say something she wasn't supposed to.

As we examine this simple fourth-grade story in the light of Frances' performance on tests of creative thinking and her career as a research scientist, we get the feeling that the story is somehow symbolic of the forces that caused her to sacrifice her creativity at an early age. On her autobiographical inventory in the fourth grade, she indicated that she could not recall ever having used a household article for some different purpose in her play activities. She was attracted to well-structured problems that can be solved by logical thinking.

## Tammy Debbins: Creativity Lost on the Way to the Fourth Grade

The creativity of Tammy Debbins was still alive when she entered first grade. In fact, she was one of the most creative children we tested in the first grade and her estimated IQ was 177. Her teacher and parents, however, were quite concerned that she still had imaginary playmates and they worked to rid her of this behavior. She was one of the children who lived in "The Project" (low-income housing), and the school social worker was called upon to help regarding the imaginary playmates. By the third grade, Tammy's creativity scores were a little below average and her IQ was a modest 110.

From our records we cannot know with certainty what happened to Tammy to diminish her. In her followup questionnaire she tells us that she dropped out of school in the tenth grade to help with the younger members of her family. She was married at age nineteen and is the mother of three boys. She reported no high school creative achievements. Concerning the primary frustrations of her life, she wrote: "I don't think I'm very smart." If she could do or be whatever she chose in the next 10 years, she would like "to finish high school and maybe go into nursing, something that really interests me."

Let us turn now to some of Frances' and Tammy's peers whose creative giftedness survived, despite learning disabilities in other areas.

## Mack Jamison: Superabundant Creativity

Mack Jamison was one of the most precociously and abundantly creative children in the study. He expressed his creativity in so many ways that almost everyone who knew him was aware that he was highly creative. In the second grade, his drawings approached the quality of a professional illustrator and in the third grade his science fiction and space age dramas were produced by his classmates. Despite his having an IQ in excess of 150 and exceptionally high creativity scores, Mack still suffered a number of learning disabilities. At least a part of this problem is reflected in the following excerpt from an article by his fourth grade teacher (Myers 1981):

> For his first two weeks in a fourth-grade class of gifted children, Mack drew dinosaurs on his binder, napkins, and the back of his left hand. His teacher attempted to involve Mack in the curricular tasks he had set for the class of 25 lively and competitive 9-year-olds, but it was useless. Once,

after making what he imagined to be a highly motivating introduction to a social studies unit, the teacher was taken aback to find Mack at his elbow, proudly showing his latest version of a brontosaurus on a paper towel.

Overcoming an urge to scold Mack for completely ignoring the task that was set for the class, the teacher hesitated and mumbled something to the effect that the pencil sketch was a good rendering of a brontosaurus.

Mack never did complete the social studies unit, and he continued to draw dinosaurs and scenes about twenty-first century space travel. Today he is a successful novelist, specializing in science fiction. Subsequent teachers in elementary and high school had indifferent success in getting this keen-minded youngster to perform "to his capacity" in the classroom — and fortunately, they were unable to prevent Mack from dreaming, drawing, and writing.

Mack himself described this fourth grade teacher as the most important mentor in his life, commenting as follows: "In many ways he provided an impetus to synthesize in what is, I'm told, my radical brain. Fourth grade ended but his influence has been permanent. I have continued to try to synthesize aspects of the sciences, arts, and humanities."

It was in the sixth grade that Mack got the insight that gave his career direction and focus. His teacher had commented favorably on an abstract realist painting Mack had made of the Oedipus cycle that he had done outside of class. Mack wrote of this incident in the following words: "This teacher's comments encouraged my interest in synthesizing the elements of literature and painting; and I have continued to draw across universes of discourse like that ever since."

While in high school, Mack founded the Minnesota Science Fiction Society, its amateur magazine, and its annual convention which has been continuing. He completed his Ph.D. degree with a dissertation on utopian political theory. His list of awards, publications, creative performances, musical compositions, business entrepreneurships, and art works is most impressive. His struggle has continued to be one of searching for strategies that will permit him to "play his own game," using his greatest strengths. It is even a part of his future career image. When asked what he would do, if he could do or be whatever he chose in the next ten years, he wrote: "A writer and musician. For me, the two are intertwined and some of the writing I intend to do is social research. If I can land a recording contract, I'll be able to develop my own route entirely in financial security."

**Robert Williams: The Inventor**

At the same time Mack was writing science fiction and drawing space vehicles and creatures in the third grade, his classmate Robert Williams was inventing things and having trouble with spelling and other language skills. In this classroom, Robert's inventions were just as apparent as Mack's science fiction and space drawings. Like Mack, Robert has earned a Ph.D., though in engineering, and has served his internship in the invention department of a corporation at the forefront in his field. At the time he completed his followup questionnaire, he expressed the aspiration of becoming an independent inventor. This would free him to "play his own game in his own way" to a greater extent. After he had returned his questionnaire, he had an inventive breakthrough which he believes will make him an independent inventor and he wrote me about the good news. He also wrote to say, "Thanks! What you've done has changed my life" and to say that he had "carefully read and enjoyed" *The Search for Satori and Creativity* (Torrance 1979) which I had sent him in appreciation of his returning his questionnaire.

**Karl David: Actor and Director**

Karl David, a classmate of Mack and Robert, did not succeed very well in his first three years of school. This was especially disappointing to his family, as both of his parents held doctorates and had been high academic achievers and his older sister had also achieved outstandingly as a student. In the fourth grade, Karl's teacher encouraged his rich talents in the arts and Karl became a "star." His parents were delighted with his unexpected flowering in the arts, especially in acting. Furthermore, his performance in the "academics" also improved now that he felt better about himself. On the followup questionnaire, Karl wrote about his fourth grade teacher as follows: "my fourth grade teacher often encouraged me to write songs—or rather, make-up songs—and then sing them for the class. I think he was *extremely* influential in developing my creative skills."

As a successful repertory actor and theater director, Karl recognizes the importance of his creativity and makes good use of it in building a successful career in the theater and has won acclaim for his acting not only in the United States but in London, Edinburgh, and other theater centers.

## Patricia Allen: Successful Creative Writer

Patricia Allen showed her creativity year after year on the *Torrance Tests of Creative Thinking* (Torrance 1974) and compiled one of the highest creativity indexes of anyone in the study. Apparently, she deliberately hid her creativity from her teachers and classmates, giving them little chance to relieve her fears and isolation. On her followup questionnaire, she describes her plight, in part, as follows:

> I am a writer today, but not until college did I realize that I had any unusual ability. My elementary school experiences were awful. I got perfect marks for organization, spelling, and punctuation, but was graded down for having lousy handwriting. I also was never told that anything I did was original. . . . My father was mentally ill and most of the things I could have written about I knew were different from what the other kids would write.

Further insights concerning her childhood struggle come from the following note to me with her questionnaire:

> Dear Dr. Torrance: I remember taking your creativity tests—I still dream about a picture of Bobby Shaftoe that I was asked to describe. I wanted to be creative, but I was terrible in art, so I thought I was a dud. I also never wrote about what I really thought about for teachers, because they wouldn't understand. If someone had told me back then that I was "creative," I would have had something to hold onto. All I knew was that I was different. I had an unhappy childhood and adolescence, but a very satisfying life as an adult. . . . It would have been nice to have been encouraged in school. Continue your work. Kids like me need someone to help.

### CONCLUSION

Almost all of the highly creative young people in our study have exciting, sometimes heartbreaking, stories to tell of their struggle to maintain and use their creativity and cope with the frustrations and sometimes shame of learning disabilities. In my opinion, they support strongly the need for expanding our concepts of both giftedness and learning disabilities. Many of them have been fortunate in having teachers, parents, or mentors who understood both their giftedness and their learning disabilities and have helped them free themselves of society's expectations of them so they can pursue the thing that they are in love with and make useful social contributions. I believe most of them would join me in giving the following bits of advice and encouragement to youngsters with learning disabilities who are gifted, especially if they are creatively gifted:

1. Don't be afraid to "fall in love with" something and pursue it with intensity and in depth. One is motivated most to do the things that they do best.
2. Know, understand, take pride in, practice, develop, use, exploit, and enjoy your greatest strengths.
3. Learn to free yourself from the expectations of others and to walk away from the games that others insist that you play. Free yourself to play your own game in such a way as to make the best use of your strengths.
4. Don't waste a lot of expensive, unproductive energy in trying to be well-rounded. Learn the skills of interdependence, giving freely from the infinity of your greatest strengths.

## REFERENCES

Kandil, S. A., and E. P. Torrance. "Further Verification of High Creative Potential among Emotionally Disturbed and Behavior Disordered Children." *Journal of Creative Behavior* 12 (1978): 280.

Langham, D. G. "GENESA: Tomorrow's Thinking Today." In S. J. Parnes, R. B. Noller, and A. M. Biondi, *Guide to Creative Action*. New York: Scribners, 1977.

Myers, R. E. "Creativity Revisited." *G/C/T,* 1981, in press.

Silver, R. A. *Developing Cognitive and Creative Skills through Art*. Baltimore: University Park Press, 1978.

Torrance, E. P. *Guiding Creative Talent,* Englewood Cliffs, N.J.: Prentice-Hall, 1962.

———. "It's Time You Learned to Eat Peas with a Fork." *Theory into Practice* 8 (1969): 332–33.

———. *Norms–Technical Manual: Torrance Tests of Creative Thinking*. Bensenville, Ill.: Scholastic Testing Service, 1974.

———. *The Search for Satori and Creativity*. Great Neck, N.Y.: Creative Synergetic Associates, 1979.

———. "Growing Up Creatively Gifted: A 22-Year Longitudinal Study." *Creative Child and Adult Quarterly* 5 (1980): 148–58, 170. (a)

———. "For Many, Being Gifted Brings Lifelong Struggle," *U.S. News & World Report,* December 15, 1980, pp. 67–68. (b)

Torrance, E. P., and R. E. Myers. *Creative Learning and Teaching*. New York: Harper & Row, 1970.

# 3

# Specific Preschool Medical Findings
# which Predict Specific Learning Outcomes

*Lawrence C. Hartlage and Cathy F. Telzrow*

E ARLY INTERVENTION with handicapped children has been demonstrated to produce the greatest degree of amelioration of the potentially devastating effects of these conditions (Gray and Klaus 1970; Horton 1974). Preschool intervention with less specific at–risk populations has also resulted in positive outcomes (Lazar and Darlington 1978). In order for these interventions to occur, systematic procedures for the identification of appropriate populations are necessary. While clinical populations are more easily diagnosed at birth (Werner, Honzik, and Smith 1968), it is the less severely involved children that represent diagnostic problems. Ironically, it is this population for whom intervention programs may produce the greatest gains.

A number of strategies for the identification of at–risk populations have been employed. One procedure has utilized specific pre- and post-natal medical variables to predict eventual learning difficulties. Such perinatal factors as hypoxia and birth trauma have been related to learning problems (Towbin 1980). Birth weight and brain circumference have been found to be related to learning difficulties by some investigators (Dobbing 1980; Kirman 1958; Nelson and Deutschberger 1970), although other evidence contradicts these findings (Babson and Kangas 1969).

Accurate prediction from specific medical indicators in the newborn has not been demonstrated (Kochanek 1980), and there is some evidence to suggest that demographic variables may provide the best predictor for at–risk status in preschool–aged children (Finkelstein and Ramey 1980), since early developmental measures have not been shown to predict well to later childhood IQ (Bayley 1939; McCall Hogarty, and Hurlburt 1972). Kochanek (1980) suggests that specific medical indicators have been found to carry less predictive weight than such social variables as socioeconomic status and mother's IQ or education. Finkelstein and Ramey (1980) utilized information on birth certificates to predict subsequent educational handicaps. Race, sex, and birth order were the demographic variables with the highest predictability (Finkelstein and Ramey 1980). Reynolds and Gutkin (1979) report demographic variables, race, and father's occupation were the best predictors of children's IQ scores.

In order to improve diagnostic procedures, thus facilitating identification of educationally at–risk populations for the delivery of specific interventions, a longitudinal investigation of the relationship between various pre– and perinatal indicators and subsequent learning difficulties is necessary. The current study provides an analysis of the relative contribution of a number of medical and demographic variables to the predictability of learning difficulties in children.

## METHOD

### Subjects

A sample of 528 children in an intensive neonatal care nursery were followed from birth through early school years. Eighty-eight percent (88%) of the sample was white, twelve percent (12%) black. The sample was approximately evenly divided by sex, with 52 percent of the sample female, and 48 percent male.

### Procedure

This investigation examined the relative predictive value of specific demographic variables and forty-two medical variables identified at birth. The forty-two medical variables examined are listed in Table 3.1. The demographic variables considered were race, mother's education, father's education, mother's and father's ages, and number of siblings.

The children were examined at six month intervals to age 2 and annually thereafter until age 6. Criterion measures included developmental inventories, intelligence tests, and other mental development milestones. The specific criterion measures and the ages at which they were administered are listed in Table 3.2.

## RESULTS

Of the forty-two medical variables examined, twelve were significantly correlated with performance on the Cattell Infant Intelligence Scale

TABLE 3.1

**Coding of Specific Medical Variables**

1. Birth weight
2. Single or multiple birth
3. One-minute Apgar
4. Five-minute Apgar
5. Drugs administered to infant
   in delivery room
6. Resuscitation in delivery room
7. Significant diagnosis of infant
8. Second significant diagnosis of infant
9. Infant operations
10. Other infant operations
11. Condition of infant on discharge
12. Incubator care in days
13. Days in hospital
14. Type of infant feeding
15. Cord status
16. Specific infant medications
17. Second specific infant medications
18. Third specific infant medications
19. Fourth specific infant medications
20. Hematocrit
21. Blood type

22. Rh factor
23. Coombs
24. Bilirubin level
25. Calcium
26. Glucose
27. Respiratory difficulty
28. Cyanoses
29. Poor muscle tone
30. Vomiting
31. Pallor
32. Excessive mucus
33. Bradycardia
34. Tachycardia
35. Tremors
36. Convulsions
37. Jaundice
38. Poor sucking
39. Edema
40. Peculiar cry
41. Lethargy
42. Hyperactivity

TABLE 3.2

**Criterion Measures and Schedule of Testing**

| Age in Months | Criterion Measures |
|---|---|
| 6 | Cattell Infant Intelligence Scale (Cattell 1960); Denver Developmental Screening Test (Frandenburg and Dodds 1975) |
| 12 | Same as above |
| 18 | Same as above |
| 24 | Same as above, plus mental development milestones (Hartlage and Lucas 1975) |
| 36 | Stanford-Binet Intelligence Test (Terman & Merrill 1960); Peabody Picture Vocabulary Test (Dunn 1965); Beery VMI (Beery 1967) |
| 48 | Wechsler Preschool and Primary Scale of Intelligence (Wechsler 1967) |
| 60 | Stanford-Binet Intelligence Test (Terman & Merrill 1960); Peabody Picture Vocabulary Test (Dunn 1965), Beery VMI (Beery 1967) |
| 72 | Wechsler Intelligence Scale for Children (Wechsler 1960) |

(Cattell 1960) and/or the Denver Developmental Screening Test (Frankenburg and Dodds 1975) on three or more repeated testings between 6 and 24 months. These medical variables were birth weight, five-minute Apgar, condition of infant at discharge, days in incubator, days in hospital, specific infant medications (vitamin K and analogues, calcium, barbiturates, digitalis type, vitamins), bilirubin levels, poor muscle tone, convulsions, peculiar cry, lethargy, and hyperactivity. Many of these variables, although consistently predicting performance on infant tests, had virtually no relationship to performance on criterion measures after age 2. Of the twelve medical variables listed, only three (birth weight, days in hospital, convulsions) are significantly related to any single test performance after age 2. Table 3.3 reports correlations of the forty-two medical variables and the criterion measures at 6, 12, 18, 24, 36, 48, 60, and 72 months.

In contrast to the findings concerning the medical variables, demographic variables became increasingly predictive of performance on criterion measures after age 2. Race was significantly correlated with performance on the Cattell Infant Intelligence Scale (Cattell 1960) at ages 18 and 24 months, and with virtually all criterion measures thereafter. Mother's age was significantly correlated with several criterion measures at all ages except 72 months. Mother's and father's education were significantly correlated with criterion performance on all measures from age 3 upward, and were among the strongest predictors. Table 3.4 provides the correlations of the demographic variables with performance on criterion measures at ages 6, 12, 18, 24, 36, 48, 60, and 72 months.

## DISCUSSION

This longitudinal followup of 528 high-risk children from birth to age 6 confirms once again that infant performance may not be predictive of subsequent intelligence test scores and mental development milestones (Bayley 1939; McCall Hogarty, and Hurlburt 1972). The data demonstrate that presence of apparent risk indicators in infancy does not necessarily predict the condition at a later age. Although specific medical variables noted at birth may provide some information about infant performance, after age 2 demographic variables such as race and parents' education represent the most significant correlations with IQ scores and other performance criteria predictive of school success.

The increasing correlations between performance on criterion measures and demographic variables (specifically race and parents'

## TABLE 3.3

### Pearson Correlations of Medical Variables and Criterion Measures‡

| Age in Months Criterion Measures§ | 6 Cat Den | 12 Cat Den | 18 Cat Den | 24 Cat Den | 36 Bin PPVT VMI | 48 WPPSI | 60 VMI Bin PPVT | 72 WISC |
|---|---|---|---|---|---|---|---|---|
| **Medical Variable by Number‖** | | | | | | | | |
| 1 | .113* .121* | .101* | .089* | | .143† | | .148† | |
| 2 | .087* | .112* | | | | .092* | .113* .087* | |
| 3 | .186* .142† | | | | | | | |
| 4 | .201† .242† | .103* | | | | | | |
| 5 | .117† | | | | | | | |
| 6 | .134† | | | | | | | |
| 7 | | | | | | | | |
| 8 | | | | | | | | |
| 9 | | | | | | | | |
| 10 | | | | | | | | |
| 11 | .127† .143† | .086* .091* | .162† | .173† | | | | |
| 12 | .271† .181† | | .121† | | | | | |
| 13 | .342† .216† | .216† .107* | .189† | .214† | .116† | | .141† | |
| 14 | | | | | | | | |
| 15 | | | | | | | | |
| 16 | | | | | | | | |
| 17 | | | | | | | | |
| 18 | | | | | | | | |
| 19 | .097* .126† | .142† | | | | | | |
| 20 | | | | | | | | |

| | | | | | | | | |
|---|---|---|---|---|---|---|---|---|
| 21 | | | | | | | | |
| 22 | | | | | | | | |
| 23 | | | | | | | | |
| 24 | .176† | .143† | | | .114* | | | |
| 25 | .136† | .201† | | | | | | |
| 26 | | | | | | | | |
| 27 | .241† | | | | | | | |
| 28 | .193† | .117† | | | | | | |
| 29 | .246† | .317† | .102* | 141† | | | | |
| 30 | | | | | | | | |
| 31 | | | | | | | | |
| 32 | | | | | | | | |
| 33 | | | | | | | | |
| 34 | | | | | | | | |
| 35 | | | | | | | | |
| 36 | .117† | .104* | | | .139† | .181† | .114* | |
| 37 | .089* | | | | | | | |
| 38 | | | | | | | | |
| 39 | | | | | | | | |
| 40 | .172† | .193† | .112* | | | | | |
| 41 | .237† | .142† | .116† | .197† | .103* | .121* | | |
| 42 | .110* | .186† | .134† | | | | | |

*$p \leq .025$

†$p \leq .005$

‡Only significant correlations ($p \leq .025$) reported

§Refer to Table 3.1 for coding of medical variables

‖Refer to Table 3.2 for list of criterion measures

# TABLE 3.4

## Pearson Correlations of Demographic Variables with Criterion Measures

| Age in Months — Criterion Measures* | 6 Cat Den | 12 Cat Den | 18 Cat Den | 24 Cat Den | 36 VMI Bin PPVT | 48 WPPSI | 60 VMI Bin PPVT | 72 WISC |
|---|---|---|---|---|---|---|---|---|
| **Race** | .092† .107† | .121‡ | .117‡ .127† | .094† .113† | .107† .184‡ .156‡ | .121‡ | .096† .113† .142‡ | .102† |
| **Mother's Age** | | | .086† | | .136‡ .127‡ | .092‡ | .087† | |
| **Father's Age** | | .134‡ | | .096† | | | | |
| **Mother's Educ.** | .121‡ | | .099† | .117‡ | .186‡ .199‡ | .204‡ | .087† .236‡ .247‡ | .246‡ |
| **Father's Educ.** | | | | .134‡ | .197‡ .121‡ .168‡ | .149‡ | .162‡ .204‡ .259‡ | .117‡ |
| **Number of Siblings** | | | | | | .134‡ | | .086† |

*Demographic Variables*

*Refer to Table 3.2 for list of criterion measures

†$p \le .025$

‡$p \le .005$

(Only significant correlations ($p \le .025$) reported)

education) after age 2 suggest that these population characteristics describe environments which contribute positively to learning potential and those that do not. Thus identification of educational at–risk status by school entry age is less related to the condition of the infant at birth than to the environment in which he spends his early years. In addition, the environmental conditions during infancy appear to have a delayed and cumulative effect, as they only become apparent as discriminators after age 2, and remain consistent predictors from age 2 onward.

Previous studies (Garber 1975) have demonstrated that intervention during the first two years by mothers whose demographic patterns are indicative of high–risk status is associated with positive outcomes for children. The present study would appear to support this as an intervention strategy. These results suggest that by age 6, children from certain demographic groupings are educationally at risk, and even systematic intervention programs initiated at this time may represent a "too little, too late" approach. It is feasible that much of the educational failure observed in children during middle childhood and early adolescence, with which this volume is concerned, is related to children's environments during the first two years. "Coming of Age" may include a reexamination of the child's learning environment during infancy.

## REFERENCES

Babson, S. G., and J. Kangan. "Preschool Intelligence of Undersized Term Infants." *American Journal of Diseases of Children* 117 (1969): 553–60.

Bayley, N. "The Predictive Value of Several Different Measures of Mental Growth During the First Nine Years." *Psychological Bulletin* 36 (1939): 571–72.

Beery, K. E. *Developmental Test of Visual-Motor Integration: Manual.* Chicago: Follett, 1967.

Cattell, P. *Manual for Cattell Infant Intelligence Scale.* New York: Psychological Corp., 1960.

Dobbing, J. "Vulnerable Period in Developing Brain." *Applied Neurochemistry,* edited by A. N. Davison and J. Dobbing. Philadelphia: Davis, 1968.

Dunn, L. M. *Peabody Picture Vocabulary Test: Manual.* Circle Pines, Minn.: American Guidance Services, 1965.

Finkelstein, N. W., and C. T. Ramey. "Information from Birth Certificates as a Risk Index for Educational Handicap. *American Journal of Mental Deficiency* 84 (1980): 546–52.

Frankenburg, W. K., and J. B. Dodds. *Denver Developmental Screening Test.* Denver: Ladoca Press, 1975.

Garber, H. L. "Intervention in Infancy: A Developmental Approach." In *The Mentally Retarded and Society: A Social Science Perspective,* edited by M. J. Begab and S. A. Richardson. Baltimore: University Park Press, 1975.

Gray, S. W., and R. A. Klaus. *The Early Training Project: A Seventh Year Report.* Nashville: John F. Kennedy Center for Research on Education and Human Development, George Peabody College for Teachers, 1969.

Hartlage, L. C., and D. G. Lucas. *Mental Development Evaluation of the Pediatric Patient.* Springfield, Ill.: Charles C. Thomas, 1973.

Horton, K. B. "Infant Intervention and Language Learning." In *Language Perspectives: Acquisition, Retardation, and Intervention,* edited by R. L. Schiefelbusch and L. L. Lloyd. Baltimore: University Park Press, 1974.

Kirman, B. H. "Early Disturbance of Behaviour in Relation to Mental Defect." *British Medical Journal* 2: 1215.

Kochanek, T. T. "Early Detection Programs for Preschool Handicapped Children: Some Procedural Recommendations." *The Journal of Special Education* 14 (1980): 347–53.

Lazar, I., and R. B. Darlington. *Lasting Effects after Preschool.* Washington, D.C.: U. S. Dept. of HEW, 1978.

McCall, R. B., P. S. Hogarty, and N. Hurlburt. "Transitions in Infant Sensorimotor Development and the Prediction of Childhood IQ." *American Psychologist* 27 (1972): 728–48.

Nelson, K. B., and J. Deutschberger. "Head Size at One Year as a Predictor of Four-Year IQ." *Developmental Medicine and Child Neurology* 12 (1970): 487–95.

Reynolds, C. R., and T. B. Gutkin. "Predicting the Premorbid Intellectual Status of Children Using Demographic Data." *Clinical Neuropsychology* 1 (1979): 36–8.

Terman, L. D., and M. A. Merrill. *Stanford-Binet Intelligence Scale.* Lombard, Ill.: Riverside, 1960.

Towbin, A. "Neuropathologic Factors in Minimal Brain Dysfunction." In *Handbook of Minimal Brain Dysfunction,* edited by H. Rie and E. Rie. New York: John Wiley, 1980.

Wechsler, D. A. *Manual for the Wechsler Intelligence Scale for Children.* New York: Psychological Corp. 1960.

———. *Manual for the Wechsler Preschool and Primary Scale of Intelligence.* New York: Psychological Corp., 1967.

Werner, E. E., M. P. Honzik, and R. S. Smith. "Prediction of Intelligence and Achievement at 10 Years from 21 Months Pediatric and Psychologic Examinations." *Child Development* 30 (1968): 1063–75.

# FAMILY AND SOCIAL SYSTEMS

# 4

# Making Practice Perfect

## Pointers for Parents

*Theresa E. Laurie and George E. Maitland*

Mᴏsᴛ ᴘᴀʀᴇɴᴛs assist with school work at various points and to varying degrees during their child's educational career. Most often this assistance is limited to help in preparing for the weekly spelling tests, completing a homework assignment, mastering basic addition and subtraction facts or times tables, and studying for tests.

However, many parents of youngsters experiencing learning difficulties usually assume an even greater responsibility for promoting their child's academic learning at home. The need for such involvement by parents of youngsters with learning difficulties seems unquestionable. These children often require: (1) great effort to keep afloat in the mainstream; (2) repeated individual practice to master skills that most youngsters master with only moderate effort; (3) a consistent effort (including non-school months) to maintain skills they have developed during the year.

Some parents of learning disabled youngsters would like to assist their child but choose not to because of feelings of inadequacy. These parents feel unprepared and untrained to deal with "school learnings." Many other parents who do work with their children report feelings of frustration coupled with desperation when they have attempted homework assistance or tutoring. These parents' experiences suggest that mixing parental instruction and learning disabilities is like mixing oil and water.

Both of these groups of parents (those who haven't tried and want to and those who have tried and wish they hadn't) need assistance. In this chapter some simple, yet effective, teaching procedures will be described for parents to use to make their work sessions with children more productive. Specific strategies will be shared for facilitating memorization of spelling words, math facts, and content area facts, and promoting the development of reading skills.

47

## THE WORK SESSION IN THE HOME

There are some preliminary things to consider before we begin a discussion of strategies for teaching children. The conditions of the work session itself can play a critical role in how much a child benefits from parental assistance.

### The Setting of the Work Session Must Be Selected with Care

Although no rules can be established which match the uniqueness of every household, the activities should occur in a location where both the parent and child are free from other distractions. Some parents find it useful to work in the child's room with the door closed or in the dining room to guarantee privacy. By labeling a certain place in the house for work to occur, the parents can begin to model good study habits for their child to follow in later years.

### The Time of a Work Session Must Be Given Some Thought

If a parent and child are engaging in a more informal work activity, such a session could occur during any time slot (e.g., when nothing good is on television). However, if the activity is a homework assignment, the time of the session deserves careful consideration. As Lovitt (1977) suggests: "Almost anything can interfere with teaching if it is allowed to intrude. Since teaching and learning have so long been associated with punishing circumstances, [many] activities compete with instruction. Such competition is more difficult if a set time is scheduled."

In addition many parents wish to teach children that homework *must* occur before watching television or engaging in other recreational activities. They therefore select a consistent time each day to work with their child.

*The length of time of the work session must be matched to the child's age and own abilities to concentrate.* Research indicates that for adults and children short intervals of practice spaced out over a period of time (a week) are better for learning than extremely long practice times where everything is studied at onece. Therefore, if a child has twenty spelling words to learn by Friday the parent could help the child study five each night during 10–15 minute sessions. At each session the new words could be practiced and tested along with the words from the previous night. This would be better than spending 30 minutes on Wednesday and Thursday trying to memorize the entire list.

Another reason for structuring the practice time into shorter work units, is to guarantee that neither the parent or the child will work longer than "patience" will allow. If both parties can remain calm and productive more will be accomplished and both will be more likely to sit together again to tackle the next activity. If patience is lost and the session becomes a power struggle little of the task will be learned. Instead both parties might learn to dread these times.

*The tone of the work session is critical to its success for the child and the parent.* It is important to maintain a positive tone. This can be accomplished by setting realistic goals for the session, and by accepting the child's limitations. If the child has a hard time reading, one must be ready for a slower, word by word performance which will be dotted with mistakes. By accepting the facts about their children, parents can avoid non-productive struggles by asking the child "why he/she makes errors", or stating judgements like "if you slowed down or tried harder you'd do better." It is important to remember that the child is performing an activity which is extremely hard for him/her. Constant praise and support and understanding will make the child more willing to try. In fact, some parents find it useful to follow a work session with some reinforcing event for the child (i.e., "You worked so hard let's play a game or go for a walk or have some hot chocolate").

If the tone of the session is tense and negative the session may need to be terminated, even if the task *has not* been completed. If a parent cannot interact calmly and in a supportive tone during homework, perhaps the job needs to be given to another family member, a neighbor or abandoned until the parents can come to a better understanding of their child.

*Finally, if the work session is focusing on assigned homework it is important to clarify, for one's self and the child, the role the parent is taking in the homework session.* The parent should take on the role as helper or a supervisor who is available to help the child complete his/her responsibility. The parent shouldn't become the person who will do all of the work. The parent can supervise the homework session by sitting with the child to go over the directions, then leaving the child to work independently. The child may only be in the next room or across the table, but it is important that the child learn to complete some of the task without an adult. Although the parent may return in 5 minutes to check the child's work or to conduct a practice test, the child is learning to do *his or her* homework.

It is critical for parents to share the responsibility for homework with the child, and be a homework monitor rather than a homework partner. Whether the child is in a special class or in the regular grades he/she will be expected to work independently for increasingly longer periods of time. By doing everything for and with their child, a parent is missing an opportunity to teach an important school and life survival skill, and may be fostering unrealistic expectations in their child which no teacher can fulfill. If the preliminary factors for a successful work session are carefully considered, a parent can then begin the task of working with their child.

## MEMORIZING INFORMATION

Parents are oftentimes encouraged by teachers to help their child memorize new information like: weekly spelling words, math facts, sight words, new content area vocabulary and facts (e.g., science vocabulary, state capitals, etc.). Unless these practice activities are structured correctly they may not lead to the old adage: practice makes perfect. To make the most of these sessions it is useful if the parents can have an understanding of the stages a learner goes through in memorizing new information.

Let's look to an example from adult learning to understand what it takes to commit new information (like the telephone number of the local pizza shop) to memory. Certainly the first time we use the number we may need to look at it several times to be sure that we have the correct numbers, repeat it over and over, or actually read it as we dial. Unless our memory for numbers is extremely good, we probably won't remember the number the next time we make the call. Consequently, we may resort to looking in the telephone book, repeating the number, writing it down, or creating some gimmick to help us remember (e.g. converting the digits to letters). In time as we continue to use the number it becomes memorized. We know when we have memorized the number because we no longer need to look back and check and the information is automatically recalled. However, if we don't use the number for a long period of time we may need to begin our practice again. From this example we can observe that memorization occurs as a result of repeated exposure to the new information.

If we keep this example in mind it can help us create structured practice experiences for children which may be more likely to result in learning.

### Common Mistakes in Practice

Parent: "Tommy these are your math/spelling/reading flash cards. Let's go over them."

Step 1: (Shows child the card and says "This is giraffe, quart, or $2 \times 3 = 6$, $3 \times 4 = 12$, etc.)

Step 2: "Now tell me this word (shows child word) or how much is $3 \times 3 = \underline{\hspace{1cm}}$ (shows card).

The child may make a mistake and be given the correct response and the adults will start the process over again. This procedure, unlike our example of an adult learning a telephone number, gives the child a limited opportunity to be exposed to the new information. The practice becomes a *test* of the child's memory, rather than an opportunity for the child to become familiar with the new information.

### Following a Sequence in Practice

Although the purpose of practicing math facts, spelling or sight words or new facts is to have the child be able to commit the information to memory, the practice sequence should not begin by asking the child to remember the new information (What is $3 \times 2 - ?$). Just as an adult learns to memorize a new phone number by looking back, writing it, saying it, and using it repeatedly, children, especially children with learning difficulties, will need to be given the similar opportunities to memorize new information.

Research has reinforced this assumption. It has been found effective to break complex tasks into smaller more manageable tasks, and to order these tasks in sequence from easy to hard. Studies have suggested learning of the harder tasks in the sequence is facilitated if practice is first provided on the lower level, simpler tasks. The practice sequence outlined below is based upon such a hierarchy. Initial practice is given in which the child is not required to remember the new information. Eventually the demands on the learner increase and in the final steps of practice the child is expected to have the new information committed to memory.

### Step 1: Provide a Lot of Practice Using the New Information

In the early stages of practice, activities need to be designed in which the child uses, *looks* at, *copies,* and *repeats* the new information.

For example: Instead of simply showing the child new sight words, spelling words, math facts, etc. it is helpful if:

The child copies the information from the flash cards or text book, and the adult states the new information.

The parent goes over the spelling list word by word, the child says the word, copies the word directly from the model, and checks to make sure the written word is copied correctly.

The parent shows the child the math fact ($3 \times 2 = 6$, $3 \times 4 = 12$, etc.). Child writes them, (onto a blackboard etc.) while looking at the flash cards.

Parent and child review the list of the names of 4 states and capitals, child writes them, but is allowed to look at the list.

Child is given two sets of flash cards and matches the two that are the same, repeating the word after the adult says it.

| the | grandmother |
|-----|-------------|
| grandmother | the |
| firetruck | firetruck |

Child makes flash cards from a word list, and draws pictures to help remember meaning.

Child traces on top of new word(s) or math fact and says names of letters, word, or numerals.

By having access to the actual words or facts during this first practice, the child is becoming familiar with the information. Just as the adult learning a new phone number may need to look at the number while dialing the phone, the child needs the opportunity to have the new information available to check and look as he/she responds.

### Step 2: Practice Finding or Selecting the Correct Answer with the New Information Still Available

As we move the child to committing the new information to memory the practice becomes more difficult. At this point the child still isn't expected to give the right answer from memory.

Read this word (grandmother).

How much is $3 \times 2 = $?

What is the capital of Virginia?

but is expected to select the correct answer from several choices, with the understanding that he/she can check back and look at the text book or the flash cards.

For example:

*Spelling:* With the spelling list in front of him/her (on the individual word in question) the child is asked to pick the word which is spelled correctly.

| Task 1 | teh | the | hte |
|--------|-----|-----|-----|
| Task 2 | grindmother | grondmother | grandmother |

*Sight Words:* Look at your flash cards and tell me which of these words says cap?
(on paper)

|  | can | cat | cap |
|--|-----|-----|-----|

*Math Facts:*

Facts: $3 \times 2 = 6$  $3 \times 3 = 9$  $3 \times 4 = 12$

Parent: "Circle the correct answer. Check the facts before you answer."

| $3 \times 2 =$ | 7, | 9, | 6 |
|----------------|-----|-----|-----|
| $3 \times 3 =$ | 10, | 8, | 9 |
| $3 \times 4 =$ | 12, | 10, | 15 |

Facts: "The capital of Virginia is Richmond, Cleveland? Check back before you answer."

Each time the child looks back or checks the book or flash card, he/she has a chance to become more familiar with the information. If an error is made the parent may redirect the child to copy and trace or say the word, letters, etc. again.

### Step 3: Practice Finding or Selecting the Correct Answer, without Looking before Making a Decision

In this step the task becomes a bit more difficult. The child is now expected to recognize the new information. Instead of allowing the child to look at the list, book, or flash cards, for the first time the child is encouraged to make a decision from memory.

The same activities used in the previous step can be used during this step but the flash card or book is not available to the youngster.

For example:

Spelling: Show the child the following:

| Task 1 | teh | the | eth |
|--------|-----|-----|-----|
| Task 2 | qurt | quart | qaurt |

Parent says: "Circle the word which is spelled correctly."

| *Sight Words:* | Display several flash cards: | | |
| --- | --- | --- | --- |
| | grandmother | firetruck | the |

*Parent says:*   "Point to firetruck."
                 "Point to grandmother."
                 "Point to the."

*Math Facts:*

Circle the right answer

| $3 \times 4 =$ | 10, | 12, | 15 |
| --- | --- | --- | --- |
| $3 \times 2 =$ | 6, | 9, | 8 |
| $3 \times 3 =$ | 15, | 10, | 9 |

*Facts:*

The Capital of Ohio is:
(Cleveland, Akron, Youngstown)?

By having experience with the new information in previous steps, it is likely that the child will have no trouble selecting the correct answer. After the child responds the child should check his or her response by using the book or flash cards.


### Step 4: Recalling/Remembering the New Information without the Model


Finally, the child is given practice reproducing or recalling the new information by saying it or writing it from memory. Since the child has already had exposure to looking, tracing, copying and selecting the new information, this step should be easier for both parent and child. Traditional practice activities described earlier which test the child's knowledge are appropriate at this step.

For Example:

*Math:*

Parent shows the child flash cards and asks for answer

$$3 \times 3 = ?$$
$$3 \times 4 = ?$$
$$2 \times 6 = ?$$

*Spelling:*

Parent dictates practice test and child writes word.
"Write the word 'giraffe'."
"Write the word 'the'."

*Reading:*

Parent shows child flash cards and asks
to read them.

| the | firetruck | was |
| --- | --- | --- |

*Facts:*

Parent says name of state, child writes
or says the name of the capital.
Parent:      "Virginia"
Child:       "Richmond"

The condition of this final phase of practice should be matched to
the conditions that the child will be expected to perform the target
behavior in the classroom. If the child is going to be expected to write the
answers to the 3's tables very quickly, then the parents should make
these same demands before terminating practice on these skills. Similarly, the condition of the child's weekly spelling test should be modelled. If the teacher dictates the test quickly and out of order the parent
should have the child write the words under these conditions in a
practice test. (Many parents have children say their spelling words, but
the weekly test requires a written response.)

It is also useful to have the child practice these new skills in other
materials to guarantee that the information is truly learned. For example, a child could use the spelling words in a scrabble game; demonstrate
knowledge of math facts in a card game, and read the new sight words in
a book, or the newspaper. By practicing the new information in this way
the parent can help guarantee that the skill will be carried over into the
other materials and situations.

## SUMMARY

By using this outline as a guide parents can build in success during the
homework sessions designed to help a child memorize new information.
There are certainly many less formal opportunities for parents to enrich
a child's skill development without homework, which cannot be over-
looked, i.e. playing games, or reading and talking together. In the next
section of the paper some ideas will be shared for promoting growth in
reading during such informal practice sessions in the home.

### Promoting the Development of Reading Skills

Parents and educators are concerned about helping children with reading problems improve their skills. Proficiency in reading requires a well developed sight vocabulary, good word attack skills, and ability to comprehend or understand the meaning of a printed passage. Although parents frequently sit and listen to their children read, they rarely make use of such opportunities to improve their child's skills. Many teaching procedures have been identified to promote growth in these skills, and knowledge of several of these would seem useful in helping parents to make the most of reading activities with their children.

### Selecting Appropriate Reading Materials

The reading materials selected by or for children to practice reading (or for enjoyment) should be both challenging yet within the child's ability (instructional) level. The following guidelines often suggested and used by reading teachers can help parents pick appropriate materials for children to read.
1. Select a 100 word passage in the book, magazine, etc. under consideration (for a younger child, 25–50 words may be more appropriate).
2. Have the child read the passage orally.
3. Count the number of words read incorrectly or words unknown. Incorrect words might include omissions, hesitations longer than 5 seconds, mispronunciations, etc.
4. If the child misses 5–7 words (in the 100 word passage) the passage is appropriate. If more than 7 words are missed the materials should be reconsidered. It is likely that the material would be too difficult.

### Improving Sight Vocabulary Through Error Correction

Research studies have been conducted to determine the best method for correcting children as they make errors in oral reading (Larson and Jenkins 1979). After investigating several strategies, the following simple procedure was found to be most effective in correcting children's reading errors.

STEP 1:  The child reads a passage.

STEP 2:  When an error is made or when the child requests a word the parent supplies the word, instead of coaxing the child to sound it out, and makes a note of the unknown word.

STEP 3:  After the entire passage is read the unknown words are written on words cards.

STEP 4:  The child is asked to read the word. Words read correctly are removed from the pack. Those words which the child is unable to read are read by the parent and retained in the pack.

At first, the missed words are presented in this manner until the child reads the entire deck correctly.

STEP 5:  At the next session the child rereads the passage and the parent can observe progress.

### Improving Word Attack Skills

In addition to reading whole words from memory, children must learn how to unlock the unfamiliar words they meet while reading. A child cannot rely on another individual to tell them every unfamiliar word. Many parents are uncomfortable in teaching children to sound out words because they don't have a solid understanding of phonics.

Gerald Glass (1971) has researched an effective method to analyze words into parts which doesn't require knowing the difference between consonants and vowels. This simple method (with minor modifications) as outlined below can be used to help children see clusters or small sounds units in the sight words they have already learned in new words that they meet in guided or independent readings or preselected (by parent or child) word lists.

STEP 1:  *Present the Whole Word*

In the Glass procedure a whole word is presented to the child.

Parent:  "This word is ground" (show written word) "What is this word?"

Child:  Child says word, if an error is made parent repeats the word.

STEP 2:  *Present the Word Parts*

Parent:  "In the word ground the "gr" makes the gr—r—r sound. In the word ground the "o-u-nd" makes the ound sound. (Show child parts)

STEP 3: *Child Provides Letters for Sounds of Word Parts*
  Parent: "In the word ground what letters make the sound 'gr'
  Child responds, if incorrect parent says: "g + r"
  Parent: "In the word ground what letters make the "ound" *sound?*"
  Child responds, if incorrect the parent says: "o-u-n-d"

STEP 4: *Child Provides the Sounds for the Word Parts*
  Parent: "In the word ground what sound do the letters g-r make?"
  Child responds, if not, parent corrects.
  "In the word ground what sound do the letters o-u-n-d make?"
  Child responds or parent corrects.

STEP 5: *Child Reads Word*
  Parent: "Says this word?"

By practicing the parts or clusters of a word, the parent can help a child learn a strategy to take unknown words apart and sound them out. This process of word study is useful and can be used even if a child doesn't know individual letter sounds (since they are modeled by the parent) or has trouble with traditional phonics programs. This strategy, if coupled with the error correction procedure discussed previously, provides an economical way to promote growth in a child's sight vocabulary and word attack skills.

## IMPROVING COMPREHENSION

Finally, the most important reading skill which must be developed is a child's ability to glean meaning from the printed page. Although few techniques have been defined as effective in increasing a child's comprehension skills, one method, Directed-Reading-Thinking Activities (Betts 1946) is cited frequently by reading experts. This method can be used to help readers of any age have an increased understanding of what they read (newspapers, magazines, library books, text books). To turn a reading session (oral or silent) into a Directed-Reading-Thinking Activity, a parent would do the following.

### Step 1: Pre-Reading

Before beginning to read a passage, time is spent helping the child develop a purpose and an interest in the materials to be read. The parent can do this by guiding the child to look at the title or any subtitles, pictures, etc. and leading a discussion to form questions and predictions about the contents of the story.

For example, a child may be reading a story entitled *The Escaped Convict*. Although brief, the title provides important clues regarding the story. The parent could create interest by asking the child what he or she thinks the title means—"What does *escape* mean? What is a *convict*?

These questions can help stimulate the child's curiosity. In addition, the pictures can help the child set predictions about what will happen. Perhaps one picture shows a boy chasing a dog in the woods, and another shows the boy with a man who appears to be pushing or grabbing the boy. To further promote interest the child is asked to guess who the convict in the title refers to: the boy? the man? or the dog? and to guess why an escape is happening.

### Step 2: Directed Reading

With the child's interest and a purpose for reading clearly defined, a part of the passage is read (orally or silently). While the child reads, he/she is looking for information to answer the questions that were generated and to determine if the guesses made previously are accurate. Any unknown words encountered by the child are provided by the parent.

### Step 3: Evaluating and Proving

At the end of the passage a discussion is held with the child to determine if his/her questions have been answered and if the predictions were right. For each answer the child gives, he/she is asked to refer to the passage to find evidence to prove and support his/her answer.
For example:

Parent: "Were you right about your prediction? Who is the escaped convict?

Child:  "I thought it was the man but it's the dog."
Parent: "Where in the story did you discover this fact?"
Child:  "Right here (points) the dog stole the man's newspaper.
The boy locked the dog in the garage but he escaped."

### Step 4: Revising Questions and Predictions

Using the new information gathered from the story the child is encouraged to look ahead in the story (at titles and pictures). He/she formulates new questions and makes another set of predictions about what might happen.

This process can help children become more involved in the story and increase the possibility that children will attend to, remember, and understand what they read.

## SUMMARY

All three of the strategies presented can be easily integrated into a half hour reading practice session. If these ideas are applied by a parent, a child's growth in all areas can be promoted.

## CONCLUSION

Parents of children with learning difficulties play an important role in fostering growth and development of their child's knowledge of basic skills. In both formal homework sessions and informal work activities this impact of the time spent with a child can be heightened if some of the ideas outlined in this paper are used as a guide.

# 5

## Effectiveness of Paraprofessional Counselors in a Structured Self-Concept Enhancement Program for Children with Learning Problems

*Mervyn Skuy and Michael Marcus*

S TUDIES of the effectiveness of using paraprofessionals in the therapeutic process have been inconclusive but have pointed to their potential usefulness in improving the functioning of various groups of people (Gruver 1971; Skuy and Solomon 1980).

In the study by Skuy and Solomon, two groups of people lacking in formal qualifications — namely university students and parents — were used in an attempt to improve the adjustment and scholastic perform-ance of children with learning problems. While the hypothesized effects of intervention were not statistically demonstrated, improvements in functioning were suggested for some children. In examining the reasons for the variability of outcome, the authors found that the performance of the different university students involved (or, as they were called, Youth Counselors) varied immensely from one to the other. As one of the prospective remedies suggested for this, the authors proposed that a more structured program of training and supervision should be provided for youth counselors (YCs).

Tied up with more specific training and guidelines for intervention is the need for a more definite, specific and clearly-defined goal than has been provided in the past for YCs and their clients. The goal of self-concept enhancement is a particularly important one for children with learning problems. Psychologists and educators (for example, Purkey 1970; Rogers 1969; Staines 1958) have suggested in their studies and writings that a person's self-concept is closely connected to how he behaves and learns. Purkey (1978) quotes substantial evidence which indicates that low performance in basic school subjects, as well as the misdirected motivation and lack of academic involvement characteristic of the under-achiever, the dropout, the culturally disadvantaged, and the failure, may be due in part to negative perception of the self. Difficulty in succeeding at or mastering the tasks at school may, in turn, lead to increasing feelings of incompetence (cf. White 1959) or negative self-concept, which would lead to further failure. There is thus a continuous interaction between the self and academic achievement.

Numerous experimental programs have been devised to enhance a student's self-concept and thus improve his school achievement. Many of them have yielded positive findings (for example, Brookover, Patterson, and Thomas 1964; Pine 1976; Staines 1958). Other studies have found no relationship between enhanced self-concept and improved academic performance. For example, Marx and Winne (1976) reported that programs of self-concept enhancement improved self-concept without any gains in academic achievement. Among the reasons advanced for contradictory findings is the questionable efficacy of certain intervention programs. Levitan and Kiraly (1975) point out that self-concept intervention programs are not structured or clearly defined. Thus, self-concept programs themselves require explicit definition, a framework for which could be provided by devising an improved, more structured program of paraprofessional intervention.

Accordingly, this study aimed to engage undergraduate psychology volunteers in a systematic, task-oriented self-concept enhancement program for children with educational difficulties. It was predicted that this form of intervention would be more effective, relative to a non-structured program, and to non-intervention, in improving self-concept, and hence academic achievement and adjustment.

## METHOD

### Subjects

The sample comprised thirty-six boys and girls who were attending a university Education Clinic for children with learning problems. Subjects were randomly selected from among those on the waiting list who were of at least average intelligence (as measured on the WISC-R) and of broadly middle-class socioeconomic status. They attended regular elementary schools and their age range was 8–12 years.

Subjects were randomly divided into three equal-sized groups, two experimental (E1 and E2) and a non-intervention control (C). Children in both experimental groups were exposed to the psycho-educational program run by undergraduate psychology student volunteers and referred to as the "Youth Counseling Program" (Skuy 1975). However, while children in E1 followed the previous non-directive, unstructured approach (Skuy 1975; Skuy and Solomon 1980), those in E2 underwent a self-concept enhancement program.

## Forms of Intervention

Group E1 provided for a one-to-one relationship between a child and a YC. The relationship was to be based on the Rogerian principles of congruence, empathy and unconditional positive regard. The YC became actively attuned to the total child, his/her school and home life, attitudes and activities, assets and problems. Emphasis was placed on spontaneity, flexibility, informality, and individuality by encouraging the YC to engage in interaction and activity with the child at times and places congenial to both. The YC was, however, expected to see his/her child for at least three hours per week over a period of six months. Informal learning activities and experiences could be selected from a booklet entitled *Guidelines for the Youth Counselor* (Skuy 1975) or devised by the YCs themselves. Professional supervision and a pre-intervention orientation program were provided by a team comprising a psychologist, a remedial educationist, a social worker and graduate students in these fields. Weekly meetings led by these professionals provided an opportunity for YCs to share feelings and ideas.

The intervention devised for E2 was the same as above in all respects but one: In E2 the specific goal of intervention was the enhancement of self-concept, an objective spelled out to YCs. They were given a set of specially-designed strategies aimed at improving their children's awareness of and satisfaction with self. These techniques were adapted from different psychotherapeutic and educational approaches, and are elaborated below.

1. *Art* materials provided a nonverbal medium for posing and clarifying questions the child had about himself and his environment, and pointed to some options he might choose for more constructive participation in creating his life conditions. The role of the YC in these activities was to demonstrate acceptance of the child, to provide the opportunity for self exploration, and to serve as a model for self acceptance. Specific techniques employed included:

### The self box

Using a cardboard box, scissors, glue, a pile of old pictures, magazines, and poster paints, the child was asked to make something he felt was representative of himself in terms of size, depth and breadth. He could cut openings that allowed other people to see inside. He was asked to represent his feelings, fears, hopes *etc.* via magazine pictures or paint. He could determine what he wanted to keep on the inside and what he chose to show on the outside. The child was thus encouraged to experience himself in an active way and to acknowledge and accept his self-perceptions;

### Family sculpting

Using plasticine, the child sculpted his family members, including himself. The child was meant to gain insight into family relationships and to symbolically express his feelings about his position in the family;

### Finger painting

The child was asked to paint the way he felt, how he would like to feel, *etc*. Expression of feelings through painting was intended to provide the child with an opportunity to externally perceive his feelings and thus evaluate them;

### Collage

Here the child was asked to pictorially represent both positive and negative aspects of himself and his interests.

2. *Drama,* like art, was used as a technique for the symbolic expression of aspects of the self. Here, the child could express feelings and practice behavior in the secure setting of the counseling "theater." The YC could take part in various ways, for example, by being cast in complementary roles by the child, or by depicting a realistically positive *alter ego* for the child.

3. *The Feeling Chart* was a technique adapted from the Transactional Analysis concept of "strokes." On the Feeling Chart, 'strokes' were denoted by different-colored stars, given in relation to interactions with significant others, and filled in weekly by YC and client jointly. For example, if a child was derided by the teacher that week and made to feel angry, YC and child would stick a red stamp in the space allocated to the teacher. This weekly exercise yielded a graphic representation of the perceived quality of interactions between the child and significant others. It also helped him to determine how he saw himself in relation to others and how others related to him. If the quality of an interaction was negative, the child was encouraged by the YC to initiate action to improve the interaction. In this way and by collecting more positive

stars, he experienced positive input about his ability to exert some effect on his environment.

4. *A Problem Solving* technique aimed at enhancing creativity. In this exercise the child was asked to draw on his imagination and design an abstract machine (e.g. a happiness or laughing machine). This process was meant to enable the child to break free from the rigidity of his previous thought processes and explore various alternatives and possibilities. It aimed to provide him with more positive feelings about his ability to solve problems.

5. *Growth Games* involved YC and child in using bodily movement, including mime and charades, and were aimed at enhancing self-awareness. Extensive use was also made of all sensory modalities, in an attempt to provide children with a fuller appreciation and more effective use of their senses.

## Measures

Before and after the intervention program, all subjects were tested on the Draw-a-Person Self-Concept Scale (DAPSC) and Wide Range Achievement Test (WRAT), while an Adaptive Behavior Rating Scale (ABRS) was completed by their parents (mother and father together, where applicable) and their teachers. The DAPSC (Bodwin and Bruck 1960) is said to measure self-confidence, freedom to express appropriate feelings, liking for oneself, satisfaction with one's attainment, and feelings of personal appreciation by others. The WRAT (Jastak and Jastak 1965) served to assess the child's performance in reading (word recognition and pronunciation), written spelling, and arithmetic computation. The ABRS (Skuy 1975) was selected as a measure of the child's adjustment which had been standardized on a comparable South African sample. It assessed interpersonal relationships, emotional strengths and weaknesses, temperament, learning patterns, practical skills, and family interaction. Skuy reported an interrater reliability of .89 and an internal consistency of .7 for the ABRS.

## RESULTS

Separate one-way analyses of variance for each variable were used to test whether there were any significant differences between E1, E2, and C on the measures prior to intervention. No significant differences were found between the three groups on the pre-test measures, thus cor-roborating the assumption of random allocation to groups. Change scores yielded on the measures following intervention were also sub-jected to separate ANOVAS.

As shown in table 5.1, the differences between changes yielded on the DAPSC for the three groups were significant, and in the expected direction. A Sheffe post-hoc comparison demonstrated the significant difference to be between E2 on the one hand, and E1 and C on the other. Thus, the self-concept enhancement program was significantly more effective than either the nondirective YC program or the control group in improving the self-concept of the study's subjects.

TABLE 5.1

**Mean Change, Standard Deviations, and F Values
for the DAPSC**

| Group | X | SD | F | P |
|-------|------|-------|------|-------|
| E1 | 1.25 | 6.09 | | |
| E2 | 7 | 10.31 | 3.96 | < .05 |
| C | −0.75 | 7.27 | | |

On the ABRS, two of the five subscales completed by parents yielded significant differences between the three groups, namely Emo-tional Strengths and Weaknesses, and Temperament. The results for the other subscales, although non-significant, were all in the expected direc-tion. Four out of five subscales showed tendencies to *negative* change for the control group. In every case, the change score of E2 was in a positive direction and tended to be higher than that of E1. The results for the ABRS (parents) are presented in Table 5.2.

From the above table it can be seen that of all the subscales of the ABRS, the results were in the expected direction. On both the Emo-tional Strengths and Weaknesses, and Temperament subscales the dif-ferences between changes yielded for E1, E2 and C were significant. A Sheffe post-hoc comparison demonstrated the significant difference to lie between E2 and C. Significant findings in favor of E2 were not in evidence in the teachers' responses to the ABRS.

Thus, there was partial support for the prediction that a self-concept enhancement YC group would be effective in improving ad-justment.

TABLE 5.2

**Mean Change, Standard Deviations, and F Values for Parents' Ratings on the ABRS**

| ABRS Subscale | E1 | | E2 | | C | | |
| --- | --- | --- | --- | --- | --- | --- | --- |
| | $\overline{X}$ | SD | $\overline{X}$ | SD | $\overline{X}$ | SD | F* |
| Interpersonal Relations | 2 75 | 20.00 | 8.92 | 32.44 | 1.00 | 8.37 | 0.40 |
| Emotional Strengths & Weaknesses | 3.42 | 16.52 | 19.58 | 31.83 | −5.08 | 18.40 | 3.47 |
| Temperament | 1.67 | 11.94 | 18.33 | 32.22 | −1.5 | 9.01 | 3.37 |
| Learning Patterns | 3.17 | 12.47 | 15.67 | 37.00 | −1.91 | 14.78 | 1.69 |
| Family Interaction | 4.83 | 14.51 | 9.41 | 30.86 | −0.58 | 13.07 | 0.67 |

*Critical value of F at the .05 level (d.f. 11/2) = 3.33

Finally, there were no significant differences between the three groups on the WRAT reading, arithmetic or spelling tests. However, on each subtest, the difference between change scores of E2 and the other two groups tended to favor the former.

The quantitative data collected in this study were complemented and supported by qualitative evaluations based on YC reports. Analysis of these reports generally reflected positive attitudes, feelings of accomplishment and a sense of fulfillment. However, a dimension not reflected in E1 reports emerged from the reports presented by those YCs who had been in the self-concept enhancement program (E2). The structured tasks appear to have provided a more secure setting for both YC and child. As compared with the YCs in the non-directive program, those in the structured program expressed less anxiety, since they were not as inclined to feel that excessive demands had been made on their own technical expertise in developing programs, and appeared to feel less vulnerable about their lack of formal training. YCs in the unstructured program, on the other hand, more frequently complained of ambiguous and uncertain role expectations, both on the part of themselves and on the part of the children and their parents.

## DISCUSSION

The significant change in self-concept scores achieved by the self-concept enhancement group was predicted, and demonstrated the efficacy of providing student paraprofessionals with specific techniques of intervention to implement with children experiencing learning problems. It also supported the assumption, made in this study, that a congenial therapeutic relationship, while being a necessary part of self-concept enhancement, is not sufficient in and of itself to produce desired change in self-concept. To improve self-concept, conditions had to be specifically set up so as to provide experiences that were self-enhancing. These comprised the structured task-oriented program with which the YCs were equipped. Apart from the effectiveness of the tasks *per se,* this task oriented program appears to have bolstered the confidence of the YCs, enabling them to perform more adequately and successfully.

Regarding the choice of self-concept measure used, apart from Bodwin and Bruck (1960), who developed an apparently valid scoring system for the test, Kamano (1960) *inter alia,* found the Draw-a-Person to be representative of the drawer's perceptions of himself. Furthermore, in light of the varying ages, levels of academic competence, reading, and comprehension among subjects, the use of this measure was considered to be parsimonious.

The centrality of self-concept to adjustment—suggested by various theorists and the findings of numerous experiments—led to the expectation that improvement in self-concept would be associated with a corresponding change in adjustment. Yet the findings in this regard were not *generally* significant or conclusive. The reasons for this could be associated with shortcomings in the measure of adjustment, or could be due to the fact that changes in self-concept did not have sufficient time to effect changes in overt behavior which were clearly discernible by the observers. It is likely that a combination of both these factors prevented the findings, which were *partially* significant, and all in the expected direction, from reaching overall significance. Where significant changes *were* found, the fact that they were yielded for E2 but not for E1 suggests that such change was not merely a reflection of parental *expectation* of change following intervention.

With regard to the teachers' ratings on the ABRS, the resuls on this measure may have failed to reach significance not because of the failure of subjects to change *per se,* but because of the relative stability and resistance to change of teacher expectations (see Dworkin 1979). Consistent with this is the possibility that teachers were not disposed to viewing the children's adjustment differently in the absence of improvements in academic performance.

Neither the self-concept nor the non-structured group had any significant success in improving scholastic performance, as measured by the WRAT. This finding is in line with the findings of earlier studies of the Youth Counseling Program (Skuy 1975; Skuy and Solomon 1980). A number of interacting factors may account for it. For one thing, the self-concept enhancing tasks implemented here were of a general nature and specific school related activities were not included. Consistent with this, the self-concept tests measured general self-concept and did not assess that aspect which could be referred to as academic self-concept.

On a more general level, an associated reason for failure of intervention — both directive (E2) and nondirective (E1) — to affect school performance, could be the failure of behaviors possibly acquired during the program to transfer to other settings, due to the dissimilarity of stimulus conditions (see Wahler 1969). This problem could be overcome in future by providing for the self-concept intervention to be based, in part, in the school setting too, and by involving the teacher more directly in the program, so that YC and teacher might collaborate, and coordinate their activities and efforts.

Time is another possible factor militating against significant change in scholastic performance. As discussed above, the effects of improved self-concept may need time to manifest themselves in inter-personal behavior. This may also be true with regard to academic functioning. Follow-up testing is thus required.

Further testing may not, however, reveal academic improvements. For one thing, academic achievement may not be considered by some subjects as desirable, or important in their feelings of self-worth (see Curtis, Zanna and Campbell 1975). Again, the learning problems of some children are relatively resistant to specific improvements (see Yule, Rutter, Berger and Thompson 1974). For those children, then, self-concept may improve without a corresponding improvement in academic performance. This improvement would in itself be valuable since children must learn to cope with life and to assert themselves, despite continuing scholastic weaknesses. If self-concept is not inextricably bound up with academic performance, a child with a relatively irreversible difficulty can nevertheless develop positive feelings about self in relation to society and life in general.

Questions regarding the interrelationship of self-concept, learning ability, attitude to school, and scholastic achievement suggest certain areas for further study. For one thing, a follow-up study of self-concept enhancement using paraprofessionals should control for type and severity of learning problem. For another, an assessment of attitudes to school and school achievement, and intervention methods leading to change in attitude, should be conducted.

In discussing the limitations of the study, and possible avenues for further investigation, the success of the structured YC group in improving self-concept should not be forgotten. The gains made here are encouraging, and support the effectiveness of systematic training for paraprofessionals. The fact that the growing use of paraprofessionals in the mental health profession has not been matched by systematic procedures to train them has been noted, *inter alia,* by Avery (1978). The provision of a specific goal and of clearly defined intervention strategies in the present study can be seen as a step in this direction.

## REFERENCES

Avery, A. W. "Communication Skills Training for Paraprofessional Helpers." *American Journal of Community Psychology* 6 (1978): 583.

Bodwin, R. F., and M. Bruck. "The Adaptation and Validation of the Draw-a-Person Test as a Measure of Self-Concept." *Journal of Clinical Psychology* 16 (1960): 427–29.

Brookover, W. B., A. Patterson, and S. Thomas. "Self-Concept of Ability and School Achievement." *Sociology of Education* 37 (1964): 271–78.

Curtis, R. C., M. P. Zanna, and W. Campbell. "Sex, Fear of Success, and the Perceptions and Performance of Low School Students." *American Educational Research Journal* 12 (1975): 287–97.

Dworkin, N. E. "Changing Teachers' Negative Expectations." *Academic Therapy* 14 (1979): 517–31.

Gruver, G. "College Students as Therapeutic Agents." *Psychological Bulletin* 76 (1971): 111–27.

Jastak, J. F., and S. R. Jastak. *The Wide Range Achievement Test: Manual of Instructions.* Rev. ed. Wilmington, Del.: Guidance Associates, 1965.

Kamano, D. K. "An Investigation on the Meaning of Human Figure Drawing." *Journal of Clinical Psychology* 16 (1960): 429–30.

Levitan, H., and J. Kiraly. "Achievement and Self-Concept in Young Learning Disabled Children." *Academic Therapy* 10 (1975): 453–55.

Marx, R. W., and P. H. Winne. "Self-Concept and Achievement: Implications for Educational Programmes." *Integrated Education* 13 (1975): 30–31.

Pine, M. A. "Self-Concept, Informal Education and Reading Achievement in Grade I." Paper presented at the Annual Meeting of International Reading Association, Anaheim, California, May 1976.

Purkey, W. *Self-Concept and School Achievement.* Englewood Cliffs, N.J.: Prentice-Hall, 1970.

——. *Inviting School Success: A Self-Concept Approach to Teaching and Learning.* Belmont, Calif.

Rogers, C. R. *Freedom to Learn.* Columbus, Ohio: Merrill, 1969.

Skuy, M. S. "Definition and Measurement of Adaptive Behaviour in a Psycho-Educational Setting." Doctoral thesis, University of South Africa, Pretoria, 1975.

Staines, J. W. "The Self-Picture as a Factor in the Classroom." *British Journal of Educational Psychology* 28 (1958): 97–111.

Wahler, R. G. "Setting Generality: Some Specific and General Effects of Child Behaviour Therapy." *Journal of Applied Behaviour Analysis* 2 (1969): 239–46.

White, R. W. "Motivation Reconsidered: The Concept of Competence." *Psychological Review* 66 (1959): 297–333.

Yule, W., M. Rutter, M. Berger, and J. Thompson. "Over and Under-Achievement in Reading: Distribution in the General Population." *British Journal of Educational Psychology* 44 (1974): Part I.

# 6

# A Structural Family Therapy Approach to the Treatment of Learning Disabilities

*Ann M. Varna Garis and Laura A. Green*

STRUCTURAL FAMILY THERAPY, developed by Minuchin (1974), is both a theoretical and an applied approach for the diagnosis and treatment of family dysfunctions. This orientation can be applied to a variety of symptomatic behaviors and presenting problems. In their work with psychosomatic families, Minuchin and his colleagues further developed the theory by articulating several patterns characteristic of psychosomatic families (Minuchin, Rosman, and Baker 1978). We believe that several of the patterns described in *Psychosomatic Families* are particularly relevant to the problems experienced in many families with learning disabled members.

As we know, it is often a difficult and challenging task to raise an LD child, and parents may feel confused about appropriate child-rearing practices. Some professionals may advise the family to seek treatment for only the LD child, or they may proscribe practices of raising LD children which differ substantially from treatment accorded to other siblings or which conflict with the parents' general parenting style. For example, parents with a laizzez-faire parenting style are often advised to be very structured with the LD child, even though they utilize their more comfortable, less structured parenting style with the other siblings. These practices may unwittingly serve to give the LD child and others in the family such messages as: "You are the problem in this family" and "You're the only one around here who needs help."

In contrast, structural family therapy views management of the learning disabled child from a family systems perspective, rather than singling out the one child as the sole target for intervention. This approach differs from others in that the entire family becomes involved in the therapeutic process; learning disabilities are considered, in Betty Osmond's words, to be a "family affair" (Osmond 1979). Structural family therapy attempts to describe dysfunctional and problematic patterns within the structure of the family and then to change the family's manner of interaction. Such changes will alter the experiences of individuals within the family and, in particular, can then effect behavioral change in the LD child. Although other sources (Gardner 1973; Abrams and Kaslow 1976; Haring and Bateman 1977; Rowan 1977; Kronick 1978; Osmond 1979) have explored the practical and heuristic value of a family orientation for the treatment of learning disabilities, to date there has been no application of a structural family therapy approach in this area.

Before citing specific examples of dysfunctional patterns from a structural family therapy perspective, three points must be clarified. First, none of the identified situations are unique to families with a learning disabled member. Indeed, many families experience such difficulties, but the family with an LD child may be more susceptible due to increased levels of stress and frustration. These situations are viewed as problematic, as potentially harmful for the child and the family, but *not* as pathological. That is, families exhibiting such difficulties are viewed as distressed, but not necessarily as disturbed. This distinction is important because the labels "pathological" and "disturbed" do not, in fact, accurately reflect the family situations in most cases and serve only to heighten the guilt and apprehension experienced by many parents of LD children.

Second, family therapy is not intended to take the place of a thorough diagnostic work-up or of psychoeducational services given to the child. Rather, family therapy is recommended as another important aspect of the total diagnostic and therapeutic process.

A third point involves the school system and, in particular, the classroom teacher. Although family therapists identify and describe functional and dysfunctional patterns within the family context, parallel situations occur within the school setting. Especially within the self-contained classroom, a family-like grouping develops as the school year progresses. Teachers often perform parent-like functions, such as the organization of tasks and the distribution of rewards and sanctions. Similarly, students often demonstrate sibling-like relatibnships. With the advent of PL 94-142, mandating that an LD child be placed in the least restrictive environment, many LD children function in regular classrooms very well. At times, however, additional stress may be experienced by the LD child, by the classroom teacher, or by other students. As a result of such stress, some dysfunctional patterns may develop and be perpetuated within the school system. Thus, the teacher's ability to recognize and to change dysfunctional patterns within the school setting will be of great benefit to all of the children, but particularly to the LD child.

When there are dysfunctional patterns existing in the family, a child may become especially vulnerable to similar situations which occur in the classroom. In fact, he or she may contribute at times to these dysfunctional patterns by setting up particular relationships in the class-room which replicate the interactions in the family. Thus, changing dysfunctional patterns within both family and school settings must be considered in an optimal treatment program.


## A STRUCTURAL FAMILY THERAPY APPROACH

When a family with a learning disabled member enters structural family therapy, all of the members of the household are initially seen as a unit to determine the functional and dysfunctional patterns that may exist. The therapist assesses the family's functioning on the basis of performance across three dimensions. Notably, the model assumes a traditional view of what constitutes healthy family functioning. Parents are expected to maintain clear authority to carry out executive functions with the children, such as limit–setting. Children, on the other hand, are viewed as having their own particular roles and developmental needs. It is assumed that all family members need a certain amount of physical and psychological space to develop as independent, actualized individuals. The three dimensions that would be assessed during the initial phase of family treatment are boundaries, balance, and alliances/coalitions.


## BOUNDARIES

Boundaries can be thought of as invisible membranes which need to exist between the parent and child subsystems and around each individual in the family. These boundaries must be explicit, but permeable, so that there is communication between individuals and between subsystems and yet enough separation to allow for privacy and autonomous functioning. There is a continuum of boundary permeabilities ranging from very porous, diffuse boundaries, forming an enmeshed system where no one has privacy, to very rigid, impermeable boundaries, creating a disengaged system in which a person would have to go to behavioral extremes in order to be noticed.

All families fall somewhere on the continuum, with optimal functioning falling within the middle range. The families with diffuse or rigid boundaries would be expected to experience difficulty and to show symptoms in one or more family members.

## BALANCE

Balance refers to the distribution of power and status between individuals. The notion underlying the concept of balance is that individuals in a subsystem should have power and status as is appropriate to their roles and developmental stages. For example, both spouses would be expected to have approximately equal status, and the children would be expected to have less power than the parents. Balance may become evident as a problem area when, for example, one child assumes power equal to or greater than that of one of the parents.

## ALLIANCES AND COALITIONS

Alliances are patterns of cohesion formed by family members when they support one another across a variety of situations. Coalitions are created when at least two individuals team up against a third member of the family. Alliances and coalitions become problematic when they occur across generations, disrupting the boundaries between the parent and the child subsystems, and disturbing the balance within the subsystems. They become particularly troublesome when they rigidly and consistently exist for an extended period of time.

## DYSFUNCTIONAL PATTERNS IN THE FAMILY SYSTEM

As mentioned earlier, Minuchin *et al.* (1978) described several patterns characteristic of psychosomatic families which, we suggest, are applicable to certain families with learning disabled members. These dysfunctional patterns include overprotectiveness, enmeshment, and lack of conflict resolution. They are not independent of one another, but rather, these patterns constitute overlapping dimensions which are often present in problematic family situations.

## OVERPROTECTIVENESS

Overprotectiveness can occur when a parent or another sibling attempts to take care of the LD child in an intrusive way that inhibits his or her independent functioning. Typically, the LD child is viewed as fragile and incompetent by the family member who believes that he or she is acting in the child's best interests.

When a parent is overprotecting the LD child, a cross-generational alliance emerges which has secondary gains for both sides. The parent naturally has an inclination to protect the disabled child from the world, and the child, perhaps feeling vulnerable, gladly accepts this attention and support. This pattern becomes problematic when it disrupts balance both in the sibling and the spouse subsystems. The other siblings may resent the increased attention and reduced demands placed on the LD child, and sibling conflict may result with hostility typically being directed toward the "special" child. The other spouse, more typically the husband, may also resent losing his share of attention and support. He may respond by distancing himself from his wife and/or family, or alternately, by expressing his anger at the child. In either case, the overprotective parent will interpret such behavior as a direct threat to or a lack of support for the LD child, and will increase the protectiveness, thereby strengthening the dysfunctional pattern.

A sibling may also behave in an overprotective manner toward the LD child, thereby functioning as a quasi-parent. This parental child may attempt to take special care of the LD child because this behavior gains parental recognition and makes the "little parent" feel important. At times, the parents may feel relieved that a child has assumed this responsibility, since they may feel overburdened. This case more typically arises in one-parent than in two-parent homes or when one parent is away from home a good deal of the time. There are two sides to this situation. On one hand, the parental child may actually be contributing and helping the LD child. On the other hand, when the pattern becomes established and the parents begin to expect this behavior from the parental child, the child may rebel against this responsibility, particularly if he or she is acquiring interests in friends outside of the home. However, since it is sometimes difficult to be openly angry with one's parents, the parental child's resentment may get directed toward the LD child.

From the perspective of the LD child, having a parental sibling is often a hindrance because there are, in effect, three parents to please. The implicit message to the child is that the learning disability has rendered him or her less equal or conpetent than his or her siblings. This message is certainly the opposite of what one would hope to convey to the child.

What can be done about overprotectiveness of the LD child? First, a structural family therapist would attempt to get the parents to assume full and equal parental functioning. At times this goal might be effected by asking the over-involved parent to take a break from attending to the

LD child, and by encouraging the underinvolved parent to participate in activities with the child. The overinvolved parent might be asked to spend time alone with his or her spouse or in activities with the other children. Second, a structural family therapist would instruct the parents to discourage, rather than to reward, parental behavior in one of the siblings. The sibling subsystem could be strengthened by involving all of the children in activities and by highlighting the strengths, abilities, and contributions of each child.

## ENMESHMENT

Enmeshment occurs in a family system when there are diffuse boundaries between family members, and in particular, when there is a diffuse, ineffective boundary between the parent subsystem and the child subsystem. Enmeshed families handle conflict in one of two ways. They either avoid it completely or they fight constantly. If they avoid conflict, arguments are not tolerated, and family members block or discount an individual's attempt to voice a differing opinion. When this process occurs in an LD family, there is little opportunity for family members to exchange information, to correct misconceptions, and to express feelings about problematic situations related to the learning disability.

When enmeshed families handle conflict by fighting all the time, arguments never get settled. For example, the parents may start arguing about finances, and the LD child may hear one parent complaining about the cost of the speech and language therapist, the educational specialist or the psychologist. The child may then start screaming, "Why do I have to go to that stupid lady anyhow? I don't want to go!" The siblings might jump in with, "Jimmy, if it wasn't for you, Mom and Dad would have enough money to get us new bikes!" Then the parents may start yelling at the children, and in the course of a few minutes, everyone is screaming, nagging, and whining with greater and greater intensity. Family members feel angry and at times out of control.

Both of these family situations are potentially damaging for the LD child. When families do not allow differences of opinion, the child quickly gets the notion that his or her feelings and ideas are not valuable. On the other hand, when there is constant conflict in the family, the child's self-esteem is also negatively affected because he or she will likely be receiving little positive regard from family members.

What can be done to help an enmeshed family? First, a structural systems therapist would work to get family members to tolerate differences of opinion and to resolve arguments before they escalate. In effect, boundaries would be restablished in the family. The second step would involve strengthening the executive or parent subsystem. If the family is involved in a cycle of escalating conflict, then the parents are instructed to back one another up and provide a united front.

The parents are also instructed not to get involved in any arguing back and forth with the children because such arguing encourages and maintains the disruption of boundaries. Each parent is instructed to share any conflictual concerns about discipline with his or her spouse in private. Also, the parents are encouraged to use the same rules, applied with the same consistency, for all of the children.

## LACK OF CONFLICT RESOLUTION

Enmeshed families typically have the most difficulty with conflict resolution. However, when any family has not learned appropriate problem-solving strategies, or when existing marital issues are being avoided by the spouses, dysfunctional family patterns can emerge, whereby all conflict is detoured through the LD child. As a way of avoiding their marital issues, the parents may focus their concern exclusively on this child, since he or she if often viewed as the family member requiring greatest attention. There is no escaping the fact that conflictual issues inevitably arise in any marriage. Additional stress is placed on a marriage and on a family unit when there is an LD member. Parents often feel frustrated by the financial expenses that are incurred or by the child's behavioral problems which appear to be resistant to management techniques. When parents have had little adult rest and release time, or when they are trying to balance their needs for professional and personal growth with their parenting responsibilities, conflicts can readily emerge and quickly escalate. If the parents deny the marital issues that exist and consider the LD child as the only troubled family member, then their exclusive focus on the LD child is suspected of serving a detouring function. Within this context, two dysfunctional patterns may emerge: protective detouring and detouring through attacking (scapegoating).

Protective detouring is a variation of the pattern of protectiveness. It occurs when both parents become so protective and concerned about the LD child's problems that all spouse issues go underground. This pattern is evident when the spouses virtually focus all of their communication with each other around the problems of the LD child. If the parents are asked what differences exist among family members or what problems the family is having, they talk exclusively about the LD child's difficulties. In effect, they are overfocused on the child's prolems to avoid open recognition of their own marital issues. The problem with this pattern is that there is an implicit message to the child: Continue to have problems so that Mom and Dad don't fight. This implicit message feeds the child's fantasies that he or she is responsible for keeping the family together. This child is given incredible power, which is anxiety-provoking and quite burdensome for him or her. The boundaries between the adult and the child subsystems become unclear and troublesome when the child is worrying about keeping the family or the parents together.

Detouring through attacking (scapegoating) does not appear to occur in psychosomatic families. Perhaps the decreased visibility of the handicap in the LD child renders him or her more vulnerable to attack, while a medically at-risk or visibly disabled individual would be a less socially accepted target for family frustration.

Detouring through attacking occurs when the LD child is viewed as the sole cause of all problems within the family. Often, such scapegoating is not an explicit phenomena in that the child does not appear to be an outcast or to be picked on. However, telling symptoms of this pattern are when parents and teachers find themselves saying privately, " — If it weren't for you we wouldn't have this situation," or when a family myth prevails which goes something like "Our family is not like other families because of you." It is, perhaps, most damaging when the message is implicit or unspoken, and when family members deny that they feel this way. Yet, parents may compain aloud, "Where am I going to get the money for the therapist?" or "If I have to miss another day of work for this, I may get fired!" In effect, the child receives a double message about his or her role in the family, and will typically respond by believing that he or she is, in effect, to blame for all problems. The child is also receiving the message that it is not all right to talk about feelings of frustration directly with family members. Thus, detouring through attack does not just refer to overt hostility expressed to the child, but also to the implicit, indirect, or unarticulated message: "You are the cause of all problems." The child may then act out his or her attributed role as the family troublemaker, which then serves to strengthen the view that he or she is a problem. Or, the child may begin to feel that he or she cannot do anything right, and may then become depressed or withdrawn. In either case, the child will develop a poor self-image.

What can be done about dysfunctional patterns of detouring in a family? First, a structural family therapist would attempt to get the parents to assume full and equal parental functioning and to recognize the difficulties that exist in their marital relationship. At times, this goal might be facilitated by working with the parents in marital therapy sessions. Second, an educational approach would be taken with the entire family to explore the detouring pattern and to receive the child of his or her real or imagined responsibility for marital harmony and family stability. Specifically, in the case of detouring through attacking, the therapist would proceed in other ways. The therapist would carefully and systematically go about challenging the notion that all family problems come from one member. Family members would be asked to examine and state how they contribute to central difficulties.

When the scapegoating is more implicit and is conveyed in nonverbal ways to the child, the therapist might first work with the family's ambivalence and frustration about having an LD member. When a therapist legitimizes the expression of feelings and tells the family that it is natural to feel sad and angry at times and inadequate at other times, individuals typically feel a good deal of relief. Parents in particular often harbor these emotions for years, disliking themselves for having these feelings. Given an opportunity to express the anger and frustration in therapy, to grieve, in effect, for the LD child's lack of perfection, family members gain a greater sense of perspective and learn how to express feelings, to accept the LD child, and to accept themselves. Parents' feelings of anger and frustration often arise from the sense of being greatly overburdened and alone. A support network will go a long way in reducing the intensity of these feelings. A relative who can come in and give the parent an afternoon off, or other parents who are members of a support group or local chapter of ACLD, trading off babysitting services with another and getting together for joint activities are examples of helpful support networks.

## DYSFUNCTIONAL PATTERNS WITHIN THE SCHOOL SYSTEM

The dysfunctional patterns of overprotectiveness, enmeshment, and lack of conflict resolution occur in the school setting as well as in the family system. Several examples of these parallels will be discussed.

## OVERPROTECTIVENESS

Overprotectiveness can occur in a classroom when a teacher feels that he or she must protect the LD child from his or her peers, and in effect, develops an alliance which the other children quickly pick up on. Instead of integrating the LD child and helping him to make friends, this alliance serves only to create peer resentment, further isolation of the child, and overdependency on the teacher. When this pattern occurs, a teacher must be able to help the children recognize one another's strengths and contributions to the classroom and then back off from overinvolvement.

The parental child can also exist in the classroom, emerging as a child's way of coping with peer rivalry. The parental child in the classroom is the one who is always telling other children to sit down, be quiet, listen to the teacher. When an LD child is in a classroom, another student may assume parent–like behavior by telling the LD child and others when and how, what to do. This behavior gives the LD child the message that he or she is less equal to and less competent than other students, and inhibits the development of his or her independent functioning. In this case, the teacher must be able to gently discourage the parenting behavior and to encourage equality and supportive friendships among the children.

## ENMESHMENT

One example of enmeshment in a school system occurs when a well-meaning LD specialist becomes so involved with the child that the regular teacher is viewed as being unable or unwilling to give the child what is needed. Instead of functioning as a consultant, the LD specialist assumes a meddling role and fights constantly with the classroom teacher, with the child suffering as a result of this conflict. At times, a third party may be needed to negotiate the difficulty and to get the professionals to work together.

## LACK OF CONFLICT RESOLUTION

A form of scapegoating may also occur in a classroom when a teacher feels reluctant about having an LD child in his or her class. Teachers may feel overburdened and unable to give the child specialized instruction or attention. They may want to do a good job, but may feel inadequate and threatened. This situation may readily occur when the LD child, who perhaps believes that he or she is the cause of problems at home, appears to adopt the role of classroom troublemaker. When other things are not going well in the classroom, it is all too easy for a teacher to feel, "If it weren't for this child . . . " The difficult aspect of this process is for the teacher to recognize these feelings and to accept, rather than deny, the anger and frustration. The next step is to ask for the support and the backup needed from the resource teachers and special education administrators. Thus, the legitimate feeling of being overburdened gets directed at the right people, and importantly, does not get misdirected toward the child. Since most teachers want to do good work and to be recognized for their efforts, it would be helpful if resource personnel and administrators not only took the first step in providing support, but also publicly acknowledged the teachers' positive efforts.

The dysfunctional patterns which can occur in both the family system and the school system are caused, in part, by the additional stresses which naturally arise with an LD child. When the complexity of these patterns is recognized, it is no small wonder that singling out the LD child as a sole target for intervention may provide limited results. Only by looking at the larger picture, by truly considering learning disabilities as a family affair and as a school affair, will our efforts to help the learning disabled child be comprehensive and fruitful. Within this context, structural family therapy provides both a road map of the complexities of the system and guideposts for positive intervention.

## REFERENCES

Abrams J., and F. Kaslow. "Learning Disability and Family Dynamics: A Mutual Interaction." *Journal of Clinical Child Psychology* (Spring 1976): 35–40.

Barragan, M. "The Child-centered Family." In *Family Therapy/Theory and Practice*, edited by P. Guckin. New York: Gardner Press, 1976.

Gardner, R. *MBD The Family Book about Minimal Brain Dysfunction*. New York: Jason Aronson, 1973.

Haring, N. G., and B. Bateman. *Teaching the Learning Disabled Child*. Englewood Clifts. N.J.: Prentice-Hall, 1977.

Kronick, D. The Family and Learning Disabilities. *Learning Disabilities: Information Please*. Montreal: Quebec ACLD, 1978.

Minuchin, S. *Families and Family Therapy,* Cambridge, Mass.: Harvard University Press, 1974.

Minuchin, S., B. Rosman, and L. Baker. *Psychosomatic Families/Anorexia Nervosa in Context*. Cambridge Mass.: Harvard University Press, 1978.

Osman, Betty. *Learning Disabilities/A Family Affair*. New York: Random House, 1979.

Rowan, Ruth. *Helping Children with Learning Disabilities*. Nashville: Parthenon Press, 1977.

# DEVELOPMENT OF MENTAL
# PROCESSING ABILITIES

# Serial Order Behavior

## To Understand It, a Scientific Challenge, an Educational Necessity

### *William H. Gaddes*

T HE HISTORY of psychology has been marked, not surprisingly, by segmental and cross-sectional studies of behavior since they are relatively easier to manage experimentally. This situation, no doubt, was related to the almost complete neglect by psychologists of the temporal aspects of human behavior, until very recently. Philosophers, of course, had, for a long time, concerned themselves with holistic and complex aspects of human behavior, no doubt because they were less constrained by their methodology than the experimental psychologists by their laboratory procedures. Immanuel Kant, 200 years ago, struggled with the metaphysical exposition of both space and time, and by concluding that different spaces are coexistent and different times are successive (Kant 1952, p. 26) he laid the groundwork for current theories of simultaneous and successive processing of information by the brain (Luria 1973) and for some recent theories of cognitive function in children (Das et al. 1979).

Until the mid- or late 1950s, psychologists concerned themselves mainly with isolated or discrete patterns of behavior such as memory for nonsense syllables, reaction time, tapping speed, color blindness, auditory memory, and so on. That many of these performances happened to include a sequential component was incidental and usually ignored or neglected.

At the beginning of this century, following the original work of Einstein (1905), it became a popular investigation among physicists to enquire into the relation of time and space, but this interest was slow to show itself in psychology. Von Monakow, a Russian neurologist, in 1914 was one of the first to address the problem of the time factor in behavior,

The experiments described in this paper were first presented at the first European meeting of the International Academy for Research in Learning Disabilities in Amsterdam, May 17, 1978.

but little interest was taken in the questions he asked until Lashley in 1948 presented his classic paper on "The Problem of Serial Order in Behavior" at the Hixon Symposium (Lashley 1951). Prior to Lashley's statement, simple neuropsychological theories of serial order behavior had appeared by Washburn in 1916, John B. Watson in 1924 and Bekhterev in 1932. These theories explained the phenomenon in terms of associative chain theories. But Lashley showed this theoretical approach to be untenable by recognizing that known velocities of neural impulses made the explanation impossible in many types of rapid sequential behavior like piano playing. Because he recognized serial behavior as "the most important and most neglected problem of cerebral physiology" (Lashley 1951, p. 114), he attempted to explain it in neurological and behavioral terms. He conceived of "elaborate systems of inter-related neurons" which provide a sequential control of the animal's effectors. These controlling systems which Lashley did not attempt to localize, he thought contributed to "every perception and to every integrated movement" (p. 128), and these systems were believed to involve both spatial distribution and temporarl sequence.

It is significant that although serial order behavior is central to all classroom learning, and hence possesses pivotal importance to the educator, the major research into its nature and function has not been produced by educators. It was Lashley, as we have seen, an eminent neuropsychologist, who initiated interest in this very complex behavioral phenomenon. Hebb, another neuropsychologist, gave great impetus to its investigation in the late 1950s by stimulating a number of his graduate students at McGill University to turn their attention and energies to its experimental examination. During the past twenty years there has been an increasing interest, particularly by neuropsychologists, in examining how the brain processes both verbal and nonverbal sequential material.

Because the brain is specialized in processing verbal material (which is sequential) and nonverbal, pictorial, or spatial material (which is perceived holistically or simultaneously) researchers have tended to group sequential stimulus material and sequential response behavior into a verbal-nonverbal dichotomy. Examples of different types of sequential receptive and expressive behavior are inferred from the tests and activities that activate them (see Table 7.1).

In this chapter I propose to examine the processes of both verbal and nonverbal sequencing, their relation to reading, writing, and arithmetic, and the possible locus of brain structures that mediate them. But before proceeding, we will define our terms and concepts.

1. All stimuli examined in this study are *outside* the perceiving subject. Bakker (1972, p. 14) has described this type of perception as "an

## TABLE 7.1

**Examples of Verbal and Nonverbal Tests to Measure Serial Order Processes in Behavior**

| | Serial Order Behavior |
|---|---|
| *Nonverbal* | *Verbal* |
| VISUAL: Sequential Light Patterns | VISUAL: Two or More Single Letters on Tachistoscope; Two or More Short Words or Numbers on Tachistoscope; Reading, Writing, Spelling. |
| AUDITORY: Tonal Memory, Tapping Patterns | AUDITORY: Dichotic Listening, 3 Pairs of Words; Digit Span, Fwd. & Rev.; Morse Code; Sentence Repetition |
| TACTILE: Tapping Patterns on $S$s Back | TACTILE: Writing on Hand or Fingertip with a Stylus. |
| COMPLEX: Walking through a House, Driving a Car | COMPLEX: Oral Spelling; Spelling Words Backwards; Reciting Numbers, Days of the Week, Months of the Year, Fwd. & Rev. |

N.B.: Serial order behavior has receptive and expressive aspects, which normally function simultaneously and reciprocally.

*inter-individual* relation in which especially the temporal moment of the physical thing (the tone) is the object of perception.'' He has contrasted this type of perception with what he calls an *intra-individual* relation in which the experiencer and the thing experienced belong to the same category (e.g., a subject describes "yesterday" or some period of time through which he has lived).

2. A serial or temporal order is an ordered succession of at least two stimuli with an inter-stimulusinterval of more than about 20 milliseconds. This minimum was chosen as being the lower limit for most children of elementary school age to discriminate the succession of two

tones as opposed to simultaneity (Lowe and Campbell 1965), although in exceptional cases a threshold of only 2 milliseconds has been reported (Gengel and Hirsh 1970).

3. Inter-individual relationships may be varied and hence offer an experimental variable which can be managed (Bakker 1972, p. 15), and this type of experimental management is what we will examine here. Intra-individual relationships are not directly manageable by the Experimenter, and hence will not be looked at in this review.

4. Bakker (1972, p. 15) has discriminated between temporal order and succession. Temporal order implies the ordered succession of stimuli which are different in some way so that they can be identified individually (e.g., the succession of doh, me, sol, or tones of different frequencies or pitch). By contrast, succession includes the presentation of two identical stimuli (e.g., similar tones or light flashes with a certain interval between them). Below the perceptual sequential threshold they are perceived as one tone or light, and above the threshold, as two separate stimuli in succession. But in this latter case it is not possible to identify which tone or light was heard or seen first, since they are identical, so that while the second stimulus succeeds the first, that is all that can be said about it. Bakker's definitions might be stated another way: If the ordinal position of the individual stimuli in a temporal sequence can be described verbally or indicated spatially, then the stimuli are said to be in temporal order. If they cannot be identified either verbally or nonverbally, then they are said to be in succession. The difference then is not in the pattern of stimuli but in the ability or inability to report them in particular ways.

5. Bakker (1972, p. 15) has considered the response to serial order stimuli as being of two types, *imitation* and *explication*. Repeating digits forward is an example of imitation; repeating them in reverse order is an example of explication, because the subject is required to recognize the position of each digit and respond in a way specific to this serial recognition.

While these two modes of responding to sequential stimuli are behaviorally and introspectively different, neuropsychological knowledge suggests that they are not basically different processes. It might be hypothesized that both require serial order processing by the brain, but imitation is largely unconscious and presumably partially subcortical, while explication demands cognitive attention and analysis, a largely cortical function.

## PLAN

First, I want to examine some experiments of verbal and nonverbal sequencing carried out in our laboratory during the past fifteen years, then to look at their possible relation to academic learning, and finally to observe how these findings might contribute to our knowledge of neurological mechanisms underlying serial order behavior.

### NONVERBAL VISUAL SERIAL ORDER PERCEPTION

In the early 1960s, as a direct result of reading Lashley's classic paper, I looked for a test of nonverbal visual sequencing in which the exposure times of the stimuli and the inter-stimulus intervals could be controlled by the Experimenter. Since we could find no such test, we decided to construct one. I took the idea from the Seashore Tonal Memory Test (Seashore et al. 1939) and translated it to a visual model. The apparatus which we called the Dynamic Visual Retention Test, or DVRT, includes a programming unit and a display screen on which sequential patterns of lights appear (Gaddes 1966, 1967). The Experimenter can control the exposure times of the lights, the intervals between lights and between groups and patterns of lights. The subject is asked to detect spatial differences in a second pattern by comparing it with his memory of the first or standard pattern. Using Bakker's categorical system, this type of serial order behavior appears to be a form of nonverbal explication (that is reconstructing mentally the serial order pattern and recognizing which light has changed position). The light patterns are usually run at 1 of 2 speeds in the clinic. The "slow" speed includes a light exposure of 1. sec. and an inter-light interval of 1. sec. The "fast" speed includes a light exposure of .1 sec. and an inter-light interval of .4 sec. When other speeds are used for experimental purposes they are specifically indicated.

Our first study with the DVRT showed that brain damaged subjects in 4 groups (Group 1, ages 9 and 10; Group 2, ages 11 and 12; Group 3, ages 13 to 18; and Group 4, adults) all performed at a significantly inferior level compared with normal subjects of the same age (Gaddes 1966). While the test appears to be highly sensitive to cerebral dysfunction, this study provided us with no knowledge of the possible locus of Lashley's "ordering systems." These systems presumably control serial order behavior and are independent of the specific neural traces on which the order is imposed.

Consequently, the next step was to investigate brain lesion cases with specific localization, to see if receptive serial order behavior, in this case visual retention as measured by the DVRT, was any worse when the lesion was posterior or anterior. To study the use of the DVRT in examining brain lesion cases, we selected two experimental groups which included 10 subjects with known frontal damage or dysfunction, and 10 subjects with nonfrontal (posterior) damage. Both brain damaged groups were matched for age and intelligence. An analysis of variance showed that the frontal group performed significantly poorer than the nonfrontal group, and both groups did more poorly than normals (Gaddes and Tymchuk 1967). While the study was limited by the small sample sizes, it did suggest that serial order behavior as measured by the DVRT, may be controlled at least in part by mechanisms in the frontal cerebral areas. This finding also supported Luria (1973) who, to paraphrase him in simple terms, saw the posterior parts of the human cortex concerned with spatial aspects of perception, and the frontal lobes with temporal ordering..

Having probed the frontal-posterior pattern, our next step was to investigate the possibility of laterality differences (Gaddes and Tymchuk 1967). A total of fifty-one brain damaged subjects, ranging in age from 9 years through adulthood, were tested on the DVRT. Three groups of 17 subjects each were selected to include left hemisphere lesions, right hemisphere lesions, and bilateral lesions. Each subject was compared with the performance of a normal subject of the same age.

Since the DVRT demands spatial-perceptual responses, we had expected that the right hemisphere lesion cases would have done worse than the left sided lesion cases, as Milner had found with the Seashore Tonal Memory Test (Milner 1962). However, we found the reverse. Our left hemisphere lesion cases did significantly worse than the right sided group, and the right sided group was inferior to the bilateral group. This evidence suggested to us at that time that the verbal mediation normally executed by the left hemisphere in language functions may be so closely meshed with the sequential ordering systems that the serial component of the DVRT task was stronger than the spatial demands. Milner found her subjects more right hemisphere involved because the Seashore Tonal Memory Test can be processed nonverbally (i.e., spatially and holistically). We found our subjects more left hemisphere involved because they counted the lights or processed the problem verbally. Efron, in his many interesting experiments (1963, 1967) found the same. In tasks demanding language analysis or tasks permitting "internal language" in a so-called nonverbal response experiment, Efron concluded that the sequencing is maximally controlled by the left hemisphere.

## SEQUENCING AND ACADEMIC COMPETENCE

Although our original development of the DVRT was to aid in localizing brain lesions, and it showed itself to be sensitive and useful in doing this, we soon became curious about its possible use in diagnosing learning disabled children. Since most or all of the children whom we saw with cerebral dysfunctions also had various types of learning problems, the DVRT offered an opportunity to study the relationship between sequencing and academic learning.

To give us a quick measure of this, we reviewed the performance of brain damaged children (i.e., those with "hard" neurological signs), of minimally brain dysfunctioning children (i.e., those with "soft" signs), and neurologically normal children. The first group, the conclusively brain damaged, showed themselves to be severely impaired on thirteen neuropsychological tests, of which eleven contained strong sequential demands. The whole sample, or 100 percent of the 83 subjects, was below average on sentence repetition and visual-motor trail making with a pencil. The DVRT, at the slow speed, showed 94 percent of the sample to be below average. Memory for tonal patterns showed deficits on 87 percent, and finger tapping for both hands, 85 percent.

The second group, those with "soft" signs, showed a below average performance on nine neuropsychological tests, and of these, seven were heavily loaded with serial order skills. In this group, the DVRT failed more subjects than any of the other tests; 92 percent of the sample of 29 were below average and 58 percent below minus one standard deviation. Below average percentages of the next four tests included: finger tapping with the dominant hand, 79 percent; trail making, one series, 76 percent; tonal memory, 72 percent; and trail making, two series, 71 percent. In both of the above groups the serial order tests predominated and suggested that they are strong indicators of central nervous system dysfunction.

The third group, those children with persistent learning problems but no neurological signs either "hard" or "soft," showed below average performances on thirteen neuropsychological tests. Of these, ten had marked serial order demands. Speech perception was done worst; 89 percent of the sample had below average scores. Since this test requires a discrimination between two phonetic sounds, it is not primarily a sequential test, but this finding supports the importance of auditory phonetic perception for academic success. Still, sequencing skills are also important for this group. Failure scores of the top five serial order tests were: tonal memory, 87 percent; trail making, one series, 86 percent; trail making, two series, 86 percent; and DVRT, slow speed, 83 percent.

While we have reported only the "top five" tests for each of the three groups, that is those most vulnerable to failure, the fact that the DVRT appeared in each of the three disabled groups provided confidence in the hypothesis that nonverbal sequencing failures are reliably correlated with learning problems, and that the DVRT is a useful indicator of both neurological dysfunctions and learning disabilities.

To examine this problem more systematically we studied forty-two normal children in Grade 2, and thirty-nine in Grade 5 (Gaddes and Spellacy 1977). The two groups were matched for Wechsler (WISC) Performance IQ (Grade 2, mean PIQ = 112.4, range 89 to 142; Grade 5, mean PIQ = 112.6, range 82 to 146). Each group had an average age of their typical grade (Grade 2, mean age 7 years, 7 months; range 7–0 to 8–3; Grade 5, mean age 10 years, 7 months; range 9–10 to 11–10). We planned to examine the relationship between a number of sequential skills and academic achievement in reading, spelling, and arithmetic (both oral and written). We selected the two groups to provide information on any possible developmental changes in serial order abilities between the ages of 7½ and 10½.

The sequential tests included five nonverbal and two verbal tests, the nonverbal tests included measures of:

> 1. Visual Receptive Serial Order. This was measured by the DVRT at two speeds.
> 2. Visual Expressive Serial Order. This was measured by a device that included a telegrapher's key connected to a battery-powered 14-volt lamp. The experimenter tapped out a serial pattern of lights and the child was asked to remember the pattern and tap it out immediately by imitation.
> 3. Auditory Receptive Serial Order. The child listened to two serial patterns of taps presented on a tape recorder and was required to say whether the second pattern was the same or different from the first.
> 4. Auditory Expressive Serial Order. Following the perception of a pattern of taps presented on a tape recorder, the child was required to remember and imitate it with a drum stick on the edge of the table.

The two verbal sequential tests included (1) the Spreen-Benton Sentence Repetition Test (Spreen and Benton 1969), and (2) the Wechsler Intelligence Scale for Children, Digit Span Reversed subtest (Wechsler 1949). These were chosen as a reference against which the nonverbal tests could be compared, since numerous researchers including Bakker (1972) have found verbal sequencing more strongly related to reading ability than nonverbal sequential tests. As well, they both require "verbal explication" (Bakker 1972, p. 17).

Our first multivariate analysis of this data included canonical correlation. Since this concept reflects an optimal relation between a first factor in one set of data and a first factor in another set, it seemed an appropriate method for examining the possible relationship between a number of sequential skills (in this case seven) and a number of academic skills (in this case four).

The Grade 2 data revealed a first canonical variable representing Spelling and Sentence Repetition. This correlation was .66, significant at <.01 level, and accounted for 43.6 percent of the variance. The second canonical variable represented Reading and the DVRT at the slow speed. This correlation measured .65 with only borderline significance of <.056 and accounted for forty-two percent of the variance. This evidence suggests that verbal serial order tasks are only a little more strongly related to academic success than nonverbal sequential skills when speed is introduced in the presentation of the latter. The fact that the DVRT at the slow speed was the first of the four nonverbal tests to emerge in the analysis also suggests that seven-year-old children are still reading in a slow, segmental, and sequential way. The DVRT light patterns at the slow speed evidently are making a partially similar demand.

The Grade 5 data provided no significant canonical correlations. To try to identify the developmental changes between age 7½ and 10½, we then used a step-up multiple regression analysis, and comparisons were made for reading, spelling, and arithmetic for both groups, Grades 2 and 5.

Reading in Grade 2 showed the highest correlation with the DVRT at the slow speed (R = .52, p < .0005). When the Visual Expressive Test was added in step 2, a multiple correlation of .58 was found (p < .005). Further additions in the step-wise analysis failed to produce any significant increase in the relationship.

Reading in Grade 5 revealed three steps yielding statistically significant R's. The three tests in the order of their emergence were Visual Expressive (R = .47), Auditory Expressive (when combined with the first test, R = .58), and DVRT at the slow speed (when combined with the previous two tests, R = .61). The change from Grade 2 to 5 showed a shift from an emphasis on slow visual sequential perception to a more integrated visual and auditory processing. There was also a greater shift to expressive sequential skills at the older age level (see Figure 7.1). This evidence suggests that nonverbal sequential skills are intimately involved in learning to read and that they show a shifting developmental pattern during the child's first five years of reading.

When Spelling was analyzed by the multiple regression step-up analysis, the multiple correlations were lower than in Reading. In Grade

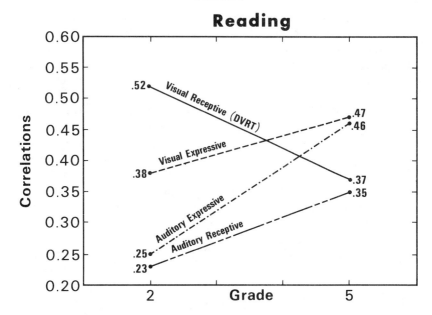

FIGURE 7.1. Progressive changes in correlations between reading and various sequencing processes from grades 2 to 5.

2, the DVRT at the slow speed showed the highest correlation with Spelling (R = .45, p < .01), and additions of tests occurred in the following order: Visual Expressive (when combined with DVRT, R = .49, p < .01), Auditory Expressive (when combined with the previous two tests, R = .52, p < .01), and DVRT at the fast speed (when combined with the previous three tests, R = .55, p < .01). Compared with the reading data, this evidence suggests that spelling draws on auditory sequential skills earlier than reading, which is not surprising since most children learn to spell by a phonetic method, while many at this age can read by a sight method.

Spelling at Grade 5 showed a different pattern. The highest single correlation was with the DVRT at the fast speed (R = .42 p < .008), and the next strongest relation was with the Auditory Expressive Test (which when combined with the DVRT at the fast speed showed a R = .43, p < .025), and then the DVRT at the slow speed (which when combined with the previous two tests gave a R = .44, p < .053). This evidence suggests that spelling includes visual sequential skills fairly strong with auditory expressive abilities, but since the multiple correlations are not high, ranging from .42 to .44, other skills not tapped by our tests are no doubt operative. Speculation suggests that a strong component not measured in this study includes kinaesthetic-sequential motor patterns, so much a part of writing. The developmental changes in sequential skills in Spelling are shown in Figure 7.2.

Arithmetic in Grade 2 was tested for both oral and written performance. Each showed a different pattern of nonverbal sequential skills. Oral arithmetic produced significant R's with three of the tests, the DVRT at the slow speed (R = .43), Auditory Receptive (with the DVRT, R = .48) and the DVRT at the fast speed (with the previous two tests, R = .51). By contrast, written arithmetic showed only one significant correlation and it was low, the DVRT at the slow speed (R = .32, p < .05). This probably means that written arithmetic at this age concentrates the child's attention more on spatial memory and the perceptual mechanics of reading and writing. Possibly oral arithmetic frees the child to give his attention more to number concepts, and hence the stronger relation of both auditory and visual sequential processes.

Only written arithmetic was tested in Grade 5, and it showed a markedly different pattern of sequential skills. The Auditory Receptive Test showed the strongest relationship (R = .44, p < .01), and the second

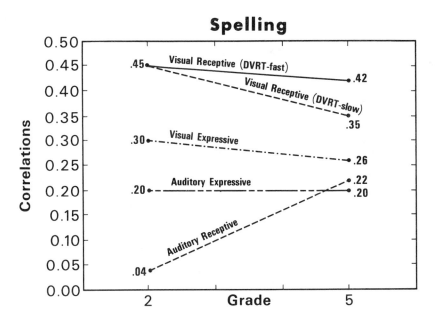

FIGURE 7.2 Progressive changes in correlations between spelling and various sequencing processes from grades 2 to 5.

step-up revealed the DVRT at the slow speed (combined with the Auditory Receptive Test, R = .51, p < .01), and the next step-up showed the Auditory Expressive Test (combined with the previous two tests, R = .53, p < .01). Where the DVRT slow dominated the sequential processes of the arithmetic learning of the 7½ year old, by age 10½ it had receded to the bottom of the list (see Figures 7.3 and 7.4). The evident ascendency of the auditory sequential skills may mean that the older child conceptualizes arithmetic more in oral and subvocal language, and has now automatized many of the visual-motor skills required in reading and writing.

In summary, an examination of the relationship between three academic skills (reading, spelling and arithmetic) and seven sequential skills (two verbal and five nonverbal) showed a slightly stronger correlation generally between reading and the verbal sequential test of Sentence Repetition than with the nonverbal sequential tests. Even so, the latter group did show significant multiple correlations with all three academic skills at both age groups, 7½ and 10½ years. Visual and

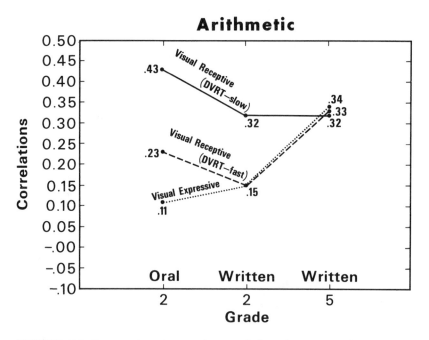

FIGURE 7.3. Progressive changes in correlations between oral and written arithmetic and visual sequencing processes from grades 2 to 5.

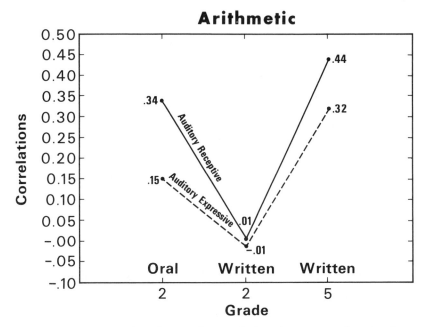

FIGURE 7.4. Progressive changes in correlations between oral and written arithmetic and auditory sequencing processes from grades 2 to 5.

receptive tests showed the strongest partial correlations in beginning learning (Grade 2) and shifted to more expressive functions in reading and more auditory sequential memory in spelling and arithmetic at the older age level (Grade 5).

## IS SERIAL ORDER BEHAVIOR TASK SPECIFIC?

The following two experiments were stimulated by the work of Bakker (1972) in Amsterdam. Throughout his book he repeated the observation that on his serial order tests, the *verbal* sequential tests discriminate between good and poor readers, and *nonverbal* sequential tests do not. As described in the study with the Grade 2 and Grade 5 children, we did find significant, middle-range, positive correlations between scores on the DVRT and reading, but we had never examined its function in relation to good and poor readers. We decided to do this in two experiments, one with children and one with adults.

Split-brain experiments have made it clear that the speed of cerebral processing is an important discriminating variable, and since Bakker's temporal order experiments included slow rates of presentation (each picture was exposed for one or two seconds), it seemed reasonable that this might have accounted for the failure of his nonverbal tests to disciminate between good and poor readers. Even so, he was cautious on this point by concluding that "verbal-temporal perception is related to language behavior, whereas nonverbal-temporal perception is not, *or less related to it*" (Bakker 1972, p. 30). To study nonverbal-temporal perception at different fast speeds, the DVRT offered an excellent opportunity.

## CHILD STUDY

An exploratory pilot study was carried out with an experimental group of eight reading-retarded boys and a control group of ten average or above average readers. The two groups were matched for age (mean age of the retarded readers, 13 years 3 months, and of the normal controls, 13 year 10 months) and Performance IQ as measured by the Wechsler (WISC). The mean PIQ of the retarded readers was 95.4, and of the controls, 95.1. The ranges of the PIQ for the two groups were close (Retarded, 87 to 105, and Controls, 82 to 104).

The two groups were measured on (1) a nonverbal visual sequential test (the DVRT at three different speeds) and (2) a verbal sequential test (tachistoscopic exposure of a series of three single letters at the same three speeds). The speeds were: (1) light or letter exposure, 100 milliseconds, interstimulus interval (I.S.I.) 100 milliseconds; (2) light or letter exposure, 100 milliseconds, I.S.I. 400 milliseconds; (3) stimulus exposure 1. second, I.S.I. .8 second. For the verbal test, eight capital letters (A, E, L, P, T, W, X, Z) were selected from a chart prepared by Kinney et al. (1966) as those letters least confused perceptually.

A multivariate test of speed was highly significant (p < .009). The "very fast" and "fast" speeds differed (p < .02) and the slow speed differed from the combined fast speeds (p < .004). The main effect of learning disability was found to be highly significant, i.e., LD and control children performed significantly different on the DVRT (p < .001), a test ostensibly designed to be a nonverbal visual sequential task.

On the verbal sequential test (the perception of sequences of single letters) the two groups did not show an overall significant difference (p < .091). However, the multivariate test of speed was found to be highly significant (p < .002). The very fast and fast speeds differed (p < .013) and the two fast speeds combined differed from the slow speed (p < .002).

At first, these findings would seem to contradict Bakker's conclusion that nonverbal visual sequential tasks do not discriminate good and poor readers, and that verbal ones do, because we found the reverse. The reasons for the differences appear to be several: (1) The DVRT is a nonverbal task but to answer it the child is asked to count, thus requiring some verbal mediation. (2) The rapid speeds require a type of cerebral processing quite unlike the slower tasks of Bakker's research. (3) The horizontal movement of the lights on the DVRT made the visual perceptual task much more difficult than the tachistoscopic test where all three letters appeared sequentially on the same spot on the screen. (4) The lack of the T-scope test to discriminate the two reading groups probably stems from the fact that single letter recognition is a simple task and easy for both groups (i.e., it showed a ceiling effect). To add to the ease of the task, the letters were selected for their ease of recognition from Kinney's chart, while Bakker's list was more difficult. It included C and G, which tend to be confused by dyslexics. (5) Our sample of reading retarded subjects was heterogeneous. It included two audiles (subjects stressing phonetic recognition), three visiles (subjects stressing visual form recognition) and three mixed.

## ADULT STUDY

In Canada, until very recently, very little research has been carried out with learning disabled adults, and for that reason a comparative study with adults was appealing. A group of eight dyslexic adults was compared with a matched group of eight normal adult readers. All subjects were more than 19 years of age, and the dyslexics were selected for failure to read above a Grade 5 level on at least two of the following reading achievement tests: Wide Range Achievement Test, Gates-McKillop Test, Neale Word Accuracy Test, and the Neale Oral Comprehension Test. All of the dyslexics had been referred to remedial reading programs for adults.

The two groups were matched for age (mean age of dyslexics, 27.9 years, range 20 to 37; and of normal controls, 28.7 years, range 23 to 34) and Wechsler Performance IQ (mean PIQ of dyslexics, 112.6, range 94 to 133; and of the controls, 112.2, range 95 to 121).

The results of a multivariate repeated measures analysis of variance showed a significant group by test interaction on the DVRT (p < .03). The dyslexics, while inferior to the normals at all speeds, had particular trouble in perceiving visual sequences at 100 millisecond intervals. When the stimuli were slowed to 400 milliseconds, performance was markedly improved for the dyslexics, but little difference was seen at slower speeds. By comparison, the normal readers could handle the light sequences equally well at all three speeds. No significant improvements in control group performance were observed as the speeds were slowed.

The tachistoscope test included two scores, *memory* and *sequencing*. Differences between the groups only occurred at the very fast speed, but these were not significant. However, memory ability ("Tell me the letters you saw in any order") was found to be significantly better than sequencing ability (p < .005) for both groups ("Tell me the letters in the same order that you saw them"). This seems to indicate that perceptual registration is easier than temporal ordering one's perceptions. Other researchers have made this same observation (Tzortzis & Albert, 1974). This suggests a sequencing deficit rather than an impairment in short term memory.

## DISCUSSION

What can be concluded from this series of studies? As is evident from the historical account of my own investigations into serial order behavior, our knowledge has increased in recognizing the complexity of perceptual and motor sequencing. During the 1960s it became popular to study sequencing but most of the researches, like my own, were segmental and based on partial knowledge. Frequently this led to contradictory findings. Where Efron in 1963 concluded that "temporal analysis of sequence, interval and simultaneity is performed in the left hemisphere in right-handed subjects, as well as in the majority of left-handed ones" (Efron 1963), by contrast, Milner reported in 1962 that the perception of sequential tonal patterns, as measured by the Seashore Tonal Memory Test, was a right hemisphere function.

In the mid 1960s, like many others, we were searching for *the* cerebral locus of sequencing and in 1966 I thought it was in the left frontal lobe. It was not until the early 1970s that Bakker's very fine doctoral dissertation appeared and provided a synthesis of the rapidly increasing body of neuropsychological knowledge that had accrued from studies of lesion cases, dichotic listening, tachistoscopic half-field studies, carotid amytal injections, electrophysiological studies, split-brain experiments, comprehensive batteries of neuropsychological tests, longitudinal studies of aphasic patients, traumatically brain injured persons, and those with developmental learning disabilities. Ideas and techniques originally designed for a clinical understanding of the brain-behavior relationships were rapidly being recognized for their new-found value in understanding and treating children with learning problems.

Bakker's basic conclusion was that "perception of temporal order is mediated neither exclusively left- nor exclusively right-cerebrally and it depends on the verbal or nonverbal character of the temporally ordered material which hemisphere is primarily involved in the processing of the information" (Bakker 1972, p. 78). He supported this theoretical conclusion with a number of original studies and in particular with an ingenious research of sequential finger localization. A group taught to identify their fingers by number (i.e., verbal identification) were better in localizing fingers on their right hands; those with no such pre-test training and who pointed to the fingers on a drawing of a hand (i.e. spatial identification) had better scores on fingers of their left hands.

While this seems to be true of the visual and tactile sense modes, it is not a clear finding in auditory perception.

We have found that the Seashore Tonal Memory Test does not correlate strongly with the DVRT. While the DVRT does correlate with reading, spelling and written arithmetic, the Tonal Memory Test does not. It seems to be much more variable in that academically bright students usually do well on the DVRT but not necessarily on the Tonal Memory Test. Another possibility is that musical tonal patterns lend themselves more to global interpretation (right hemisphere function) and clinical studies of amusia reveal a greater incidence of right hemisphere damage or dysfunction. Certainly this seems to be true in recognizing simple tunes, or of the responses of subjects untrained in music. A recent study (Hirshkowitz et el. 1978) supports this view. While listening to music, non-musicians had more right hemisphere activity as measured by the EEG, while experienced musicians had more left hemisphere activity. Trained musicians usually report that they analyze music sequentially; novices probably listen naively and uncritically to the general effect. This suggests that hemispheric specialization in the perception of music is related to perceptual processing and experience, and not to fixed properties of the physical stimuli or supposed invariant brain functions.

Davis and Wada (1977) using spectral analysis of visual and auditory evoked potentials, found that flashes stimulated the occipital lobes more than the temporal, and that auditory clicks had the reverse effect. From this they concluded that the typical cerebral pattern of activity did depend on the stimulus modality. However, when they studied these changes relative to speech dominance they concluded that the dominant and nondominant hemispheres are respectively involved in the analysis of temporally and spatially ordered information. The particular "lateralized processing of a given stimulus depends on its relative amounts of spatial and temporal information and on the subject's intention or ability to extract the information" (Davis and Wada 1977). Their findings propose a fine dynamic integration of structural predispositions and experience and training.

O'Connor and Hermelin (1973) have also reported a study which stressed an interaction of experience, training, personal learning strategies and central nervous system function. They found that when given a choice of remembering three digits temporally or spatially, normal children tended to respond in temporal order, while deaf, autistic and some mentally retarded children recalled or recognized the spatial or left-to-right order. Again this suggests that visual sequencing is not necessarily a left or right hemisphere function, but that "the order chosen by each subject would appear to be an elected strategy rather than a fixed mechanism" (O'Connor and Hermelin 1973).

Buffery (1976) in a developmental study of boys and girls between five and eight years, found that hemispheric processing can be manipulated by the level of difficulty of the task. Children in this age range tend to process easy-to-verbalize problems in their left hemispheres; difficult-to-verbalize tasks shift the processing more to the right.


## CONCLUSION


The findings from these experiments suggest the following conclusions:

1. Visual sequential perception is sensitive to brain dysfunction anywhere in the brain, although this holds more for congenital brain lesion cases. Localized traumatic damage is usually more impairing to serial order behaviors when the damage is in the left hemisphere.

2. Sequential perception is a discrete ability and while associated with normal perception and memory, it possesses its own functional integrity and can be independent of other cognitive functions under certain conditions.

3. The speed of cerebral processing is a significant aspect of serial order behavior. The DVRT and tachistoscope have enabled us to examine perception and memory of visual stimuli, both verbal and nonverbal, at various speeds of less than a second. This has revealed deficits in visual-sequential skills of retarded readers which are missed at slower rates of presentation. This data and similar testing procedures can be used by school psychologists to select those dyslexics with a perceptual processing problem that is related to their impaired reading.

4. Serial order perception is usually task specific, varying with the degree of verbal or nonverbal quality, the level of difficulty, or the sense mode of the task.

5. There is no fixed cerebral locus for sequencing. Both hemispheres are involved depending more or less on the nature of the sequential task, although they tend to involve the left hemisphere more than the right in right-handed subjects.

There is a very real need for educational diagnosticians to recognize serial order behavior as an essential function in classroom learning, and to employ sensitive testing procedures for identifying and assessing it. While it is also essential to measure the child's language development and various linguistic skills, it is equally important to know if there are any perceptual processing deficits present, and to know whether these include some aspect of serial order behavior. This is a complex clinical procedure that I have discussed in detail elsewhere (Gaddes 1980), and one that every school psychologist should acquire if he or she is to do a complete and competent assessment.

### REFERENCES

Bakker, D. J. *Temporal Order in Disturbed Reading.* Rotterdam: Rotterdam University Press, 1972.

Bekhterev, V. M. *General Principles of Human Reflexology.* Translated 4th Russian Edition. New York: International Publishers, 1932.

Buffery, A. W. H. "Sex Differences in the Neuropsychological Development of Verbal and Spatial Skills." In *The Neuropsychology of Learning Disorders: Theoretical Approaches,* edited by R. M. Knights and D. J. Bakker. Baltimore: University Park Press, 1976.

Das, J. P., J. R. Kirby, and R. F. Jarman. *Simultaneous and Successive Cognitive Processes.* New York: Academic Press, 1979.

Davis, A. E., and J. A. Wada. "Hemispheric Asymmetries in Human Infants; Spectral Analysis of Flash and Click Evoked Potentials." *Brain and Language* 4 (1977): 23–31.

Efron, R. "Temporal Perception, Aphasia and Déjà vu." *Brain* 86 (1963): 403–25.

Efron, R. In *Brain Mechanisms Underlying Speech and Language,* edited by C. H. Millikan and F. L. Darley. New York: Grune & Stratton, 1967. Pp. 30 ff.

Gaddes, W. H. "The Performance of Normal and Brain-damaged Subjects on a New Dynamic Visual Retention Test." *The Canadian Psychologist* 7a (1966): Inst. Suppl., 313–23.

――. "A New Test of Dynamic Visual Retention. *"Perceptual and Motor Skills* 25 (1967): 393–96.

――. *Learning Disabilities and Brain Function: A Neuropsychological Approach.* New York: Springer-Verlag, 1980.

Gaddes, W. H., and F. J. Spellacy. "Serial Order Perceptual and Motor Performances in Children and Their Relation to Academic Achievement." Victoria, B.C.: *Research Monograph No. 35,* Department of Psychology, University of Victoria, 1977.

Gaddes, W. H., and A. J. Tymchuk. "A Validation Study of the Dynamic Visual Retention Test in Functional Localisation of Cerebral Damage and Dysfunction." Victoria, B.C.: *Research Monograph No. 33,* Department of Psychology, University of Victoria, 1967.

Gengel, R. W., and I. J. Hirsh. "Temporal Order: The Effect of Single versus Repeated Presentations, Practice, and Verbal Feedback." *Perception and Psychophysics* 7 (1970): 209–11.

Hirshkowitz, M., J. Earle, and B. Paley. "EEG Alpha Asymmetry in Musicians and Non-musicians: A Study of Hemispheric Specialization." *Neuropsychologia* 16 (1978): 125–28.

Kinney, G. C., M. Marsetta, and D. J. Showman. "Studies in Display Symbol Legibility. Part 12. The Legibility of Alpha Numeric Symbols for Digitalized Television." Beford, Mass.: The Mitre Corporation ESD-TR-66-1117, 1966.

Lashley, K. S. "The Problem of Serial Order in Behavior." In *Cerebral Mechanisms in Behavior, The Hixon Symposium,* edited by L. A. Jeffress. New York: Wiley, 1951.

Lowe, A. D., and R. A. Campbell. "Temporal Discrimination in Aphasoid and Normal Children." *Journal of Speech and Hearing Research* 8 (1965): 313–14.

Luria, A. R. *The Working Brain.* Harmondsworth: Penguin, 1973.

Milner, B. "Laterality Effects in Audition." In *Interhemispheric Relations and Cerebral Dominance,* edited by V. B. Mountcastle. Baltimore: Johns Hopkins University Press, 1962.

――. "Brain Mechanisms Suggested by Studies of Temporal Lobes." In *Brain Mechanisms Underlying Speech and Language,* edited by C. H. Millikan and F. L. Darley. New York: Grune & Stratton, 1967.

O'Connor, N., and B. M. Hermelin. "The Spatial or Temporal Organization of Short-Term Memory." *Quarterly Journal of Experimental Psychology* 25 (1973): 335–43.

Seashore, C. E., D. Lewis, and J. G. Saetveit. *Manual of Instructions and Interpretations for the Seashore Measures of Musical Talents.* Camden: Educational Department, RCA Victor Division, Radio Corporation of America, 1939.

Spreen, O., and A. L. Benton. *Neurosensory Center Comprehensive Examination for Aphasia.* Victoria, B.C.: Department of Psychology, University of Victoria, 1969.

Tzortzis, C., and M. L. Albert. "Impairment of Memory for Sequences in Conduction Aphasia." *Neuropsychologia* 12 (1974): 355–66.

Washburn, M. F. *Movement and Mental Imagery.* Boston: Houghton Mifflin, 1916.

Watson, J. B. *Behaviorism.* New York: Norton, 1924.

Wechsler, D. *Wechsler Intelligence Scale for Children, Manual.* New York: Psychological Corporation, 1949.

# 8

# Visual Selective Attention and the Learning Disabled Child

## Implications for Word Recognition Abilities

*Ronald W. Schworm*

T HE PURPOSE of this study was to investigate and clarify the role of visual selective attention in word recognition by beginning readers and to determine if selective attention is a factor in the diagnosis of reading problems of children who are beyond the beginning stages of reading but who are not making satisfactory progress. Earlier research (Schworm 1979a, 1979b) revealed that specific visual attending strategies may be related to specific word recognition abilities. A comprehensive study combining the procedures and activities of the previous investigations was needed to determine if specific attending strategies are developmental and related to word recognition.

### SELECTIVE ATTENTION AND DECODING

The research studying selective attention as a construct that separates children in performatory skill learning has been conducted several ways (Anderson, Holcomb, Doyle 1973; Keogh and Margolis 1976; Mercer 1978; Ross 1975; and Tarver, Hallahan, Cohen, and Kauffman 1977). However, examining the relationship between visual selective attention and reading requires a reexamination of the construct to insure that it matches the demands of the task. Selectively attending, as Gibson and Levin (1975) imply, means identifying the critical information. Attention is, by definition, accompanied by inattention so that the important information is given less consideration. When learning to recognize a word, all of the information is essential; however, the research on learning to read has identified several stages of word recognition behavior through which beginning readers progress (Carroll 1976; Filp 1975; Juel 1980, Samuels 1970). For example, beginning readers appear to recognize single and initial letter sounds before they recognize and produce consonant and vowel clusters. Children who do not eventually direct their attention to the medial position of words are often limited in the amount of progress they make in the skill of reading (Schworm 1979a). As Rubin (1978) indicates, the most important information occurs in the medial position of the word and it is to this information that the learner must eventually attend.

Although not always direct, the implications of the role of visual selective attention in the reading process have been alluded to through various kinds of studies. Gibsons' hypotheses (Gibson and Gibson 1955); Gibson 1969, 1971) in particular, provide a theoretical base that implies that beginning readers perceive and select relevant units in words and use them to recognize unfamiliar words. This suggests that beginning readers develop stimulus selection strategies which direct visual attention to letter clusters that appear in the medial positions of words. Discussion and research by Venezky and Calfee (1970), Smith (1971), and Cunningham (1976) concur with Gibson's (1971) contentions that beginning readers identify various graphic units of words that are useful for later word pronounciation. Although the individual theories may differ on how words are recognized, all agree that beginning readers abstract and store in memory graphic units that are retrieved to help pronounce unfamiliar words (Cunningham 1976). The constructs of these theories allude to and indicate that failure to attend to the correct stimulus or stimulus set will affect the abstraction and retention of the relevant cues needed to mediate complex words and may inhibit the transition from one stage of reading skill acquisition to another.

## IMPLICATIONS OF SELECTIVE ATTENTION AND WORD RECOGNITION ABILITIES

Selective attention has been described as a factor essential for word recognition (Bateman 1979; Ross 1975); however, the influences of the process on skill development are still undetermined. Learning how to recognize words involves a series of deliberate self-directed visual strategies. Attention, when it is used as an active process in word recognition, facilitates the conscious and the nonconscious abstraction of functional spelling patterns that are both distinctive and invariant (Schworm, 1979a). The supposition of this study is that visual selective attention plays a prominent role in the development of children's word recognition strategies. Selective attention as a facilitating variable is imperative in some aspects of memory search and decision making when beginning readers deal with letter identification and later retention of intraword detail.

Gibson's definition of attention (Gibson 1969, Gibson and Rader 1979) more so than other definitions, is more akin to the attentional deficits of children who have severe learning problems (Schworm 1979b; Schworm and Ableseth 1978). As described by Gibson, attention is an active process, influenced by intention, motivation, and the accomplishment of some goal. Specifically, attention is "a process of extracting information from ongoing events in a selective, active, economical way" (Gibson and Rader 1979, p. 3). Task learning requires self-directed, voluntary attending behavior. It is hypothesized that it is this kind of attending behavior that children with learning problems do not engage in, or do so with difficulty.

The hypothesis that beginning readers advance through specific stages leading to word identification implies that the learner must begin to control attention, recognize the distinctive elements of the word, and shift attention serially from one relevant dimension to another. The initial consonant or consonant-vowel pattern is used to establish word identity. However, because of the multitude of words that begin with the same letter or letter patterns, visual attention must systematically transfer to other elements. As purported by the second stage of the hierarchy, beginning readers shift their attention to the final patterns of words. Ultimately, words become more complex, necessitating further analysis. Most words assume their distinctiveness because of their medial elements. All of the elements of a word are essential for word identification, however, because letters serve as cues, some letters, when in combination with other letters serve as cues, some letters, when in combination with other letters, become more relevant. The expectation is that the beginning reader will learn all of the relevant dimensions of a word but place more emphasis on the medial dimensions and their relationships with beginning and ending letter patterns. The importance of this process of word identification increases as words become complex.

A particular way of determining if visual selective attention is a facilitating variable in word recognition is to study the learner's visual propensity for selecting redundant relevant cues. A study conducted by Schworm (1979b) revealed that accelerated acquisition of word recognition ability was directly related to the learner's ability to identify those patterns that occur frequently in words. The beginning reader samples visually all of the elements of a word, assigning higher values to those letter patterns that are relevant for generalization.

The development of visual selective attention in word recognition can be related to the role of discrimination learning in rudimentary feature discrimination and generalization. The role is active, beginning at an undifferentiated level and proceeding to a differentiated level that leads to recognition of higher ordered units. What the beginning reader learns, how the beginning reader learns, and the variables that influence both how and what the beginning reader learns during the acquisition of word recognition skill have been repeatedly investigated or inferred from related research. It is the position of this study that word recognition stages are directly related, in part, to a sequence of alternative hypotheses identified in discrimination learning. A review of the correlaries between word recognition and discrimination learning illustrates the influence of visual selective attention on the development of advanced or automatic word recognition behavior.

Trabasco and Bower (1968) identified several hypotheses in discrimination learning that can explain, with adaptation, the possible strategies the beginning reader uses to recognize words. Three of the hypotheses: configural, cue-dominance, and pattern component transfer, are related to the transitional stages of word recognition skill development; configuration, use of initial and ending letters, and use of medial letters and letter clusters.

The first hypothesis presented by Trabasco and Bower (1968), the configural hypothesis, implies that the beginning reader makes paired associations of symbols and sounds based on relevant visual cues as they are grouped together. The whole is not analyzed into its parts. All of the cues are perceived as a concept that relate specifically to a combination of features. Omission of a relevant cue, alteration (reversal) of relevant cues, or the addition of an irrelevant cue would result in incorrect pattern perception and visual-auditory association, and reduce retention.

The cue-dominance hypothesis implies that the individual restricts attention to one dimension at a time. Once a relevant dimension is located and the learner feels that the dimension solves the problem, further search and identification is discontinued. Beginning readers apparently rely on initial or ending letter patterns to help with word recognition. Many beginning readers overselect; that is, they identify one letter or letter pattern and discontinue further analysis. Consequently, one dimension of the word dominates, often resulting in chance responses to whole words.

The pattern-component hypothesis, explained by Trabasco and Bower (1968) as the "conditioning both of stimulus patterns and of components within patterns" (p. 21), describes the process the beginning reader increasingly uses during the advanced stages of word recognition skill. It is this process, it is hypothesized, that is acquired quickly by the learner who develops word recognition skills at a younger age without apparent instruction. Intraword letter patterns, the relevant and redundant vowel-vowel teams and vowel-consonant combinations are abstracted by the advanced beginning reader during the configuration and cue dominant stages of word recognition. The beginning reader who acquires word recognition skills at a slower rate or the beginning reader who must be deliberately taught patterns does not, as a rule, make associations to novel patterns as quickly or as easily as the advanced learner.

A fourth hypothesis, by comparison the most advanced hypothesis in discrimination learning, is the habit-distribution hypothesis. This hypothesis implies that the learner will transfer what is learned regardless of the context in which it is acquired. For example, this hypothesis assumes that the reader can identify spelling patterns in isolation as well as in the whole word. The habit-distribution hypothesis provides the basis for the test of the objective of this study. Some children are better readers because they have advanced through the acquisition stages, and can, on demand, distribute their knowledge of spelling patterns by identifying them in varied contexts.

A stage or hierarchial concept of word recognition acquisition is developmental; any of the four hypothesis can explain some facet in the development of the word recognition process. Taken as a collective, the hypotheses illustrate a progression in perceptual learning that is plausible and logical and one that has some empirical support. Because the progression infers a developmental hierarchy, it can help explain or support various causes of word recognition problems. Each hypothesis is related to specific deficits, deficits that could interfere with the development of automatic word recognition skill.

It was the hypothesis of this study that some children experiencing difficulty learning how to recognize and retain words may not develop the same selective attention strategies as children who are not having or who have not had problems. Specifically, the objective of this study was to determine the kinds of attentional deficits that may interfere with word recognition ability.

## METHOD

### Subjects

Sixty-four children from first (n = 28) and third (n = 36) grades were selected from seven classrooms and two elementary schools. Classroom teachers were requested to identify randomly a representative sample of high, average, and low achieving students to acquire a cross-section of ability and performance levels. The learning disabled children (n = 40) represented a sample of students who were referred to and evaluated at the Diagnostic Clinic for Developmental Disabilities, Department of Pediatrics, Strong Memorial Hospital, Rochester, New York.

High and average achieving children were those whose reading scores were at or above grade level at the time of evaluation. Low achieving students were those whose reading scores were below grade level, however, their reading problems did not require special instruction or remedial assistance. The average reading score of the low achieving group was six academic months below the expected grade level standard. All learning disabled children (n = 40) displayed more than one academic year's delay in reading ($\bar{X}$ = 1.6), exhibited learning problems in more than one subject, demonstrated difficulties in learning early in their schooling, and were referred to the clinic for comprehensive testing and evaluation. All children had full scale intellience scores within normal range. Children with sensory impairments or emotional disturbances were excluded from the study.

### Procedures

The test of selective attention, referred to as the Select-A-Figure-From-Many (SAFFM) test, was used as the measure of attending ability. The initial development of the test was based on a task used by Gibson and Gibson (1955). Three protocols were used in the present study. The first protocol was used as a warm-up task. The warm-up task consisted of shapes that represented familiar objects. The remaining two protocols were categorized by the similarity and dissimilarity of shape. The SAFFM test of dissimilar figures (A1) and similar figures (B1) were developed as tasks that require multiple medial or peripheral cue selection for correct responding. The target cards for the two tests used in this study are presented in Figure 8.1.

Each deck consisted of fifteen stimulus cards, five of which were exactly the same as the target card. The other ten cards were distractors, containing designs that were highly similar to or very different from the target card. To administer the SAFFM, the evaluator displayed the target card and instructed the student to look at it carefully. The student was told that the card would be embedded in the deck and that the objective of the task was to tell the evaluator when he or she saw a card that was exactly the same as the target card. Students were instructed to

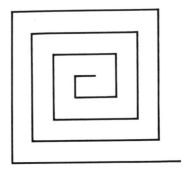

Stimulus Card
A1

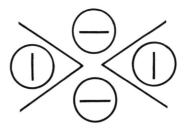

Stimulus Card
B1

FIGURE 8.1. Stimulus cards for SAFFM decks A1 and B1

say "yes" when they saw the target card and "no" when they saw a card
that differed. Criteria, or successful performance was achieved when
the student responded yes to all target cards and no to all stimulus cards.
The task was repeated until the student responded accurately for three
consecutive trials. If the student selected or identified a distractor card
as a target card during the independent or baseline trials, he or she was
informed that they had made a mistake and they were "getting the cards
mixed up" or "confused."

A child's performance on the SAFFM was measured by determining the interaction level that existed between the student and the task
during the initial experience or exposure. An interaction level can be
described as a particular learning strategy or set of learning strategies
that the student uses to solve a problem (Schworm and Abelseth 1981). If
a student fails to respond correctly to the task at an independent level,

(i.e., the responses are initiated correctly and consistently after a simple command or direction) it is assumed that the child has not selected and utilized the important features and properties of the task. To determine if the child has not utilized the correct features and properties, the evaluator changes the amount and kind of information provided for the child, and gives specific prompts to help focus the child's attention. This external information source cues the child to attend specific features, properties, and events that define the problem and is referred to as information feedback. If selective information is a critical factor, as supposed, and if the child is not adequately responding with an established set of attending strategies, then the addition of various forms of information feedback that direct the child to attend to the salient and critical aspects of the problem should result in a change in performance. It was hypothesized in this study that children at various achievement levels could be differentiated by the amount of interaction they needed to efficiently devise a strategy and solve the task. Lower achieving children would require more interaction as compared to average and high achieving children. It was also suspected that older, lower achieving children would respond like younger, average children, that is their problem-solving strategies would require the same amount and degree of augmented information feedback. As noted, each interaction level provided a child with more information about the task. There were five interaction levels used to add information and direct attention. Those levels were student description, teacher explanation, teacher demonstration, and imitation. The sequence and description of each interaction is illustrated in Figure 8.2.

The *Spelling Pattern Tests* were developed and used in previous studies (Schworm 1979a, 1979b). The patterns consisted of vowel-vowel combinations that predominately appear in the medial position of the word and which have an invariant pronounciation. They were presented in three formats: in isolation, with ending consonant cues, and with beginning and ending consonant cues (see Table 8.1).

The first test consisted of nineteen two-letter vowel-vowel and vowel-consonant combinations that predominately appear in the medial positions of words. These spelling patterns were isolated from any cues that could assist pronounciation. The second spelling pattern test consisted of eight vowel-vowel combinations selected from the first test. The combinations were attached to a consonant to form a three letter pattern. These spelling patterns resembled word parts. The consonant was added to determine if it aided pronounciation. The third test was comprised of nonwords containing the vowel combinations used on the first and second tests. The nonword format simulated whole words and provided a beginning and ending cue.

Sequence of Instructional Interactions

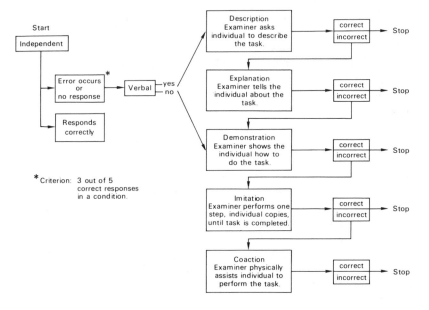

FIGURE 8.2.  Sequence of Instructional Interactions

The Wide Range Achievement Test (Jastak and Jastak 1965), Word Recognition, Level 1, was used to acquire a grade level score for each student and to determine the number of words each student could pronounce automatically.

Each student was administered the Select-A-Figure-From-Many, the Spelling Pattern, and the Word Recognition tests. Each subject was seen individually. Test order was randomized for each student for control for practice and fatigue. Before testing, practice cards were used to insure that each student understood the directions. Students were allowed five seconds to pronounce each vowel combination or nonword. If there was no response the tester turned to the next card. Correct answers or reinforcement were not given by the evaluators.

The SAFFM tests were administered following the directions described earlier. The warm up or practice task preceded the remaining two tests. The order of administration of A1 and B1 was randomized for each student to insure that presentation was not a factor in overall results. Each student was debriefed after performing the SAFFM test to determine the kinds of cues they used to help retain the target figure

TABLE 8.1

**Spelling Pattern Tests**

| Two-letter Spelling Patterns | Three-letter Spelling Patterns | Nonwords |
|---|---|---|
| ai (bait) | ain | taib |
| ea (each) | eal | fean |
| ee (bleed) | eep | deel |
| ou (ounce) | oup | nout |
| oo (boot) | oot | bool |
| au (cause) | aut | faup |
| oi (coin) | oin | boin |
| oa (boat) | oan | tay |
| ay (day) | | bown |
| ow (own/cow) | | sird |
| ir (bird) | | terb |
| er (term) | | furt |
| ur (burn) | | nenk |
| ut (rut) | | fut |
| ip (tip) | | kop |
| en (mend) | | bap |
| op (hop) | | parn |
| ap (tap) | | toan |
| ar (barn) | | |

while sorting through the deck of distractor cards. The cues for the dissimilar card deck, referred to as A1, were medial cue, configuration, medial and ending cue. The cues for the similar card deck, referred to as B1, were size of circle, direction of line, length of line, circle and lines, and configuration.

### Analysis

Initially, scores from the SAFFM test and the spelling pattern tests were used to determine if the attending strategies of different groups of children were similar. If the two tests represented the same construct, the test results for different groups of children should have covaried (Butterfield and Dickerson 1978); for example, higher achieving students should have passed both and lower achieving students should have failed both.

In addition, a series of multiple regression analyses were used to examine the relationships between the spelling pattern and selective attention results and the reading scores. The primary analysis was a comparison of reading achievement, spelling pattern pronounciation, and the number of trials needed to complete the SAFFM test. Multiple comparisons were made between the individuals' test scores and other variables. The type of strategy used by each student was coded and used as a criterion variable to determine the kind of attending strategy employed on the SAFFM test. Attending strategies were represented by codes for multiple cue selection, single cue selection, medial cue selection, peripheral cue selection, and configurative responding. Scoring of attentional strategies for each stimulus deck was based on the following criteria.

### Deck A1

*Single or multiple cue selection.* Based on the number of properties of the target card used by the student to identify the target card.

*Medial cue selection.* Based on the student's indication that the middle line of the card was used as the primary care.

*Peripheral cue selection.* Based on the child's indication that the outer line or that the corners were used as criteria for selection.

*Configurative.* Based on the child's indication that the number of lines, "the boxes"—the maze—was used to aid retention.

### Deck B1

*Single or multiple cue selection.* Based on the number of properties of the target card used by the student to identify a target card.

*Medial cue selection.* Based on the indication that the direction and size of lines and the size of circles were used to help with identification.

*Peripheral cue selection.* Based on the indication that the size of circle, circle only, or the slanted lines were used to help with identification.

## Configuration

Based on the indication that the general shape of the design was used, for example, circles and lines were used but not differentiated by size or direction.

Correct identification of the target card for Deck B1 required multiple cue responding. Attention to the size of circle and to the direction and size of the line was required for correct retention. Repeated recognition of the target card of Deck A1 required multiple cue identification and use of medial or peripheral cues, for example, the line in the middle of the maze or the curvature of the outside lines.

Results of the debriefing and the coding of attending strategies, were used to analyze the type of responses of high, average, and low achieving learning disabled readers. Scores were related to group and individual performances on the spelling pattern and word recognition tests. Based on the previously stated hypotheses, it was assumed that higher achievers would use multiple, medial cues for Decks A1 and B1, and would also recognize more medial spelling patterns presented in isolation. It was further assumed that use of multiple, medial, and peripheral cues would be related to recognition and pronounciation of medial components of words.

## RESULTS

The initial analysis substantiated the hypothesis that identification of isolated medial letter patterns was related to the the learner's ability to solve the selective attention task by identifying and retaining peripheral and medial cues. The letter pattern test results of readers selected from regular classrooms correlated with their test results on the SAFFM test, $r = .72$ for the two letter and dissimilar task, B1. These results indicate that better readers identified more spelling patterns than average or lower achieving readers and completed the SAFFM tests in fewer trials. The significant correlations ($p > 05$) indicate that both tests are, in part, measuring the same construct. Better achieving, and older students completed both tests with greater accuracy and in fewer trials than younger, beginning readers, or older, lower or average achieving readers. The correlation between both tests of selective attention, A1 and B1, was $r = .83$, indicating that the measures were intercorrelated, and based on the same principles. Students who did well on one measure also did well on the other.

Comparisons between the learning disabled readers and the low, average, and high achieving readers selected from the regular classrooms revealed that these two groups did, in fact, represent different populations. Two separate analyses were completed. The first compared performance of the learning disabled group to the performances of all non-learning disabled children and the second compared the performances of third grade students only to the performances of all learning disabled children. Removing the first grade student scores from the second analysis was done to provide better balance between both groups in terms of age and years of reading instruction. The learning disabled group consisted of children who were predominantly either in the last half of second grade, or were in third, fourth, or fifth grades. All third grade students were tested in the first half of the school year. Separate analyses of variance, repeated measures of test scores of all students revealed that significant differences existed between the performances of both groups on the two letter pattern, $F(2,101) = 5.58, p < .05$, and three letter pattern tests, $F(2,101) = 4.67$, p $< .05$. The results of the nonword test were not significant, $F(2,101 = 2.89$, however, the $F$ test does approach significance at the .05 level, $F(2,101) = .09$, when the nonword test scores of third grade students were significantly higher than the nonword test scores of all learning disabled students.

Failure of the nonword test to discriminate between both groups of students is due, in part, to the scores of the beginning first grade readers who were included in this analysis. All learning disabled students were able to recognize some words, however, many of the first grade students, a sample that may have included some children with potential reading disabilities, were unable to pronounce nonwords. The significant differences between groups on the two- and three-letter spelling pattern test reveal that ability to recognize medial letter patterns, or ability to pronounce letter patterns by relying on fewer cues, can discriminate between those students who are making satisfactory progress in reading as compared to those who are not.

To determine if performance on the selective attention tests could discriminate between learning and non-learning disabled readers, an analysis of variance, repeated measures, was used to examine the difference between performances on the two selective attention tasks. The third grade students required fewer trials ($\overline{X} = 6.8$, $SD = 4.6$) than the learning disabled group ($\overline{X} = 8.9$, $SD = 6.7$) to complete the task A1, $F(2,71 = 5.92$, p $< .01$ and fewer trials ($\overline{X} = 8.9$, $SD = 5.7$) than the learning disabled group ($\overline{X} = 12.4$, $SD = 7.2$) to complete the task B1, $F(2, 71) = 4.70$ p $< .05$. These results indicate that learning disabled students required more evaluator interaction, more trials, and more prompts before recognizing the relevant cues needed to identify the stimulus card.

To answer the question, do learning disabled children use different visual attending strategies than nonlearning disabled children, an analysis was made using the results of the debriefing, results which indicated if a student completed the selective attention task by relying on multiple or single cues, and medial or peripheral cues or configurative responding. Types of cues or responding used was determined by asking the students what they attended to to help identify the target card, by noting the kinds of distractor cards selected on each trial, or by the kinds of interactions that changed the students responding from incorrect to correct.

An analysis of the scores of students from the regular classrooms revealed that higher achieving readers, readers who also recognized more medial spelling patterns, used multiple cues and either medial or peripheral cues to help identify and retain the target card, and completed both tasks in less than five trials without the assistance of the evaluator. Average achieving students relied on multiple cues, however, they predominantly used peripheral cues to identify and retain the target cards. Lower achieving students, in either first or third grades, and all average achieving first grade students relied on a single peripheral cue or configurative responding to identify and retain the target card. Multiple linear regression revealed that number of cues, type of cues, and degree of interaction needed by a student were good predictors of reading achievement ($R = .83, R^2 = .69$), two letter spelling-pattern identification ($R = .89, R^2 = .79$), and three letter spelling-pattern identification ($R = .83, R^2 = .69$), as well as performance on the selective attention test A1 ($R = .83, R^2 = .70$) and selective attention test B1 ($R = .78, R^2 = .62$).

## DISCUSSION

The results of the analyses validated the initial postulations that significant differences would exist between the performances of learning and non-learning disabled readers on the selective attention and spelling pattern tests. As hypothesized, the data revealed that many learning disabled readers do not use the same visual selective attention strategies as nonlearning disabled readers when they attempt to pronounce unknown words. The strategy of attending to the middle of target cards was significantly related to the kind of cues, the number of trials, and the degree of interaction needed to complete successfully the selective attention tasks. Higher and average achieving readers identified more medial spelling patterns, pronounced more words, and completed the selective attention tasks in fewer trials than the lower achieving and learning disabled readers by using multiple, medial, and peripheral cues. Many of the learning disabled readers, regardless of age, performed like younger, beginning readers. They relied on single cues, reportedly using configuration to identify and retain the target cards. In essence, the results indicate that visual selective attention may indeed be developmental, and its use and deployment may be observable, measurable, and related to a specific stage in the learn to read process.

Visual selective attention, as an operation, refers to the strategies used by a learner to recognize and recall functional, relevant properties needed to make decisions about the integrity and identity of a stimulus. Although it has been difficult to define the term selective attention as a behavior (Alabiso 1972), consistent research has shown that children become better at detecting differences and selecting relevant cues in task related activities as they become older (Hale 1979). Older children use more economical, flexible visual response patterns, and identify relevant, functional cues needed to discriminate one stimulus from another. It was the contention of this study that words, as tasks or stimuli, consist of components that have different values with certain components more functional than others. The results reveal that a lag in the development of a strategy or some type of interference, may impede the child's use of economical, efficient search procedures needed to enhance word recognition ability. Performances of learning disabled and non-learning disabled readers on the visual selective attention and the spelling pattern tests revealed that a relationship exists between the specific perceptual learning hypotheses and the stages of word recognition skill.

Beginning readers and many learning disabled readers relied on configuration, or global responding to complete the selective attention task. They were not analytic, and they did not attend to medial or peripheral cues unless instructed to do so. Their attentional strategies were inflexible, and uneconomical. They relied on a single cue to aid retention.

Children emerging in the learn to read process, and better achieving learning disabled readers relied on cue-dominance, the use of familiar, salient beginning and ending consonants to help decode unknown words. They responded to the demand to identify and remember the target cards by using single peripheral cues. They did not automatically attend to the middle of the card, the position where the most relevant and economical information was deliberately embedded.

Many children identified as average achievers, and all higher achieving readers, used multiple cues to complete the attention tasks. The cues they used were peripheral or medial, and were the most relevant of all the cues one could select to help with retention. These students also pronounced more medial spelling patterns in isolation and easily pronounced words containing those same patterns. Their ability to distribute their attention, locate, integrate, and generalize the cues or medial spelling patterns from one card or word to another was evident.

It is imperative to indicate that higher achieving beginning readers, for example, those first grade children reading content above grade level recognized the same number of medial letter patterns and used the same kinds of attending strategies as higher or average achieving, older readers. They pronounced medial spelling patterns beyond the level of instruction they had received in school or at home. Likewise, most higher achieving readers recognized patterns that had never been included in their reading instruction. Gibson's (1971) theory that beginning readers abstract, that is, perceive and select functional, relevant units and use them to identify unfamiliar words, suggests that even though children are presented with a whole word approach and encouraged to pronounce words as wholes, they still select intraword redundancies without deliberate rule learning and memorization. It is assumed that the accelerated reader learns to use advanced stimulus selection strategies, for example, learns to attend to multiple, medial, and peripheral cues, at a faster rate than other readers.

## CONCLUSION

The number of trials it took a child to complete the selective attention tests corresponded to the degree and type of interaction needed for that child to complete the tasks. When asked to describe the pattern, many beginning readers discovered important components that they did not realize when they responded independently on earlier trials. Some children responded correctly after they listened to the evaluator describe the design. Emerging readers, those who recognized words more frequently than other beginning readers, responded to their own descriptions or the evaluator's explanations.

The younger beginning reader, and those learning disabled readers with the greatest discrepancies between expected reading achievement and actual scores required demonstration or imitation before they attended to the relevant tasks. Gibson and Rader (1979) indicate that improvement in "economical perception and attentive behavior is not a capacity change or a stretching out of a span. The change does not depend upon a mysterious increase in a reservoir of power, but on cognitive growth: growth in knowledge of meaningful affordances and ordering of a knowledge system so as to use order and structure" (p. 19). Children not reacting to their own responses by detecting and correcting their errors or to the efforts of the evaluator until their specific responses were compared and contrasted may not have developed the cognitive power to use efficient attending strategies. In essence, they may not know how to learn, or know how to know.

Children having difficulty remembering the target card were not perceptually handicapped. Rather, they may not have developed the perceptual skills needed to search for, identify, and retain the relevant information, nor have they determined that one stimulus property, when in correspondence with another, has greater value in determining the structure and the invariance of an event or task. The failure of these children to attend so that they identify and extract functional information appears to relate to their lack of application of active, cognitive strategies.

## REFERENCES

Alabiso, F. "Inhibitory Function of Attention in Reducing Hyperactive Behavior." *American Journal of Mental Deficiency* 77 (1972): 259–82.

Anderson, R. B., C. Holcomb, and R. Doyle. "The Measurement of Attentional Deficits." *Exceptional Children* 39 (1973): 534–39.

Bateman, B. In *Theory and Practice of Early Reading,* edited by L. Resnick and P. Weaver. Hillsdale, N.J.: Erlbaum Associates, 1979.

Butterfield, E., and D. Dickerson. "Cognitive Theory and Mental Development." In *International Review of Research in Mental Retardation,* edited by N. Ellis. *Vol. 8.* New York: Academic Press, 1978.

Carroll, J. B. "The Nature of the Reading Process." In *Theoretical Models and Processes of Reading,* edited by H. Singer and R. Ruddell. Delaware: International Reading Association, 1976.

Cunningham, P. "Investigation of a Synthesized Theory of Mediated Word Identification." *Reading Research Quarterly* 11 (1975–76): 127–43.

Filp, J. "Relationship among Reading Subskills: A Hierarchial Hypothesis." *Journal of Reading Behavior* 7 (1975): 224–40.

Gibson, E. *Principles of Perceptual Learning and Development*. New York: Appleton-Century-Crofts, 1969.

——. "Perceptual Learning and the Theory of Word Perception." *Cognitive Psychology* 2 (1971): 351–68.

Gibson, E., and N. Rader. "Attention: The Perceiver as Performer." In *Attention and Cognitive Development,* edited by G. Hale and M. Lewis. New York: Plenum Press, 1979.

Gibson, J., and E. Gibson. "Perceptual Learning: Differentiation or Enrichment." *Psychological Review* 62 (1955): 32–34.

Gibson, J., and H. Levin. *The Psychology of Reading*. Cambridge: MIT, 1979.

Hale, G. "Development of Children's Attention to Stimulus Components." In *Attention and Cognitive Development,* edited by G. Hale and M. Lewis. New York: Plenum Press, 1979.

Jastak, J. F., and S. R. Jastak. *Wide Range Achievement Test*. Wilmington, Del.: Guidance Associates, 1965.

Juel, C. "Comparison of Word Identification Strategies with Varying Context, Word Type, and Reader Skill." *Reading Research Quarterly* 3 (1980): 358–76.

Keogh, B., and J. Margolis. "Learn To Labor and To Wait: Attentional Problems of Children with Learning Disorders." *Journal of Learning Disabilities* 9 (1976): 18–28.

Mercer, C. "Modeling and Attention of Mentally Retarded, Learning Disabled, and Normal Boys." *Journal of Special Education Technology* 1 (1978): 27–35.

Ross, A. *Psychological Aspects of Learning Disabilities and Reading Disorders*. New York: McGraw-Hill, 1975.

Rubin, D. "Word Initial and Word Final Frequencies." *Journal of Reading Behavior* 10 (1978): 177–83.

Samuels, S. J. "Modes of Word Recognition." In *Theoretical Models and Processes of Reading,* edited by R. Ruddell and H. Singer. Delaware: International Reading Association, 1970.

Schworm, R. W. "Effects of Selective Attention on the Decoding Abilities of Children with Learning Problems." *Journal of Learning Disabilities* 12 (1979a): 639–44.

——. "Word Mediation and Generalization in Beginning Readers." *Journal of Reading Behavior* 11 (1979b): 139–51.

Schworm, R. W., and J. L. Abelseth. "Teaching the Individual with Severe Learning Problems: Strategies which Point to Success." *Education and Training of the Mentally Retarded* 13 (1978): 146–53.

——. "Evaluating Instructional Interactions: How Do We Begin Teaching?" *Learning Disability Quarterly* 4 (1981): 101–11.

Smith, F. *Understanding Reading*. New York: Holt, Rinehart, Winston, 1971.

Tarver, S., D. Hallahan, S. Cohen, and J. Kauffman. "The Development of Visual Selective Attention and Verbal Rehearsal in Learning Disabled Boys." *Journal of Learning Disabilities* 10 (1977): 491–500.

Trabasco, T., and G. Bower. *Attention in Learning: Theory and Research*. New York: Wiley, 1968.

Venezky, R., and R. Calfee. "The Reading Competency Model." In *Theoretical Models and Processes of Reading,* edited by R. Ruddell and H. Singer. Delaware: International Reading Association, 1970.

# 9

# The Development of Memory Skills in Children

## Portraying Learning Disabilities
## in Terms of Strategy and Knowledge Deficiencies

*John W. Hagen and Craig R. Barclay*

T HE PROBLEMS of identifying, assessing, and educating learning disabled children continue to attract international attention. In the past
twenty years learning disabilities have become a public concern because
of the growing awareness on the part of parents and teachers that many
children have great difficulty acquiring and using knowledge through the
various language modes. It is noteworthy that, except in a few instances,
over two decades of awareness has not led to a clear understanding of
the nature of learning disabilities.

The question of whether a problem exists is no longer debated. In
fact, the estimates that from one to three percent of all children attending
school in the United States are in some way learning disabled are
considered very conservative (National Advisory Committee on Handicapped Children 1968). Ironically, a major unresolved question is how to
define precisely what a learning disability is; consequently, it is difficult
to arrive at both an accurate description of the phenomena and a reliable
estimate of the magnitude of the problem (Torgesen 1975). Most recent
definitions include the notions that learning disabled children are of
normal intelligence, they acquire certain academic skills at a slower rate
than most other children their same age, they are not developmentally
disabled in the sense of being mentally retarded, and they have great
difficulty learning and using communication skills, especially in reading
(cf. Cruickshank 1981, who takes the position that a learning disability
is independent of age and level of intellectual functioning; he also
argues that a disability is grounded necessarily in a neurophysiological
dysfunction).

The authors were supported in part by NICHD Grant 5 T32 HD07109-04 while preparing
this chapter. Appreciation is expressed to Richard Newman, who read an earlier draft of
this paper.

Consider the problems of identifying learning disabilities in broader terms. At least two issues arise if a narrow range of performance measures, like those associated with reading, are used alone to classify children. One is obvious; namely children are complex, multidimensional beings composed not only of psychological but also social and physical features which change with time. It seems reasonable to assume then, that multiple measures on many behaviors in different settings must be taken over time before identifying children as learning disabled. The second issue is not at all obvious. It is termed here the "relativity of context" problem, which means that behavior occurs and is best understood with reference to some standard or context. Examples of different contexts are the classroom, school, home, and neighborhood. Our judgements about how well children perform or the appropriateness of their behaviors are determined in large part by the contexts we use as points of comparison. A relevant case is to compare children from two different school districts. In one district, academic and intellectual performance is valued highly, while in the other, it is not. The likelihood that a child would be seen as disabled in the latter district is less than if school achievement is stressed.

Regardless of problems with definitions, descriptions, and numbers, learning disabled children have unusual difficulties with classroom tasks requiring cognitive activities needed for the acquisition and use of knowledge. Characterized in this way, the learning disabled are viewed as developmentally immature. This view need not imply, however, that these children are incapable of learning and performing effectively in the schools. Instead, by assuming that learning disabled children are deficient in the use of certain strategic behaviors, intervention programs which teach task-relevant skills should be effective. Research findings which demonstrate that learning disabled children can benefit from certain types of strategy instruction suggest that disabilities, in the sense of structural insufficiencies, are not the sole cause of performance deficits.

The arguments presented thus far are not new. There is a long and detailed history of the "production deficiency" approach to explaining performance differences among children. More specifically, a production deficiency refers to the situation in which the child does not spontaneously produce a set of effective mediational behaviors but can be trained to do so given a minimum of time and effort (Flavell, Beach, & Chinsky 1966; Paris 1978). The general conclusions drawn are that young children do not, on their own, use task relevant strategies for problem solving. However, with age and experience, effective strategies are used in appropriate situations. In the developmental literature, age related behavior change is characterized in terms of greater and greater differentiation through which the child's behavior becomes increasingly task specific.

One area in which extensive information is available regarding the acquisition of effective problem solving strategies is in the development of memory skills in children. In comparing the memory development literature with that available on learning disabilities, two striking similarities emerge. First, there is a common philosophical orientation: performance is explained in terms of differences instead of deficits among children (e.g., Torgesen 1977b). Second, both areas focus on the cognition-behavior connection. That is, the assumption is made that certain behaviors are more process oriented than under strict environmental control—in many situations, people *think* before they act instead of simply reacting.

The purposes of this chapter are to provide an overview of memory development in children from preschool to about grade 8 (13 year olds) and to use this knowledge as a context for understanding learning disabilities. Also, the instructional implications of the research on memory development for educating the learning disabled are discussed. In the first section of this chapter, the study of learning disabilities is placed in historical perspective. This is followed in the second section by a description of issues in the study of memory development which highlights the advantages of conceptualizing learning disabilities in terms of information processing components. It is emphasized that effective behavior results from the fine-tuned interaction of the person's structural features, the strategies and other control processes acquired through experience, and the task demands placed on the individual. The third section focuses on educational implications, especially on an instructional approach aimed at maximizing the maintenance and generalization of learned skills.

## HISTORICAL OVERVIEW

Placing contemporary theoretical and empirical work in perspective through a brief historical overview of learning disabilities affords a context in which ideas presented in later sections of this paper are best understood. An historical view also emphasizes how enduring many basic issues are in the study of human behavior, especially in the case of disabled children. An appreciation of these issues should facilitate future research by economizing our efforts through an access to an existing body of empirical work.

Problems of contemporary significance are found in the early work of Heinz Werner and Alfred Strauss (also see Hallahan and Cruickshank 1973, for a comprehensive discussion). The most noteworthy of these problems is associated with specifying possible causes of behavioral dysfunctions. In studies of mentally retarded children, the distinction was made between exogenous and endogenous causes. This is, persons thought to be neurologically impaired versus children whose retardation was attributable more to genetic or familial factors.

Subsequent research on neurological deficits focused on perceptual-motor functions. The assumptions of the "perceptual deficit" hypothesis are found in the seminal works of Cruickshank, Kephart, Frostig, Doman, and Delacato. Much of the pioneering work of these researchers dealt with children of normal intelligence. Also, parallel to developments in the perceptual-motor area, Orton, deHirsch, and Kirk were pursuing neuropsychological reasons for language disorders believed to underlie many learning disabilities.

The criticisms of a strict neurological approach to the diagnosis and treatment of learning disabled children are well documented elsewhere. In brief, such a unidimensional conceptualization may over-simplify the nature of learning disabilities. The heterogeneity of the population alone suggests that most dysfunctions are best characterized in terms of multiple, interactive factors. By assuming neurological deficits, convenient labels are used for categorizing children where such labels have practical significances, especially when it is necessary to identify a group of children in need of services provided through some federally funded project. Descriptive labels, however, do not facilitate remediation. In our view, a deficit approach is too narrow since it neither best characterizes most learning disabled children nor does it provide an adequate explanation of their behavior to develop instructional programs. These criticisms apply as well to strict academic or behavioral accounts of human performance (e.g., Engelmann 1969) in which psychological processes are largely ignored.

More recent theories have taken a number of different forms modelled from research on cognitive-developmental processes. A feature common to many current theories is an emphasis on the reciprocally dependent relationship between the person and his or her environment—what Bandura (1978) has termed "reciprocal determinism." In a model proposed by Adelman (1971), for example, it is argued that the maximum benefits to the child are realized when the deviations between the child's disability and an instructional program are minimized. Thus, individual differences are stressed such that each child's academic skills and interests are tailored to fit with an educational program. In other theories, more or less emphasis is placed on either the person or environment variable, for example, Senf's (1972) information integration theory.

Another theoretical position is that proposed by Torgesen (1975, 1977a), who suggests that the distinguishing feature of learning disabled children is their "inactivity" when faced with a problem. Torgesen (1977a and b) argues that even though many disabled children have problems selectively attending to relevant information or difficulty in certain memory processes, poor performance can still be considered in terms of deficiencies in problem solving strategies — instead of ability deficits. The learning disabled child is viewed as one who, first, lacks an intent to learn, and second, has not acquired the skills needed to actively participate in the learning process. Another needed element is added here. That is, the metacognitive or executive control component; the child may not know when or how to apply skills already learned or to monitor the effects of such skills on the mastery of a task.

Our position, like Torgesen's, is a cognitive-developmental one, in which the typical child is seen as an active, changing organism in a variable environment. The acquisition and use of knowledge by children results from purposeful interactions with the environment over time. Hagen (1971) expresses this sentiment in his description of the development of memory:

> In order to offer a developmental account of short-term memory in children, one must incorporate concepts for intention, verbal processes, strategies, and memory itself. The following model is proposed. The child is learning at two levels. He acquires new skills, some of which come about without his intending to learn them, and others which he sets out to attain. At the same time, he begins to realize that he is an actor in his environment as well as to reactor to it. Task demands are made increasingly upon him and more differentiated responses are required. What he is really learning is that *he* himself determines how well he does, and that he can improve his performance if he uses certain of his new skills in certain task situations. Thus the intention to remember comes about because the child has learned that remembering is both possible and desirable. He has also learned that his ever-increasing verbal skills can be put to use in a memory situation. The employment of these skills in task-appropriate strategies during the acquisition phase of a memory task results in enhanced memory performance, and he is further encouraged to use the strategies as well as to develop even more efficient ones. (pp. 267–68)

Future research on learning disabilities is needed which focuses on the development of the cognitive activities required to solve school-type tasks. In the next section of this paper, the problems associated with the acquisition of strategic behaviors are taken up within the domain of memory development.


## MEMORY DEVELOPMENT


The development of memory is often described in terms of the child's growing capacity to remember together with an ever-increasing active involvement with the environment. Memory improves because children acquire the capability to mediate their performance through the use of some symbolic system. This system, in turn, frees children from their ties to any specific environmental context (Luria 1976).

Much of the evidence to date supports the notion that age-related changes in memory are due to an increasingly sophisticated use of mnemonic strategies. Furthermore, memory development is accompanied by an ever growing knowledge system which, in orchestration with strategy use, facilitates the acquisition of new knowledge as well as the retrieval and use of existing information. The purpose of this section of the chapter is to characterize the prototypic development of memory skills in children. It is our position that the child's capacity to remember, the strategies employed to problem solve, and a general knowledge base interact with task characteristics and demands. The result of this interaction is the child's observed memory performance.

Capacity refers to the structural features of the system (e.g., short-term memory). Capacity explanations of performance assume that behavior is caused by maturation. In the case of learning disabilities, it is argued by some that limited or defective structural capabilities, either central or peripheral in nature, are the fundamental cause of memory deficiencies. Capacity, however, is also used in reference to the processing capabilities of the system. Accordingly, developmental changes are seen through the more efficient allocation of limited structural resources.

Strategies refer to the "rules" and specific behaviors used to solve problems in a means-end fashion (see Paris 1978). Strategy explanations of memory development posit that behavior change results from the acquisition and effective use of problem solving skills. This component of the information processing system is receiving increasing attention from researchers interested in learning disabilities, especially from those who view the child as an inactive learner (Torgesen 1977b).

The knowledge component is the semantic feature of the system that the organism acquires over a long period of time; that is, knowledge is used in reference to higher-order schemata which guide behavior as opposed to specific items of information stored in long-term memory. In one sense, knowledge and strategies are similar since knowledge can be viewed as the general, abstract representation of experiences, whereas strategies are instances of those experiences applied to some specific problem. Explanations of memory development are made in terms of the differing amounts of knowledge children have acquired about some class of problems. One reason why the learning disabled child may be inactive in learning new information is because of a lack of adequate knowledge about various approaches to problem solving.

Consider now the development of memory strategies in children. Flavell (1970) suggests that strategies are intentional cognitive activities which have behavioral consequences. A simple example is writing down a phone number or grocery list so that the information is not forgotten. Research has shown that with age, the child begins to use mnemonics spontaneously and becomes more capable of adapting these strategic behaviors to different tasks.

An examination of selected studies highlights the need to understand memory development in terms of what the child actually does when faced with a problem. This examination also shows that while young children can use effective strategies, strategy use alone does not account for all the developmental differences found. Apparently some additional factor, like general familiarity with a task, is needed to more accurately explain memory development.

The work of major interest deals with the child's use of language; specifically, the rehearsal of to-be-remembered information. Theoretically, rehearsal is any activity which keeps information alive in short-term memory and mediates the transfer of that information to a long term store. Also, the function of elaborative rehearsal is to enhance the child's semantic (knowledge) system through the assimilation of new information to what is already known.

The research of John Flavell and his colleagues was instrumental in providing the impetus for the extensive work in this area. In the early studies (e.g., Flavell et al. 1966) it was assumed that the poor memory performance of the young child was due to a failure to use verbal rehearsal. The young child was seen as capable of remembering well, but it was unlikely she or he would marshall an appropriate strategy. To test the verbal deficiency hypothesis, Flavell et al. (1966) studied children in Grades K, 2, and 5. A serial recall task was used in which children had to remember a set of pictures in an order determined by the experimenter.

A portion of the children were tested 15 sec. after the presentation of the pictures. The performance of these children provided the most interesting data since, during the delay, they needed to rehearse the picture names in order to remember them. A second experimenter, trained in lip reading, carefully observed the child's verbal behavior. The major findings were that the number of children observed verbalizing during the delay period increased with grade level as did their actual recall, and the amount of information remembered correlated positively with rehearsal.

In subsequent work, Keeney, Cannizzo, and Flavell (1967) showed that rehearsal and recall were functionally related. In order to demonstrate the causative relationship between verbal behavior and memory, children were trained to rehearse, which improved their recall. The relevant data are summarized in Table 9.1. It is seen that children who did not spontaneously use (i.e., "nonproducers") rehearsal performed more poorly than children who did (i.e., "spontaneous producers"). Further, on a posttest given immediately after training, the nonproducers performance was comparable to that found for spontaneous producers. However, when the experimenter stopped prompting the children to verbalize, many reverted back to their pretraining level of performance. The authors argued that one reason for this finding was that while training provided the necessary skills, it did not impart sufficient knowledge about the utility of what was learned.

In a more recent study by Kennedy and Miller (1976), this "knowledge deficiency" hypothesis was tested. If it is assumed that children abandon a trained strategy because they do not recognize the relation-

TABLE 9.1

**Proportion of Trials on Which First Graders
Were 100% Correct in Their Recall by Group and Session**

| | Session | | |
|---|---|---|---|
| Group | Assessment | Prompted Maintenance | n |
|---|---|---|---|
| Non-Producers | .40 | .61* | 17 |
| Spontaneous Producers | .65 | .67 | 12 |

*10 of these 17 children abandoned the trained rehearsal strategy during an unprompted maintenance test (Keeney, Cannizzo, and Flavell 1967).

ship between a particular strategic behavior and its mediating consequences then such knowledge should lead to the continued use of a
learned skill. Kennedy and Miller's results supported this assumption.
Thus, children will maintain purposeful behavior if they are made aware
of the beneficial effects of a particular strategy. This conclusion is also
supported by other research on mnemonic aids like self-testing and
self-monitoring skills. However, the question of generalization to other
strategies remains to be answered.

In summarizing the literature, strategic behaviors appear to develop through four related periods of change. Initially, the child is
mediation deficient since an appropriate mnemonic is not spontaneously
produced, nor can it be trained easily. Next, the child's strategic behavior results in a mediational inefficiency (Ryan, Hegion, and Flavell
1970). That is, a strategy can be trained but the behavior only minimally
enhances recall. This is followed by a production deficiency period in
which training elicits an effective skill. The final period of mnemonic
development is characterized by the spontaneous use of strategic behavior. Strategy use results from the child's awareness that a mnemonic
is needed to aid memory.

Children's awareness of the utility of strategies seems to be based,
in part, on a knowledge of the capabilities and limitations of their own
memory systems. In general, this knowledge is termed "metacognition"
or knowing about one's own cognitive systems, and in memory this
knowledge is referred to as "metamemory." Flavell and Wellman (1977)
propose a taxonomy of two types of knowledge one typically develops
about memory. The first is a sensitivity to those situations requiring
effort to remember and, the second is a knowledge of those variables
(i.e., person, task, & strategy) affecting performance. The basic findings
show that while very young children are somewhat knowledgeable
about their own memory capabilities (Ritter 1978), developmental differences are found among school-aged children and adolescents.
Further, changes in metamemory are also seen through the adult years
(Lachman, Lachman, and Thornesbery 1979).

Another approach to studying metacognition and the relationship
between knowing and acting in a purposeful manner focuses on the
effects prior knowledge has on memory. This research demonstrates
that substantial amounts of previous experience with a specific task
influences the amount of information remembered. For example, Chi
(1978) reported a developmental study in which children (mean age 10.5
years) and adults were compared on their memory for chess positions.
The children were expert chess players, whereas the adults could play
chess but did not do so competitively. The problem was to reconstruct

meaningful arrangements of chess pieces after a brief viewing period. It was found that the children outperformed the adults, thereby reversing the typical age trends reported widely in the literature.

The characterization of memory development presented here suggests that children acquire effective strategies and knowledge of the utility of what is already learned through exposure to certain types of problems. Much of the evidence supports the argument that the child's performance is not limited severely by a structural deficit. This does not imply, however, that structural capabilities are unimportant: Capacity limits exist, regardless of one's experience and knowledge.

How might the strategy and knowledge components of the human information processing system help us understand learning disabilities? The evidence for strategy use on memory tasks by the learning disabled child is fairly recent and limited. Information regarding the learning disabled child's use of knowledge to problem solve is also limited, and the available data come primarily from studies on good and poor readers.

A perusal of selected studies on strategy use suggests that many of the notions regarding the mnemonic development of normal children are generalizable to the case of children with learning difficulties. Furthermore, some researchers suggest that the disabled may also be knowledge deficient in the sense that these children are unaware of when, where, and how to deploy their strategic efforts (e.g., Torgesen 1977b). In the discussion that follows, an attempt is made, first, to cite selected studies of the disabled in which a strategy deficiency is reported; and, second, a brief review of children's knowledge about reading skills is presented.

Tarver, Hallahan, Kauffman, and Ball (1976) reported that 8–13-year-old learning disabled children did not use selective attention and rehearsal strategies on a Hagen-type Central-Incidental learning problem. This task requires that children recall both central information designated by the experimenter as the to-be-remembered material, as well as incidental stimuli. The results indicated that the disabled children remembered significantly less central information than a group of same aged non-disabled youngsters. An analysis of incidental recall showed no differences between disabled and normal children. This result suggests a selective attention deficiency among children in the disabled group (cf. Hagen and Kail 1975). In a second experiment, however, when the disabled were induced to rehearse, the older youngsters significantly improved their recall of central information.

In a related study, Torgesen (1977b) investigated the hypothesis that fourth grade learning disabled children who were identified as poor readers were deficient in the use of active short-term memory strategies. Children were presented a standard recall task, and direct observations were made of their mnemonic behavior. In comparison to normal readers, the disabled children not only recalled less information but also failed to use (observable) active memory strategies. As in the Tarver et al. (1976) study, Torgesen found that a brief instructional intervention significantly improved the performance of the learning disabled children.

In reference to a possible knowledge deficiency, studies comparing good and poor readers suggest that the disabled have difficulties monitoring their comprehension—indicating a lack of awareness of when written material is understood. For example, early research showed that good readers modified their eye movements given materials varying in difficulty and adjusted their behaviors as the task demands changed (e.g., Anderson 1937; Levin and Cohen 1968).

In other studies, readers were asked how confident they were that comprehension questions were answered correctly (e.g., Forrest and Waller 1979). Not surprisingly, older children and better readers more accurately evaluated their own performance than did younger children or poor readers. Also, children sensitive to the state of their comprehension scored well on subsequent comprehension tests and flexibly adjusted their reading strategies when needed. These results indicate an important type of awareness, since knowledge of whether one is comprehending a message is essential before corrective steps can be taken (cf. Brown and Baker 1981).

Throughout this presentation two factors have been stressed which account for effective adaptation to different task demands. These factors are effective strategies and the knowledge needed to select, monitor, and oversee cognitive efforts. In the next section, a taxonomy is proposed which uses these factors to suggest an instructional approach for dealing with the problems associated with learning disabilities.


## AN INSTRUCTIONAL APPROACH


The evidence presented here supports our claim that young children fail to adapt to certain problems for at least two related reasons. First, task-appropriate strategies are not spontaneously used. Either relevant skills are not available in the youngsters' repertoires or, the strategies are available, but inaccessible; that is, the children do not think to use what they have already learned. This finding points to the second reason why children oftentimes fail to adapt—they may lack the knowledge of when and why to behave strategically.

This analysis gives rise to a potentially useful taxonomy of information processing components which in turn, has instructional implications. The taxonomy is represented in Figure 9.1. In brief, if one asks whether performance differences are expected among children of different ages or between learning disabled and "normal" children, then a number of questions must be answered. First, are the young or disabled youngsters production deficient in the use of some strategy? If the answer is "yes," then relatively poor performance is predicted within the population of deficient children as well as between the young or disabled and a group of spontaneous producers. Second, are the children knowledge deficient? Again, if the answer is "yes," the provision of greater knowledge should lead to a higher level of performance. Note, that since these predictions are based on task-appropriate behaviors, age and diagnostic category are irrelevant.

Now consider the case in which children are given strategy training but are knowledge deficient regarding the instructional benefits. The children should do well on training problems. However, since they are unaware of why strategies are useful, these children should stop using the skills when left to their own devices. More importantly, youngsters in this category are not expected to generalize their trained strategies to new problems (e.g., Brown et al. 1979).

A final question focuses on those children knowledgeable about skill use given some classes of problems, but who do not perform strategically on all tasks. It seems that the learning disabled are often

FIGURE 9.1

| | Strategy Deficiency? | |
|---|---|---|
| | YES | NO |
| Knowledge Deficiency?  **YES** | Poor overall performance | Good performance on training problems but no unprompted maintenance or generalization |
| **NO** | Variable performance depending on type of problem presented | Good overall performance |

FIGURE 9 1. A strategy and knowledge taxonomy indicating expected performance levels given different deficiencies.

viewed as competent in some areas but not in others. Children who are strategy deficient given a specific type of task but knowledgeable of other problem solving skills are expected to outperform children deficient in both strategy use and knowledge. Through instruction, it should be possible to use the disabled child's existing knowledge base to develop generalizable strategies. According to the model proposed here, it is not assumed that instructional effects are equal for young normal and older learning disabled children. If adequate assessments of the strategy and knowledge components are made, then differential predictions would follow regarding the relative effects of any instructional program.

The instructional approach suggested here is based on assessing the child's current level of strategy use given academic problems. The reference used for assessment is either a task analysis specifying optimal performance (e.g., Siegler 1978) or the behavior of an expert, that is, a person who performs at an optimal level (e.g., Brown 1979). Next, production deficient children are instructed to use effective skills until some criteria of learning are achieved. During training, children are shown explicitly the relationship between what they are doing strategically and improvements in performance. This is followed by a testing period where children are given problems similar to those on which training was carried out but, no prompting is used. Finally, the children are given generalization tests where the trained strategies could be used effectively. It is our contention that such an instructional approach will lead to enhanced performance among learning disabled children.

## REFERENCES

Adelman, H. S. "The Not So Specific Learning Disability Population." *Exceptional Children* (March 1971): 528–33.

Anderson, I. H. "Eye-Movements of Good and Poor Readers." *Psychological Monographs* 48 (1937): 1–35.

Bandura, A. "The Self System in Reciprocal Determinism." *American Psychologist* 33 (1978): 344–58.

Brown, A. L., J. C. Campione, and C. R. Barclay. "Training Self-Checking Routines for Estimating Recall Readiness: Generalizations from List Learning to Prose Recall." *Child Development* 50 (1979): 501–12.

Chi, M. T. H. "Knowledge Structures and Memory Development." In *Children's Thinking: What Develops?* edited by R. Siegler. Hillsdale, N.J.: Erlbaum, 1978.

Cruickshank, W. "Learning Disabilities: A Definitional Statement." *Concepts in Learning Disabilities: Selected Writings.* Syracuse University Press, 1981.

Engelmann, S. *Conceptual Learning.* San Rafael, Calif.: Dimensions, 1969.

Flavell, J. H., D. H. Beach, and J. M. Chinsky. "Spontaneous Verbal Rehearsal in a Memory Task as a Function of Age." *Child Development* 37 (1966): 283–99.

Flavell, J. H., and H. M. Wellman. "Metamemory." In *Perspectives on the Development of Memory and Cognition,* edited by R. V. Kail and J. W. Hagen. Hillsdale, N.J.: Erlbaum, 1977.

Forrest, D. C., and T. G. Waller. "Cognitive and Metacognitive Aspects of Reading." Paper presented at the meeting of the Society for Research in Child Development. San Francisco, March 1979.

Hagen, J. W. "Some Thoughts on How Children Learn to Remember." *Human Development* 14 (1971): 262–71.

Hagen, J. W., and R. V. Kail. "The Role of Attention in Perceptual and Cognitive Development." In *Perceptual and Learning Disabilities in Children. Vol. 2: Research and Theory,* edited by W. M. Cruickshank and D. P. Hallahan. Syracuse: Syracuse University Press, 1975.

Hallahan, D. P., and W. M. Cruickshank, eds. *Psycho-educational Foundations of Learning Disabilities.* Englewood Cliffs, N.J.: Prentice-Hall, 1973.

Keeney, T. J., S. R. Cannizzo, and J. H. Flavell. "Spontaneous and Induced Verbal Rehearsal in a Recall Task." *Child Development* 38 (1967): 953–66.

Kennedy, B. A., and D. J. Miller. "Persistent Use of Verbal Rehearsal as a Function of Information about Its Value." *Child Development* 47 (1976): 566–69.

Lachman, J. L., R. Lachman, and C. Thornesbery. "Metamemory Through the Adult Life Span." *Developmental Psychology* 15 (1979): 543–51.

Levin, H., and J. A. Cohen. "Studies of Oral Reading: XII. Effects of Instructions on the Eye-Voile Span." In *The Analysis of Reading Skill,* edited by H. Levin, E. J. Gibson, and J. J. Gibson. Final report, Project No. 5-1213, Contract No. OEG-10-156, Cornell University and U.S. Office of Education, 1968, 254-283.

Luria, A. R. *Cognitive Development: Its Cultural and Social Foundations.* Cambridge, Mass.: Harvard University Press, 1976.

National Advisory Committee on Handicapped Children. *Special Education for Handicapped Children.* 1st annual report. Washington, D.C.: U.S. Department of Health, Education, & Welfare, January 31, 1968.

Paris, S. G. "Coordination of Means and Goals in the Development of Mnemonic Skills." In *Memory Development in Children,* edited by P. A. Ornstein. Hillsdale, N.J.: Erlbaum, 1978.

Ritter, K. "The Development of Knowledge of an External Retrieval Cue Strategy." *Child Development* 49 (1978): 1227–30.

Ryan, S. M., A. G. Hegion, and J. H. Flavell. "Nonverbal Mnemonic Indicators of Strategic Behaviors under Remember Instructions in First Grade." *Child Development* 41 (1970): 539–50.

Senf, G. M. "An Information-Integration Theory and Its Application to Normal Reading Acquisition and Reading Disability." In *Leadership Training Institute in Learning Disabilities,* edited by N. D. Bryant and C. E. Kass. *Final Report,* vol. 2. Tucson, Ariz.: University of Arizona, 1972.

Siegler, R. S. "The Origins of Scientific Reasoning." In *Children's Thinking: What Develops?,* edited by R. S. Siegler. Hillsdale, N.J.: Erlbaum, 1978.

Tarver, S. G., D. P. Hallahan, J. M. Kauffman, and D. W. Ball. "Verbal Rehearsal and Selective Attention in Children with Learning Disabilities: A Developmental Lag." *Journal of Experimental Child Psychology* 22 (1976): 375–85.

Torgesen, J. K. "The Role of Nonspecific Factors in the Task Performance of Learning Disabled Children: A Theoretical Assessment." *Journal of Learning Disabilities* 10(1) (1977): 33–41 (a).

——. "Memorization Processes in Reading-Disabled Children." *Journal of Educational Psychology* 69(5) (1977): 571–78 (b).

# 10

## Social Perceptual Processing Problems

Psychological and Educational Considerations

*Paul J. Gerber*

$\mathbf{A}$ s many learning disabled students spend more time in regular classrooms, the importance of social/interpersonal abilities becomes a matter of increased concern to special and regular educators. Despite efforts to provide for administrative and programmatic considerations in the least restrictive environment, emphasis is still focused on academics for the learning disabled child. There simply have been few formal attempts to address socio-adaptive behavior which is crucial to any mainstreaming effort. Thus for the learning disabled child, the least restrictive environment may be the least restrictive academically, but the most restrictive socially.

### CLINICAL OBSERVATIONS

Clinical observations of learning disabled children have suggested that social imperception is one of the complex variables which interferes with interpersonal processes. Lewis *et al.* (1960) stated that the mechanism that organizes behavior, enables the child to perceive social situations, and develop social awareness, fails to operate properly. Johnson and Myklebust (1967) commented that the most pronounced characteristic of this type of disability is the distortion of experience, not the mastery of academic tasks. Kahn (1969) wrote that perceptual inadequacies of learning disabled children when applied to social and interpersonal relationships involve inaccurate perception and conceptualization of social matters. Kronick (1979) stressed that the perceptual distortions and inconsistencies cause impaired feedback from the environment resulting in confusion of the learning disabled child's life space. Wender (1971) called the learning disabled child an unsuccessful extrovert. Lerner (1976) has summarized the characteristics of an individual who is socially imperceptive. She described the observable characteristics as: (1) performing poorly in independent activities expected of children of the same chronological age; (2) poor in judging moods and attitudes of people; (3) insensitive to the general atmosphere of a social situation; (4) continually doing or saying the inappropriate thing (p. 325).

## PEER STATUS OF LEARNING DISABLED CHILDREN

Prior to the adoption of the term learning disabilities, investigators uncovered problems in peer status and social acceptance among these children. Research has shown learning disabled children more rejected and less accepted than their nonhandicapped peers for a variety of reasons. Johnson (1950) pointed out that perceptually handicapped children in regular fourth and fifth grade classes were significantly more rejected and less accepted than their nonhandicapped peers. Johnson expected low academic ability to be the reason for the rejection, but his study revealed "aggressive behavior" and "the apparent inability or desire to conform to standards of group behavior" to be the determining factors.

Baldwin (1958) investigated the social position of perceptually handicapped children in fourth, fifth, and sixth grade regular classrooms. Social acceptance was again found to be lower among the perceptually handicapped children. Anti-social behavior was the major determinant of choice. Reports from peers like "he bothers us," "she's lazy," "he disturbs our class," and "he can't play" were the major complaints.

With the advent of contemporary efforts of mainstreaming, research on peer status of learning disabled children has again borne out these effects. Studies have shown the learning disabled child to be generally unpopular as Bryan (1974, 1976) found that elementary age learning disabled children were viewed as less attractive and more rejected than nonhandicapped children. Siperstein, Bopp, and Bak (1978) reported that learning disabled students were never among the most popular, but their incidence rate among isolates was similar to that of other children. Moreover, Bruininks (1978) demonstrated less popularity of elementary age learning disabled students in conjunction with other variables.

In many of the studies the investigators expressed their concern for the learning disabled children who simply did not fit in. Repeatedly and sociometric studies found learning disabled children less accepted and more rejected. This body of investigation lead to another area of inquiry. The complex dynamics and requisite skills in social relationships were explored. Efforts focused on behaviors, deficit skills, and attributes associated with low peer acceptance.

## THE UNDERLYING FACTORS OF SOCIAL PROBLEMS IN LEARNING DISABLED INDIVIDUALS

Whereas the writing of numerous investigators have put forth clinical explanations of social problems in learning disabled individuals while others have demonstrated low peer appeal, there has been little investigation into the underlying factors contributing to this social phenomenon. Bruininks (1978) found that learning disabled students had poorer self-concepts than comparison children. Moreover, they were less accurate when assessing their own social status. Bryan (1978) identified verbal communication habits to be a significant factor of social rejection as learning disabled children emit and receive more rejection statements than their nonhandicapped counterparts. Finally, in studying the comprehension of nonverbal communication in learning disabled children Bryan (1978) found that they were less skillful than their normal peers.

## SOCIAL PERCEPTUAL PROCESSING AND NONVERBAL COMMUNICATION

The issue of social perceptual processing problems in learning disabled individuals has been approached from the perspective of misinterpretation of nonverbal cues and interference in nonverbal communication by several writers. Mostly, those who have written from this perspective have addressed the problems in the learning disabled adolescent. It has been suggested that at the adolescent level the task of the socially imperceptive person is intensified because of the emphasis on the subtleties of a more sophisticated communication system. Kronick (1975) reported a cluster of problems stemming from difficulty in interpreting nonverbal cues in space and perceiving situations as a *gestalt*. She cited misuse of body in expression, difficulty in interpreting people's nonverbal messages, inability to understand the full impact of messages on others, and inability to monitor one's impact on others in conversation or social interaction as some of the major problems. She wrote: "It is almost as if the learning disabled adolescent were deaf and blind for several years, and were then suddenly thrust into a culture wherein he is expected to have mastered incredibly complex communication patterns, most of which have been internalized by others and are practiced unconsciously" (p. 69).

Siegel (1975) wrote that deficits in perceiving nonverbal cues and understanding nonverbal communication evidenced by minimally brain damaged adolescents may be the crucial factor in understanding the heart of their socialization shortcomings. He stated that the inability to perceive the true meanings of nonverbal social cues, the meanings of facial expressions and body language, emotional messages of boredom, discomfort, anxiety, and suspicion will be missed and inappropriate responses follow. Siegel attributed this to what he called a "faulty feedback mechanism." This interferes with the communication process by making it difficult for the minimally brain damaged adolescent to see the relationship between what he says and the subsequent reaction of whom he is speaking.

Siegel (1975) has attributed part of the communication difficulties from lack of experience. He commented: "In this area he (the learning disabled adolescent) needs more experience than nonhandicapped adolescents to learn nuances and subtleties of nonverbal communication and to be able to fathom the symbolic behavior which stands forwards and to begin to develop more sociocentric language, thought, processes, and conduct" (p. 37).

Experience and practice in detecting nonverbal cues and comprehension of nonverbal communication are essential components to the development of socialization and communication skills in learning disabled and nonhandicapped individuals alike. This is highlighted by the fact that many of the messages in a conversational interaction are not communicated by words alone. Mehrabian (1970) has broken down conversational interaction into its essential elements during human social communication. He found: "When an individual talks, the words themselves account for seven per cent of what he communicates; 38 per cent is conveyed by his manner of speech, and 55 per cent by facial expression and body language (as quoted in Siegel 1975)" (p.32).

In view of the problems in sensory integration that learning disabled individuals are known to have, the implications are great. The process of the ongoing monitoring of visual social stimuli like gestures, facial expressions, and body posture are confounded by the simultaneous monitoring of auditory social stimuli like voice, tone, and verbal expression. The task of integrating these dynamic social signals and generating a socially appropriate response is a complex, ongoing task. Albeit, the individual with social perceptual processing difficulties encounters failure experiences which have broader implications for self-concept, interpersonal relationships, and life adjustment.

## QUANTITATIVE AND QUALITATIVE ASPECTS OF SOCIAL PERCEPTUAL PROCESSING

One of the underlying factors that has been investigated by Gerber (1978) is social perceptual processing in learning disabled children. This by definition includes the complex skills involved in gathering information from a total social field, processing the relative importance of the data, and generating a positive interpersonal response appropriate to the social situation. In controlling for such variables as intelligence quotient, sex, race, and chronological age, comparative social perceptual processing skills were investigated in six- and seven-year-old learning disabled and nonhandicapped children, and ten- and eleven-year-old learning disabled and nonhandicapped children. The instrument used as the Test of Social Inference (Edmonson, Leland, deJung, Leach 1974). Analysis of comparative scores showed six- and seven-year-old learning disabled children to be significantly behind their nonhandicapped peers in social perceptual processing. Similarly, ten- and eleven-year-old learning disabled children were significantly below the skills of their nonhandicapped peers. In both cases the deficiency averaged two to three years, which ultimately showed the older learning disabled students in this study functioning at the level of the nonhandicapped six- and seven-year-old children. Also shown were significant increases of social perceptual processing ability from the six and seven year level to the ten and eleven year level in the learning disabled subjects. This lends credence to the hypothesis that skill deficiencies in this area stem from a lag as opposed to a deficit.

A comparative analysis of the qualitative aspects of both the learning disabled and nonhandicapped children's responses presents ample evidence about the breakdown in social perceptual processing in learning disabled individuals. When presented with pictures depicting various social situations from the Test of Social Inference response styles were in marked contrast of each other.

The nonhandicapped children were able to organize the essential elements of the social situation. They were able to discriminate relevant and irrelevant cues and generate responses focused toward the central theme. Generally, they easily ascertained the essence of the social meaning in the stimulus picture.

On the other hand, learning disabled children had problems in the organization of the social stimuli. As there was a tendency to attend to less significant cues and difficulties in conceptualizing a *gestalt,* grasping the central theme was an arduous task. A significant trend in responses was ambiguity of social inferences. However, there was not a total dissociation from the central theme of the social situation. In many cases, meaning was derived from the social situation but significant cues that modified meaning were not considered as part of the *gestalt.* The responses were comparable to those of brain injured individuals whose perceptual efficiency has been affected by organic involvement. Particularly, the literature on the response styles of various projective personality tests, most notably the Rorschach Inkblot Test, is reflective of the qualitative evidence of the Gerber study.

## PROGNOSIS FOR SOCIAL PERCEPTUAL PROCESSING DEFICITS

Upon the discovery that social perceptual processing deficits are a significant underlying problem in learning disabled individuals, the issue of remediation becomes an important consideration. As pointed out in the research by Gerber, social perceptual processing skills do increase with maturation. Yet, current research still supports the notion of lagging behind peers in this vital area. Thus far, there have been no efforts to gauge the effects of a formal curricular intervention to develop social perceptual skills in learning disabled individuals. Yet, an indication of prognosis may be borrowed from the literature on mental retardation.

Edmonson *et al.* (1972) developed and used an experimental curriculum for training social perceptual skills in educable mentally retarded and higher functioning trainable mentally retarded adolescents. Results in using various experimental groups showed significant gain in the area of social perceptual ability. Permanence of skill acquisition was questionable though.

In the absence of sound empirical data on remediation procedures, logic suggests that similar gains may be possible with learning disabled populations as well. Moreover, increased mental ability may lend to a stronger prognostic outcome.

## QUESTIONING PROCEDURE TO FACILITATE SOCIAL
## PERCEPTUAL DEVELOPMENT

Currently, there have been few attempts to address the remedial aspects of social perceptual processing problems. Because of the relative recency of this line of inquiry, only a small number of writers have proffered remedial practices and materials in the area of social perceptual functioning. Some specifically designed procedures have become available via the work of Siegel *et al.* (1978) and Minskoff (1980). Others have been borrowed from the socio-adaptive skills incorporated in curricula for mentally retarded children.

A structured questioning procedure for development of social perceptual processing skills has been formulated by Gerber and Harris (1980) to use with learning disabled children. Typically, it is used in conjunction with the picture interpretation in reading, appreciation of juvenile literature, and learning through visual aids. Its structure is derived from what is known about the response styles of learning disabled children described earlier in this chapter. Its goal is the full awareness of the *gestalt* of a social situation and subsequent socially appropriate options of behavior according to the processing of the social stimuli.

## QUESTIONING PROCEDURE TO FACILITATE SOCIAL PERCEPTUAL
## SKILL DEVELOPMENT

### Social Perceptual Cues

The purpose of the questioning is to help the child identify who is involved in the incident, what is the focus of this event, what do characters' facial expressions and body language reveal. Questions addressed to the child(ren) to elicit appropriate responses would include:
What do you see (What is each character doing)?
Who is the most important character in the picture?
What is that character doing?
Who else is there?
What is he doing? What are they doing?
How do you know?
How can you tell? Are they smiling or crying, etc.?

### Situation-Specific Behaviors

The purpose of these questions is to identify appropriate behaviors.
Questions to be asked include:
Why is he behaving this way?
What else could he do?
What happens if he does that? (possibly more than one alternative)
What is the best thing for him to do? (possibly more than one)
Why is it the best?

### Emergence of Affect

The purpose of these questions is to have children articulate what affective responses that are appropriate for the specific social situation.
If you were there how would you feel?
Why would you feel that way?

## CONCLUSION

It is incumbent for those who work with learning disabled individuals to acknowledge problems in social perceptual processing and socio-adaptive skills. An understanding of the dynamics of these problems has far reaching implications for social and emotional development, behavior management, and ultimate life adjustment.

The field of learning disabilities has begun to look towards the areas within the social domain since uncovering low peer status and interpersonal relationship problems in learning disabled individuals. Investigation of the underlying problems in social adjustment has shown that social perceptual processing problems is one of the complex components that needs to be addressed. Moreover, deficiencies in this area must be viewed across the entire continuum of development. Without consideration of this crucial element, diagnostic efforts, placement decisions, and remedial programs will fall short of their intended goals.

## REFERENCES

Baldwin, W. "The Social Position of the Educable Mentally Retarded Child in the Regular Grades in the Public Schools." *Exceptional Children* 25 (1958): 106–108, 112.

Bruininks, V. L. "Peer Status and Personality Characteristics of Learning Disabled and Nondisabled Students." *Journal of Learning Disabilities* 11 (1978): 484–89.

Bryan, T. H. "Learning Disabled Children's Comprehension of Nonverbal Communication." *Journal of Learning Disabilities* 10 (1977): 501–506.

———. "Peer Popularity of Learning Disabled Children. *Journal of Learning Disabilities* 7 (1974): 620–25.

———. "Peer Popularity of Learning Disabled Children: A Replication." *Journal of Learning Disabilities* 9 (1976): 307–11.

Bryan, T. H., and J. H. Bryan. "Social Interactions of Learning Disabled Children." *Learning Disability Quarterly* 1 (1978): 33–38.

Edmonson, B., H. Leland, and E. Leach. "Social Inference Training and Retarded Adolescents." *Education and Training of the Mentally Retarded* 5 (1970): 1969–76.

———. *The Test of Social Inference.* New York: Educational Activities, 1974.

Gerber, P. "A Comparative Study of Social Perceptual Ability of Learning Disabled and Nonhandicapped Children." Ph.D. dissertation, University of Michigan, 1978.

Gerber, P., and K. Harris. "Using Juvenile Literature to Develop Social Skills in Learning Disabled Children" (in press).

Johnson, G. O. "A Study of the Social Position of Mentally Handicapped Children in the Regular Grades." *American Journal of Mental Deficiency* 55 (1950): 60–89.

Johnson, D., and H. Myklebust. *Learning Disabilities: Educational Principles and Practices.* New York: Grune and Stratton, 1967.

Kahn, J. P. "Emotional Concomitants of the Brain-Damaged Child." *Journal of Learning Disabilities* 2 (1969): 644–51.

Kronick, D. *What About Me? The LD Adolescent.* San Rafael, Calif.: Academic Therapy, 1975.

Minskoff, E. "Teaching Approach for Developing Nonverbal Communication Skills in Students with Social Perception Deficits: Part 1." *Journal of Learning Disabilities* 13 (March 1980): 118–23.

Lerner, J. *Children with Learning Disabilities.* Boston: Houghton-Mifflin, 1976.

Lewis, R. S., A. A. Strauss, and L. F. Lehtinen. *The Other Child.* New York: Grune and Stratton, 1960.

Siegel, E. *The Exceptional Child Grows Up.* New York: Dutton, 1975.

Siegel, E., R. Siegel, and P. Siegel. *Help for the Lonely Child.* New York: Dutton, 1978.

Siperstein, G., M. J. Bopp, and J. J. Bak. "Social Status of Learning Disabled Children." *Journal of Learning Disabilities* 2 (1978): 49–53.

Wender, H. *Minimal Brain Damange in Children.* New York: Wiley-Interscience, 1976.

# NEW STRATEGIES FOR
# TEACHING READING

# 11

## Phonemic Analysis Training in the Teaching of Reading

*Lise Wallach and Michael A. Wallach*

W E BELIEVE that most of the children who have difficulty learning basic reading—whether they are called learning disabled, reading disabled, or disadvantaged—lack particular skills of quite specific kinds that are prerequisites for learning to read. The reading instruction that is typically provided at school usually tends to assume the presence of these skills for the very reason that they can indeed be taken for granted in the case of other children. Especially important in this regard seem to be skills of phonemic analysis or phonemic awareness—the ability to analyze spoken words into separate sounds. Someone who has these skills will know, for example, that "Ma" and "me" both start with the sound "mm," while "Pa" and "he" do not; and that the word "me" consists of the sounds "mm" and "ee." They can say whether "Mother" or "ball" starts with the sound "mm," and whether 'rain" or "snow" starts with the sound "ss." While readiness curricula often will include exercises on identifying and matching sounds in words, the children we are talking about are quite unable to perform such exercises, as many teachers of high risk children know. Since the procedures given are too difficult for these children, such readiness exercises already *presuppose* the skills which these children need to acquire, rather than providing instruction that delivers the needed skills.

This kind of problem with phonemic analysis is, of course, going to make learning to read extremely difficult for a child. A child who is unable to recognize the individual sounds in spoken words is precluded by that lack from making use of phonics—the relationships between sounds and letters. While such a child could learn sound-letter correspondences, this learning could not be applied in decoding print because the child would have no idea of the role of these sounds in words as heard —the spoken language already familiar to the child. Teaching the child how to recognize or identify sounds in spoken words thus seems crucial if it can be done. Such phonemic recognition or analysis might be called pre-phonics. The view has been widespread that if a child is in this

155

situation when starting school, the needed phonemic analysis skills cannot in fact be successfully established by instruction. Recent work suggests, however, that phonemic analysis is teachable.

Let us now consider each of the basic points we have asserted. Do children who are at risk for reading failure lack phonemic analysis skills that other children typically possess? Are phonemic analysis skills really of significance for learning to read? And — most crucially — are there methods by which phonemic analysis skills can be successfully taught to children who lack them?

## PHONEMIC ANALYSIS SKILL DEFICITS OF CHILDREN AT RISK FOR READING FAILURE

Consider first a study that defined risk in terms of socio-economic disadvantage. In recent work by Wallach, Wallach, Dozier, and Kaplan (1977), disadvantaged and middle class children about to enter first grade were tested with several different phonemic analysis tasks. In one such task, for instance, the child was to indicate, in the case of each of various pairs of pictures that the child could correctly name, which member of the pair of pictures started with a given sound. For example, one sound used in the task was "mm" as in "Mother." The child was told that some words start with the sound "mm," like "Ma" or "mud" or "me." Then—with the appropriate pairs of pictures displayed—the child was asked to indicate whether "man" or "house" starts with "mm," whether "book" or "mop" starts with "mm," whether "car" or "mouse" starts with "mm," etc. We tried to make the tasks as easy as possible. As can be seen, the members of each pair were quite different. Also, errors were corrected, with the critical sounds receiving emphasis and elongation.

Despite our making the tasks as easy as we could, disadvantaged children proved to be strikingly deficient on tasks of this kind, which call for identifying starting phonemes in spoken words. By contrast, most of the middle class children, though not all, performed these tasks very well. Our study also demonstrated, however, that the same children who had such trouble with phonemic analysis had no trouble *hearing* phoneme differences in words. Before receiving the phonemic analysis tasks, the children were given a test of auditory discrimination which required them to indicate, in the case of each of various pairs of pictures with similar names, the picture named by the tester. The names of the two pictures in each pair were the same except for their starting sounds, and were picked with the aim of maximizing confusability—hence this time trying to make the task as difficult as possible. For instance, one pair was "lake" and "rake," and the tester would say to point to the rake. Another was "key" and "tea," with the child to point to the key, etc.

While some investigators (e.g., Oakland and Williams 1971) have believed that disadvantaged children are lacking in auditory discrimination ability as indexed by a test of this kind, we found that if you make sure the children know the names of the pictures, almost all of them readily make the correct choices—even when the words to be discriminated have very confusable starting sounds. Thus, disadvantaged children are strikingly lacking in phonemic analysis skills when starting school, but not because of any deficiency in auditory discrimination ability. They can hear phoneme differences quite adequately.

Why is phonemic analysis so difficult? For one thing, it is a "metalinguistic" activity: to recognize that "rake" starts with "rr," one has to stop and think about "rake" itself as a word, instead of merely using it to refer to rakes. But this cannot be the entire answer. The ability to recognize separate *syllables* in words as heard also requires metalinguistic analysis, yet syllable recognition turns out to be a great deal easier for children than phoneme recognition (Fox and Routh 1975; Liberman and Shankweiler 1979; Rozin and Gleitman 1977).

The main source of the difficulty children can have recognizing phonemes in words most likely stems from the special kind of analytic task that is involved here. The analogy of hidden picture puzzles may be of help. Suppose we think of the sound "rr" in its relation to the heard word "rake" as like a simple visual figure embedded in a larger and more complicated one that serves to disguise it. Locating an embedded figure that is hidden within a larger visual unit can be a difficult task because it calls for zeroing in on part of a complex perceptual constellation that resists such analysis and compels the perceiver's acceptance as a totality. Having to determine whether a spoken word starts with a particular phoneme or not poses a similar sort of problem—only worse. It is worse, as a matter of fact, in two ways. An embedded visual figure at least can be isolated as a physical entity, and it remains constant in different visual contexts. The phonemes that comprise spoken words, on the other hand, cannot be clearly isolated, and they do not maintain their constancy in different syllables or words. Phonemes examined in terms of their acoustical properties are found to overlap in time rather than to follow neatly one after another in the sound stream, and also are found to vary acoustically in different speech contexts (Liberman, Cooper, Shankweiler, and Studdert-Kennedy 1967).

Now consider a phonemic analysis study that defined risk directly in terms of teachers' estimates of reading disability. This work was carried out by Fox and Routh (1980). The same kind of deficiency at phonemic analysis is seen to emerge for the children who are at risk. The procedure used here coaxed children to segment spoken material into as small units as possible, first asking them to segment sentences into words, then words into syllables, and then syllables into phonemes. The child was to tell the tester "a little bit" of what the tester just said, with the task made as easy as possible for the child by presenting initially unanalyzed segments again with further coaxing to tell a little bit of what just was said. First grade teachers were asked to nominate three groups of children — average readers, children with mild reading difficulties (below grade level but not in need of special help), and children with severe reading disability (in need of special instructional help and likely to repeat first grade). Those with below-average intelligence test performance were excluded from the study.

Assessed in the late spring of the first grade year, average readers and children with mild reading difficulties had perfect or near-perfect scores on the phonemic analysis task. In marked contrast, children judged to have severe reading disability could hardly do any phonemic analysis at all.

## THE IMPORTANCE OF PHONEMIC ANALYSIS SKILLS FOR LEARNING TO READ

But can we claim that phonemic analysis skills really matter in their own right for learning to read, or are they simply correlates of other deficiencies in such high risk children? In the past, when children had reading difficulties that were not readily assignable to general intellectual or motivational factors, interpretations would usually make reference to presumed visual problems, such as with visual-motor integration, visual discrimination, or spatial relations. Recently, however, there has been growing recognition of the role of langauge-related aspects of audition (Bateman 1979; Benton 1975; Vellutino 1978).

Within the last decade or so, increasingly definitive linkages between performance on a variety of tasks involving phonemic analysis and various reading achievement measures have been discerned (Golinkoff 1978; Liberman and Shankweiler 1979; Williams 1980). For example, Rosner and Simon (1971) found, for tasks requiring the child to delete a syllable or a phoneme from a spoken word, such as saying "mat" without the "mm" sound, that there were substantial correlations with the Language Arts section of the Stanford Achievement Test. These relationships were obtained in samples of children ranging through all grades from kindergarten to sixth grade, and they persisted in all but the sixth grade sample when IQ scores were controlled for. As another example, Goldstein (1976) found with four year olds that skill at segmentation of words into syllables (e.g., "kangaroo" into "kan, ga, roo") and into phonemes (e.g., "tea" into "tuh, ee"), and at synthesizing such segments into words, predicted subsequent reading achievement. Again, these results held up independent of IQ. Further indications of the role of phonemic analysis in reading achievement will be evident in our discussion below of effective teaching techniques for phonemic analysis skills.

The reasons why phonemic analysis skills are important for learning to read can be put as follows (Carroll and Walton 1979; Gleitman and Rozin 1973; Liberman and Shankweiler 1979; Rozin and Gleitman 1977; M. A. Wallach and L. Wallach 1976, 1979a, 1979b). If a child is unable to identify a phoneme as a recurring sound in different word contexts, the child has no basis for making use of the relationships between letters and sounds when trying to turn written language into the already familiar spoken language. This forces the child to have to learn each new word by rote as a unique pattern of stimuli, a strategy that becomes increasingly burdensome as words continue to accumulate and become ever harder to distinguish from each other.

It is true, of course, that correspondences between letters and the sounds they represent are far from perfect in our written language. But this does not stop such correspondences from being of considerable help for deciphering and learning new words, if the child is able to identify phonemes in spoken words and knows those letter-phoneme regularities that are typical. Despite the exceptions, after all, English still is an alphabetic language. It certainly also is true enough that attention to a word's meaning may suffer if a child is overly taxed by the mechanics of working out the sounds that correspond to its letters. But the answer to this problem, as Chall (1967) has found, is not less practice at making use of these correspondences, but more practice—until doing so becomes sufficiently fast and automatic that the child no longer has to focus on it.

Thus, without the aid to learning new words that use of letter-phoneme regularities permits, this learning would become increasingly strainful and, indeed, would never get far. But note that for such facilitation to become possible, the child has to know more than just letter-phoneme associations—traditional phonics. The child also needs what we have called pre-phonics skills—he or she must know in addition how to recognize these phonemes as they occur in different spoken words. Skills of phonemic analysis are thus a prerequisite form of ability that is needed in order to make it possible for phonics instruction to work.

## TEACHING PHONEMIC ANALYSIS SKILLS: SOME EFFECTIVE TECHNIQUES

Even if we accept the importance of phonemic analysis skills for learning to read, however, what about the widespread belief that these skills cannot be effectively taught to children who lack them? If this belief were correct, one would *have no choice* but either to put off instruction until children lacking these skills have become maturationally "ready," or to try to avoid the need for these skills by teaching words as unique patterns — even though the consequence of either of these courses of action must be that the children will fall behind. But there now are techniques of demonstrated effectiveness for teaching phonemic analysis skills. Thus, the instructional program we have developed (L. Wallach and M. A. Wallach 1976; M. A. Wallach and L. Wallach 1976, 1979a, 1979b) contains procedures which have been shown to establish phonemic analysis skills successfully for children starting school without them. Other recent work also has found ways to teach phonemic analysis skills to high risk children (see, e.g., Lewkowicz 1980; Williams 1979, 1980). The belief that phonemic analysis is unteachable to these kinds of children thus seems misguided.

Why have phonemic analysis skills so often been viewed as unteachable? One reason may well be frequent assignment of problems with phonemic analysis to deficiencies of auditory discrimination — a type of deficit that might be hard to overcome by instruction. Work based on such tests as the Wepman Auditory Discrimination Test (Wepman, 1960) and the Goldman-Fristoe-Woodcock Test of Auditory Discrimination (Goldman, Fristoe, & Woodcock, 1970) appeared to support the belief that many children, especially among the learning disabled, the disadvantaged, and others behind in reading, had a hard time hearing differences between phonemes. However, it now seems that low performance on these kinds of tests often stems not from problems with hearing, but rather from extraneous factors like using the words "same" and "different" in the test — concepts which can create difficulties in their own right—and using vocabulary with which the child is unfamiliar (Gleitman and Rozin 1973; Wallach *et al.* 1977).

Another likely reason why phonemic analysis has often been considered unteachable is the fairly widespread assumption that children will become confused by hearing the extra vowel sounds that inevitably come along with most consonant sounds if the attempt is made to pronounce them in isolation. We have found this accompanying vowel sound in fact, however, to give even high risk children little trouble when systematic practice is provided with different consonant sounds.

But the crucial reason for the belief that phonemic analysis skills cannot be effectively established by instruction must simply be the failures encountered when the teaching of these skills has been tried. Let us turn, then, to the kinds of instructional techniques that now have been shown to work. The key method for teaching phonemic analysis used in our program involves providing a strategy which the child can learn to apply for extracting starting phonemes from their word contexts. The strategy is to separate off the starting phoneme from the rest of the word by a pause. We have found no first grade children, however poor their prognosis for learning to read, unable to learn this strategy for breaking up words, first by imitating the person who models the technique for them, and then by applying it on their own. Furthermore, we have found that, once they are well practiced in using this pause strategy, all such children are able to identify starting phonemes in spoken words. Determining whether "man" or "house" starts with the sound "mm" becomes easy when the child breaks up the word "house" into "h - ouse," and the word "man" into "m - an."

Similar to this pause strategy and probably still easier for children to learn is a method reported by Zhurova (1973) in which the teacher, as in stuttering, repeats the starting sound two or three times and then presents the entire word —as, for example, "h - h - house," "m - m - man." The child first imitates the teacher and then proceeds alone. As with the pause strategy, Zhurova's method too serves the function of giving the child a way to isolate the initial phoneme from the rest of the word. Both the pause strategy and the repetition strategy seem effective in carrying the child across the crucial hurdle of learning to isolate starting phonemes in spoken words. That isolation of the initial phoneme as the best place to begin for helping children with phonemic analysis seems now to be widely acknowledged (Lewkowicz 1980).

Another method which also has been discussed (Lewkowicz, 1980) for this purpose is elongation of the starting sound, but for many consonant sounds elongation is not feasible. Further, our evidence suggests that even when it is possible, elongation is inferior to the pause and the repetition strategies. Recall that Wallach et al. (1977) used elongation as part of their error correction routine for children unable to identify starting phonemes in words, with little benefit for such children as a result. What seems necessary is a method by which the child can, as it were, "break off" the initial phoneme from the rest of the word—something that our pause strategy or Zhurova's repetition strategy accomplishes.

Two supporting methods for helping the child with phonemic analysis also are used in our program besides the pause strategy. One involves "tongue-twister" sentences that repeat a given phoneme at the start of a number of words following in close succession. The other involves a form of correction that lets the child hear the contrast between the way a word actually sounds and the way that word would sound if it began with the phoneme that the child has erroneously chosen.

To illustrate how these kinds of methods can be implemented in a systematic teaching procedure for establishing phonemic analysis skills in high risk children, we present next a summary of the instructional steps followed in the first part of our program. This part is designed most crucially to make sure the child will become proficient at identifying phonemes in the initial positions of spoken words. Also learned are letter shapes and letter-phoneme associations. The program is a tutorial procedure based on mastery learning sequences, intended for providing high risk children with supplementary tutoring in regular classrooms or in resource rooms. But teachers can adapt the types of tasks that follow for a small group as well as individual instruction of such children.

The child is taught one sound for each letter of the alphabet, proceeding through the letters in alphabetical sequence. Before showing the child any letter, however, work first is given on its sound—making use in various ways of the pause strategy and supporting methods just described. The first step carried out with each sound is to tell the child a tongue-twister sentence of the type mentioned before. Thus, for the phoneme /r/ the sentence is: "*R*uth and *R*achel *r*an after *R*ichard's *r*abbit in the *r*ain." The tutor then pronounces each of the words beginning with the critical phoneme first normally and then with the sound separated off by a pause: "Ruth, R - uth, Rachel, R - achel," etc. The child pronounces the words both ways, too, imitating the tutor.

In the next step, the child is given two pictures at a time, one whose name starts with the phoneme at issue and the other not, is asked to identify them, and then to choose which one starts with the sound being worked on. This is repeated with different pairs of pictures until the child meets the criterion of making seven correct choices in a row. A specific correction procedure is used whenever the child makes a wrong choice. For example, suppose the child was to choose which picture starts with "rr," "radio," or "bed"—and says "bed." Then the tutor says, "No. It's bed, not red. Radio starts with 'rr.' Say r - adio." Thus, the pause strategy and letting the child hear how the word would sound if it started with the wrong phoneme both are used here. If the child continues to have difficulty, the tutor pronounces the names of both pictures with the initial sound separated off by a pause to start with—"r - adio, b - ed"— and has the child do the same, only then asking which picture starts with the critical sound.

After practice on the tongue-twister sentence for a given phoneme, and then this "two-picture game," another game follows. Now the child is shown *one* picture at a time, and is to say whether or not it starts with the sound that is being worked on. Some do and some do not, in a random sequence. Again the task is repeated, with different pictures, until the child meets the criterion of answering seven correctly in a row. And again, specific correction procedures and extra help are used as needed.

After a child has met the learning criterion on both these games for the phoneme being worked on, the letter then is introduced. Each letter is shown to the child embedded in a picture whose name starts with that letter's sound, to serve as a memory aid. For example, the letter "r" becomes part of a coil of rope. The children are shown the connection between the picture's name and the sound, and then they practice tracing and drawing the letter.

A series of further games then follows, intended to assure that the child associates the letter in question with the appropriate sound and also giving further practice at phonemic analysis. Pictures of objects whose names start with various sounds are to be correctly matched to letters; and then words starting with various sounds are spoken and the child is to point to the appropriate letter. At first, the letters used are the ones built into pictures that serve as reminders of the sound; then the children must match to letters alone. Again, the pause strategy is used for extra help as needed.

In the last step for each letter, all the letters worked on to that point are presented one at a time in random order. The child is asked to give each letter's sound, and also to provide an example of a word beginning with that sound.

High risk children who lack phonemic analysis skills have been found to learn them very well when the preceding steps are followed. Such learning, with stringent criteria of mastery, typically takes high risk first graders about two and one-half months of training, using half-hour tutoring sessions five days a week by paraprofessionals (Dorval, Wallach, and Wallach 1978; M. A. Wallach and L. Wallach 1976, 1979a). An adaptation of the preceding steps for high risk four year olds, using Zhurova's repetition strategy in combination with the basic procedures just described, indicates that high risk children even as young as four are able to learn these same phonemic analysis skills to the same high criteria of mastery (Dorval, Joyce and Ramey, Note 1). In all of the studies using these procedures, learning rate for the first few phonemes is slow but then speeds up dramatically.

Having established phonemic analysis skills for starting sounds in spoken words, it turns out that identifying phonemes in other positions in words and blending phonemes to form words pose little difficulty, even for first graders expected to have trouble learning to read. Thus, the next part of our tutorial program is as follows:

The first step, a simple blending task, is to present sets of three pictures, all three in a given set starting with the same sound. The first set is "ball," "bus," and "bed." The tutor pronounces the sounds in one of these names separately—for example, for the picture of the bus, "buh - uh - ss"—and asks the child to find the right picture. When the child has correctly chosen each of the three pictures on the basis of their names being pronounced in this manner as separate sounds, the tutor goes on to the next set of three pictures. Since high risk children of the kind we have taught are often viewed as incapable of blending, it seems especially interesting that this sort of task goes easily after help on only one or two examples. Their earlier training on phonemic analysis of sounds in starting positions of words most likely explains their success at this point in blending (Lewkowicz 1980).

Next the child actually builds words from letters, and then reads the words by sounding out and blending. Again the child is shown sets of three pictures at a time—for example, one set is "gum," "bus," and "sun." Now the child also receives letter cards for spelling the names of the pictures. For each of the three pictures in turn, the tutor first has the child give its name. Then the tutor pronounces the sounds in the name separately—for instance, for the picture of the gum, 'guh - uh - mm." The child is to find the letter card for each sound and put the letters in the correct order, with help as needed. After the name is built, the tutor points to its successive letters from left to right and has the child pronounce their sounds—"guh - uh - mm." Then the tutor points more rapidly across the letters, pronouncing the sounds with shorter pauses between them, and finally pointing across the letters still more rapidly and saying "gum." Many of the children are struck by a sudden, powerful insight here into how words are spelled.

After the child has built the three words in the set and the tutor has read them this way, the tutor builds the words and has the child read them, followed by the child building them again for the tutor to read. A number of sets of three pictures are worked through in this manner, after which considerable further practice takes place with sets of spoken words for which no pictures are provided.

High risk first graders typically master the phonemic analysis and synthesis tasks of this part of the program–with considerable enjoyment –in about two or three weeks of the same type of half-hour tutoring sessions mentioned before. That this mastery is accomplished so rapidly suggests the significant role of the kind of phonemic analysis training for starting sounds in words provided by the earlier tasks described.

The remainder of our program, finally, has the child reading whatever texts are in classroom use, learning words by techniques that assure utilization of already acquired phonemic analysis, phonics, and blending skills. The new words in the text passage are first presented separately, and these steps are followed with each one: (1) When a word is built up from simpler words, the component words are worked on first. (2) The tutor gives the sound of any letter or letter combination different from what was learned. (3) Then the tutor has the child sound out the word's letters. (4) Then, unless the child has now recognized the word, the tutor sounds it out, followed by blending further and further into the word until it is recognized. If the word is "elephant," for instance, the tutor would say, "el..., ele..., eleph...," etc. When the words are mastered, the children read the passage, with discussion to assure comprehension. If they have trouble with a word in reading the text, the same teaching steps just described are repeated as necessary.

Most of the high risk children in this last phase of the program soon start sounding out words on their own initiative when they don't recognize them. They now are making use in reading, therefore, of the phonemic skills they learned earlier. Evaluation studies conducted toward the end of the first grade year suggest that this process contributes strongly to their reading achievement.

Thus, in one field evaluation (M. A. Wallach and L. Wallach 1976, 1979a), beginning first graders scoring within the bottom 40 percent on the national norms for starting first graders of the Metropolitan Readiness battery were randomly assigned from the same classrooms to tutoring with the program or were controls. Median readiness scores were at the 25th percentile in both groups. Some of these children had already been classified as learning-disabled or mentally handicapped. Using Spache's reading achievement tests near the end of the first grade year, the tutored children were strikingly superior to the controls not only in word recognition but also in reading passages with comprehension of meaning and with facility, on these standardized test materials that were unfamiliar to them.

In another field evaluation (Dorval, Wallach, and Wallach 1978), a different sample of beginning first graders again scoring in the bottom portion of the distribution on a readiness battery, in this case the Comprehensive Tests of Basic Skills, received tutoring with the program or were in several control conditions. Median readiness scores in terms of national norms were at the 25th percentile and lower for various groups. Results after tutoring during the first grade year again indicated that the experimentals were strikingly superior to the controls in reading passages with facility and with comprehension of meaning as well as in word recognition, using standardized test materials unfamiliar to them. The appropriate level of the Comprehensive Tests of Basic Skills, along with the Spache, were the reading achievement tests used in this evaluation.

Finally, another phonemic analysis training method for which evaluation recently has also been provided is based on the work of Elkonin (1973). We describe it briefly to round out this presentation of teaching techniques. Elkonin's general procedure involves movable tokens which represent the sounds in the word to be segmented. Using the tokens as markers to help make the word's phonemes more concrete, the child is to learn to say the separate sounds in the word, pronouncing it slowly and marking off the sounds in order by moving the tokens.

Williams (1979, 1980) has utilized this basic method in an instructional program for high risk elementary school children. First, children learn to move wooden squares to mark off the number and order of syllables in words, which turns out to be an easy task. Then the same method is applied to the difficult task of marking off the number and order of phonemes in consonant-vowel and consonant-vowel-consonant combinations, working first with a limited set of nine phonemes. Some of these bigrams and trigrams are real words, others are nonsense syllables. This kind of practice at segmenting the sounds is followed by work on blending them into the same bigrams and trigrams. Then comes learning of letter-sound correspondences for the phonemes at issue. After that, there is decoding of letter displays of bigrams and trigrams still made from the same nine phonemes—represented now by wooden squares that have letters on them—and there is spelling of the spoken bigrams and trigrams with the letters. Then other letter-sound correspondences are introduced and used in trigram decoding, followed by more complex units for decoding.

Designed as an instructional supplement for high risk children, the Williams program has been found (Williams 1980) to enhance not only phonemic analysis and blending, but also the decoding of new consonant-vowel-consonant combinations — both real and nonsense words—comprised of letters on which the program had given decoding training in other combinations. Thus, evaluation evidence also finds the techniques just described to be of help for high risk children. However, it is probably important for some children, as Elkonin (1973) notes, to include attention to the pronunciation of individual sounds, as by the use of the pause or repetition strategies discussed earlier. In any case, the teachability of phonemic analysis and its role in facilitating the decoding aspect of reading are once again demonstrated here for high risk children.

In sum, we have presented evidence suggesting that children at risk for reading failure have difficulty identifying sounds in spoken words — phonemic analysis — although hardly any of them have trouble with auditory discrimination. We also have examined how the lack of phonemic analysis skills seems to be a critical factor in a great deal of the trouble children can encounter in learning to read. Finally, we have described methods of teaching phonemic analysis that have been demonstrated to work effectively, along with evidence that use of such methods not only establishes phonemic analysis skills in high-risk children but facilitates their subsequent learning of basic reading as well.

## REFERENCES

Bateman, B. "Teaching Reading to Learning Disabled and Other Hard-to-Teach Children." In *Theory and Practice of Early Reading. Vol. 1,* edited by L. B. Resnick and P. A. Weaver. Hillsdale, N.J.: Erlbaum, 1979.

Benton, A. L. "Developmental Dyslexia: Neurological Aspects." In *Advances in Neurology. Vol. 7: Current Reviews of Higher Nervous System Dysfunction,* edited by W. J. Friedlander. New York: Raven, 1975.

Carroll, J. B., and M. Walton. "Has the Reel Reeding Prablum bin Lade Bear? Summary Comments on the Theory and Practice of Early Reading." In *Theory and Practice of Early Reading. Vol. 3,* edited by L. B. Resnick and P. A. Weaver. Hillsdale, N.J.: Erlbaum, 1979.

Chall, J. S. *Learning to Read: The Great Debate.* New York: McGraw-Hill, 1967.

Dorval, B., T. M. Joyce, and C. T. Ramey. "Teaching Phoneme Identification Skills to Young Children At Risk for School Failure: Implications for Reading Readiness Instruction." Chapel Hill, N.C.: Frank Porter Graham Child Development Center, University of North Carolina at Chapel Hill, 1980.

Dorval, B., L. Wallach, and M. A. Wallach. "Field Evaluation of a Tutorial Reading Program Emphasizing Phoneme Identification Skills." *The Reading Teacher* 31 (1978): 784–90.

Elkonin, D. B. "USSR." In *Comparative Reading,* edited by J. Downing. New York: Macmillan, 1973.

Fox, B., and D. K. Routh. "Analyzing Spoken Language into Words, Syllables, and Phonemes: A Developmental Study." *Journal of Psycholinguistic Research* 4 (1975): 331–42.

———. "Phonemic Analysis and Severe Reading Disability in Children." *Journal of Psycholinguistic Research* 9 (1980): 115–19.

Gleitman, L. R., and P. Rozin. "Teaching Reading by Use of a Syllabary." *Reading Research Quarterly* 8 (1973): 447–83.

Goldman, R., M. Fristoe, and R. W. Woodcock. *Test of Auditory Discrimination.* Circle Pines, Minn.: American Guidance Service, 1970.

Goldstein, D. M. "Cognitive-Linguistic Functioning and Learning to Read in Preschoolers." *Journal of Educational Psychology* 68 (1976): 680–88.

Golinkoff, R. M. "Critique: Phonemic Awareness Skills and Reading Achievement." In *The Acquisition of Reading: Cognitive, Linguistic, and Perceptual Prerequisites,* edited by F. B. Murray and J. J. Pikulski. Baltimore: University Park Press, 1978.

Lewkowicz, N. K. "Phonemic Awareness Training: What to Teach and How to Teach It." *Journal of Educational Psychology* 72 (1980): 686–700.

Liberman, A. M., F. S. Cooper, D. P. Shankweiler, and M. Studdert-Kennedy. "Perception of the Speech Code." *Psychological Review* 74 (1967): 431–61.

Liberman, I. Y., and D. Shankweiler. "Speech, the Alphabet, and Teaching to Read." In *Theory and Practice of Early Reading, Vol. 2,* edited by L. B. Resnick and P. A. Weaver. Hillsdale, N.J.: Erlbaum, 1979.

Oakland, T., and F. C. Williams. *Auditory Perception: Diagnosis and Development for Language and Reading Abilities.* Seattle: Special Child Publications, 1971.

Rosner, J., and D. P. Simon. "The Auditory Analysis Test: An Initial Report." *Journal of Learning Disabilities* 4 (1971): 384–92.

Rozin, P., and L. R. Gleitman. "The Structure and Acquisition of Reading II: The Reading Process and the Acquisition of the Alphabetic Principle." In *Toward a Psychology of Reading: The Proceedings of the CUNY Conferences,* edited by A. S. Reber and D. L. Scarborough. Hillsdale, N.J.: Erlbaum, 1977.

Vellutino, F. R. "Toward an Understanding of Dyslexia: Psychological Factors in Specific Reading Disability." In *Dyslexia: An Appraisal of Current Knowledge,* edited by A. L. Benton and D. Pearl. New York: Oxford University Press, 1978.

Wallach, L., and M. A. Wallach. *The Teaching All Children to Read Kit.* Chicago: University of Chicago Press, 1976.

Wallach, L., M. A. Wallach, M. G. Dozier, and N. E. Kaplan. "Poor Children Learning to Read Do Not Have Trouble with Auditory Discrimination but Do Have Trouble with Phoneme Recognition." *Journal of Educational Psychology* 69 (1977): 36–39.

Wallach, M. A., and L. Wallach. *Teaching All Children to Read.* Chicago: University of Chicago Press, 1976; Phoenix paperback edition, 1979 (a).

——. "Helping Disadvantaged Children Learn to Read by Teaching Them Phoneme Identification Skills." In *Theory and Practice of Early Reading. Vol. 3,* edited by L. B. Resnick and P. A. Weaver. Hillsdale, N.J.: Erlbaum, 1979 (b).

Wepman, J. M. "Auditory Discimination, Speech, and Reading." *Elementary School Journal* 60 (1960): 325–33.

Williams, J. "The ABD's of Reading: A Program for the Learning Disabled." In *Theory and Practice of Early Reading. Vol. 3,* edited by L. B. Resnick and P. A. Weaver. Hillsdale, N.J.: Erlbaum, 1979.

Williams, J. P. "Teaching Decoding with an Emphasis on Phoneme Analysis and Phoneme Blending." *Journal of Education Psychology* 72 (1980): 1–15.

Zhurova, L. Y. "The Development of Analysis of Words into Their Sounds by Preschool Children." In *Studies of Child Language Development,* edited by C. A. Ferguson and D. I. Slobin. New York: Holt, Rinehart and Winston, 1973; originally published 1963.

# 12

# Error Monitoring

## A Learning Strategy for Improving Adolescent Academic Performance

*Jean B. Schumaker, Donald D. Deshler, Gordon R. Alley, Michael M. Warner, Frances L. Clark, Sue Nolan*

T HE FIELD OF learning disabilities (LD) is experiencing an increased demand for programs designed to serve learning disabled students in secondary schools. In response to this demand, several curriculum options have been developed (Deshler, Lowrey, and Alley 1979). One of these options — the learning strategies model — has been the focus of much research and programming efforts in recent years. As described by Alley and Deshler (1979), a learning strategies approach is designed to accomplish the following goal: to teach learning disabled adolescents strategies that will facilitate their acquisition, organization, storage, and retrieval of information, thus allowing them to cope with the demands of the secondary curriculum. In short, this approach is designed to teach students "how to learn" rather than specific content. For example, the teacher may teach the LD students techniques for clustering and organizing material that must be learned for a social studies test rather than actually teaching the social studies content. Furthermore, these same strategies can often be generalized across settings, contents, and time.

The thrust of the intervention research being conducted by the University of Kansas Institute for Research in Learning Disabilities has been the learning strategies intervention model. This programmatic research effort is designed to study not only underlying assumptions of this model but also to determine the power and robustness of specific learning strategies that are designed to facilitate the secondary LD student's ability to cope with the demands of the secondary school. Such strategies as self-questioning, visual imagery, multipass (for reading comprehension), test-taking, and error monitoring are being studied. The purpose of this paper is to present data from one segment of this programmatic effort, error-monitoring, as illustrative of the techniques being developed to impact the performance of the LD adolescent.

The specific learning strategies researched by The University of Kansas Institute for Research in Learning Disabilities must meet the basic conditions. First, they must have a high probability of helping the LD adolescent cope with the demands of the secondary setting. Second, they must address deficit areas found in a large proportion of the LD adolescent population. Third, they must be based on principles of cognitive psychology and learning. Error monitoring is considered to be an important learning strategy for LD adolescents because it meets the above three conditions. The remainder of this section will discuss error monitoring in relation to the three conditions stated above.

First, the curricular requirements of the secondary school place heavy written expression demands on students. Teachers expect students to take notes during class lecture and most assignments and tests require written expression (Moran 1980). Students' written products are often judged as much for spelling and punctuation accuracy as for content (Cuthbertson 1979). Consequently, students who have strategies to monitor errors in their work before handing it in usually receive better grades. Another demand placed on students in secondary settings is to assume responsibility for their performances. Typically, junior and senior high school students do not have the close interaction with and supervision of teachers that they enjoyed in the elementary grades. In elementary school, many of the study assignments and reviews were conducted under the watchful eye of the teacher. In these highly structured situations, teachers assumed much responsibility for monitoring errors on the students' work. To succeed in secondary schools, students are expected to assume more responsibility for the correctness of their assignments. For many LD students, the absence of teacher assistance in such activities can prove devastating. In short, the demands of the secondary school require students to assume responsibility for more of their actions and performances, including the monitoring of errors in their work.

Second, research on the characteristics of LD adolescents indicates that these students have deficits in monitoring errors in their performance. Alley, Deshler, and Warner (1979) have found that LD specialists report that a deficit in monitoring errors in spelling occurs four times as often in a learning disability as in a non-learning disability population. To learn a skilled, highly integrated response and to perform in a competent, accurate, rapid, and expert fashion, one must respond to feedback data generated from one's own response and to external information. Siegel (1974) has suggested that a faulty feedback mechanism in older learning disability students may impede their ability to act appropriately in social situations. Deshler, Ferrell, and Kass (1978) have found that learning disabled high school students evidenced a monitoring deficit on academic tasks which required their detection of self-generated and externally-generated errors. On a creative writing task for example, LD students detected only one-third of the errors they committed. The repercussions of such performances in academic and future employment situations are obvious. The need to make LD adolescents aware of the quality of their performance in written work is evident.

Third, the important role of monitoring or the detection of errors in learning and performance is clearly documented in the psychological literature. Powers (1973), for example, maintains that much successful human behavior is oriented around the ability of the individual to use feedback information to monitor errors in his/her performance. Adams (1971), in summarizing his research on error monitoring, states: "knowledge of results is the foremost source of information which results in corrections that eventually lead subjects to a correct response. Thus, the monitoring of errors and the use of feedback information is a most critical variable controlling learning and performance" (p. 122). While significant attention has been given to error monitoring in psychology, much less emphasis has been given to this topic in the learning disability literature. Deshler (1974), in a review of the most frequently used textbooks in learning disabilities and special education, found only one that discussed the important role of error monitoring in learning and performance for LD populations. The neglect of this topic is ironic given the significant problems that many LD students encounter in discriminating between correct and incorrect responses. Even the general education literature has not given major attention to strategies for error monitoring. That is, most instructional techniques that deal with error monitoring do not treat it as a primary instructional goal but rather as an incidental by-product of another intervention (Hamacheck 1968; Laurita 1972). Even less emphasis has been given to error monitoring as a learning and performance variable in the learning disability literature. This is unfortunate given the curricular demands for the skill, the monitoring deficits found in LD students, and the important role of monitoring as a learning and performance variable.

The purpose of this study therefore was to determine the effect of teaching LD adolescents an error-monitoring learning strategy. A specific instructional methodology was used to teach students the new strategy. The student's ability to apply the strategy to *both* teacher-generated and self-generated written products was measured.

## METHOD

### Subjects

Nine secondary students, seven males and two females, participated. All nine students were currently being served in programs for learning disabled students. The students were selected after reviewing their school records and interviewing their LD teachers. Only those students who had IQ scores in the normal range (i.e., above 80), exhibited deficits in one or more achievement areas, and did not exhibit evidence of physical or sensory handicaps, emotional disturbance, or economic, environmental, or cultural disadvantage were asked to participate. The participating students had IQ scores ranging from 88 to 117 ($\bar{x}$ = 99), grade level reading scores ranging from 3.9 to 8.0 ($\bar{x}$ = 6.2), and grade level writing scores ranging from 2.3 to 8.5 ($\bar{x}$ = 5.3). Their ages ranged from 12.5 to 18.0 years ($\bar{x}$ = 15.8 years) and they were in grades 8 to 12 ($\bar{x}$ = 10).

### Learning Setting

The study took place in a classroom-like setting in a community center which had been converted from a school. Each student was seated at a desk or small table. The teacher circulated among the students to give them individual instruction and feedback. The teacher taught four or five students at a time.

### Instructional Materials

The teacher was provided with a manual which contained a step-by-step description of the instructional procedures. Following these procedures, the teacher developed a set of instructional materials (hereafter referred to as "teacher-generated materials"). These materials included handwritten, one-page passages into which the teacher inserted specific writing errors. In each passage, the teacher made five capitalization errors, five appearance errors, five punctuation errors, and five spelling errors. The teacher made two sets of these passages for each student such that the readability of one set of the passages was at the student's reading ability level and the readability of the other set was at the student's grade level. This was accomplished by the teacher selecting the passages from materials which had already been scored for readability,* writing the passages on lined notebook paper, inserting the specified errors, and xeroxing the pages.

*This teacher used 66 *Passages to Develop Reading Comprehension* and 88 *Passages to Develop Reading Comprehension,* by M. Gilmore, A. Sack, and J. Yourman, published by College Skills Center, 1250 Broadway, New York, to construct the teacher-generated passages. The reason she used these materials was that they contained a series of short, high-interest passages which had already been judged for readability. The readability of the passages in 66 *Passages* ranges from first to eighth grade and in 88 *Passages* ranges from sixth grade to college level.

## Procedures

*Instructional procedures*

The instructional steps used by the teacher in teaching the monitoring strategy were adapted from those suggested by Alley and Deshler (1979) and Deshler, Alley, Warner, and Schumaker (1980). They were as follows:

*Step 1: Test to Determine the Student's Current Monitoring Skills*
In this step, the teacher tested the student's monitoring skills first in the teacher-generated materials at both ability and grade level and then in a passage written by the student him/herself. After testing was completed, the teacher discussed the results with the student, affirming that the student exhibited a deficit in the way he/she monitored for errors and, as a result, left a number of errors in his/her work.

*Step 2: Describe the Error Monitoring Strategy*
Next, the teacher described the steps involved in the Error Monitoring Strategy to the student and contrasted them with the student's current checking habits. The steps included the specific behaviors in which the student should engage and the sequence of behaviors which should be followed. As each step was explained, a rationale was given for why the behavior was important and how it would help the student to produce a better written product.

*Step 3: Model the Strategy*
In this step, the teacher modelled the Error Monitoring Strategy for the student. Thus, the teacher demonstrated the strategy by acting-out each of the steps previously described to the student while "thinking aloud" so the student could witness all of the processes involved in the strategy.

*Step 4: Verbal Rehearsal of the Strategy*
Here, the student verbally rehearsed the steps involved in the Error Monitoring Strategy to a criterion of 100 percent correct without prompts. This instructional step was designed to familiarize the student with the steps of the strategy such that he or she could instruct him/herself in the future as to what to do next when performing the strategy.

*Step 5: Practice in Ability Level Teacher-Generated Materials*
In this step, the student practiced applying the strategy to successive passages written at his or her current reading level. This reduced the demands on the student such that he/she could concentrate on the application of the new strategy. As the student became proficient in monitoring, he or she was encouraged to progress from overt self-instruction to covert self-instruction while practicing the strategy.

*Step 6: Feedback*

The teacher gave the student positive and corrective feedback after he or she completed monitoring each passage. When the student reached a criterion of detecting and correcting 90 percent of the errors in a given passage, the student went on to Step 7.

*Step 7: Test on Teacher-generated Passages*

Here, the student received two tests in Teacher-generated passages, one at ability level and one at grade level. These provided measures of each student's progress in learning the strategy. If the student reached criterion on the ability level test but not on the grade level test, Steps 5 & 6 were to be repeated using grade level materials. If the student reached criterion on both tests, the student progressed to Step 8.

*Step 8: Individual Analysis of Common Errors*

For this step, the teacher analyzed with the student the types of errors the student commonly was making in his or her written work. For this purpose, the student and teacher used products the student had recently written. The result of this analysis was a list of the kinds of errors the student should be specifically careful to monitor. The list was secured in the student's notebook.

*Step 9: Practice in Student-generated Paragraphs*

The student was instructed to write a paragraph and to apply the monitoring strategy to that paragraph.

*Step 10: Feedback*

Each time the student completed monitoring a new paragraph, the teacher gave the student positive and corrective feedback about his or her use of the monitoring strategy to detect and correct errors. Steps 9 and 10 were recycled until the student's final copy of a paragraph had fewer than one error for every 20 words.

*Step 11: Test on Student-generated Paragraph*

The student was asked to write a paragraph and monitor that paragraph as a final test of the student's monitoring skills.

### Error Monitoring Strategy Procedures

As described above, the student first learned to detect and correct errors in Teacher-generated passages. For this purpose, the student followed these procedures:

1. Read each sentence separately.
2. Ask yourself the "COPS questions" (see description below).
3. When you find an error, circle it and put the correct form above the error if you know the correct form.

4. Ask for help if you are unsure of the correct form.

The "COPS questions" were questions the students were to ask themselves to cue themselves to look for four kinds of errors. These four categories of errors were devised after reviewing many samples of LD students' written work. An effort was made to minimize the number of categories while covering the largest number of errors the students were making. The "COPS" acronym, as part of the learning strategy, was chosen in light of the detecting and correcting activities involved in the strategy. The COPS questions and the errors the student looked for were as follows:

C — Have I capitalized the first word and proper names?

O — How is the overall appearance? (Here the student looked for errors involving spacing, legibility, indentation of paragraphs, neatness, and complete sentences.)

P — Have I put in commas and end punctuation?

S — Have I spelled all the words right?

Each of these categories and the types of errors subsumed under each category were fully described to the students in the Describe Step (Step 2).

When the student began monitoring his or her own work, these were the steps to be followed:

1. Use every other line as you write your rough draft.
2. As you read each sentence, ask yourself the COPS questions.
3. When you find an error, circle it and put the correct form above the error if you know it.
4. Ask for help if you are unsure of the correct form.
5. Recopy the paragraph neatly in a form for handing in to the teacher.

### Measurement Systems

Each of the four categories of errors was subdivided into subcategories of the types of errors which were emphasized with the students. There were 12 subcategories in all. For example, capitalization errors were subdivided into three subcategories: the first letter of the first word of a sentence not capitalized; proper nouns not capitalized; and capital letters improperly used. Each of these types of errors was objectively defined. Scorers became familiar with these definitions and received two hours of scoring training. This training consisted of an explanation of the scoring procedures, practice scoring actual passages and paragraphs, and discussion and feedback after calculating reliability between scorers.

For teacher-generated passages, answer keys were provided. Thus, the scorers merely had to categorize and tally the errors the students detected and the errors which they corrected correctly. Interscorer reliability was obtained by having two scorers independently score one randomly selected pre-test and post-test at ability level and at grade level for each student. The scorers' tallies were compared category by category and occurrence reliability calculated by dividing the number of agreements by the number of agreements plus disagreements. The percentage of agreement was 91.6 percent for errors detected and 90.5 percent for errors corrected.

For the student-generated passages, the scorers first had to categorize and tally all the errors the student made in his/her rough draft. Then, the errors remaining in the student's final draft were also scored. These tasks were accomplished on a tally sheet whereby the errors the student made on each line of his/her paragraph were categorized into the twelve subcategories of errors. Two independent scorers scored one pre-test paragraph and one post-test paragraph for each student. Interscorer reliability was determined by comparing their tally sheets line by line and category by category. An agreement was scored if both observers tallied an error as occurring in the same subcategory of errors and on the same line of the paragraph. Again, occurrence reliability was calculated. The percentage of agreement on errors was 75 percent. This percentage, although acceptable, is somewhat low due to the difficulty in categorizing some of the errors. For example, making a decision between whether a word was mispelled or whether it was illegible (an overall appearance subcategory) was difficult. Some words that were illegible to one scorer were readable for another scorer. The percentage of agreement when the total number of errors tallied by both scorers were compared was 85 percent.

### Experimental Design

A multiple baseline design across three students (Baer, Wolf, and Risley 1968) was employed and then was replicated twice with two more sets of three students each. The first student in each group of three students received only one set of pretests before instruction began. The second student received two sets of pretests and the third student received three sets of pretests.

## RESULTS

Figure 12.1 shows the pretest (baseline) results, the practice (or training) results and the post-test results for the first three students, $S_1$, $S_2$ and $S_3$, in Teacher-generated passages. The percentage of errors detected is shown in the closed symbols and the percentage of errors corrected is

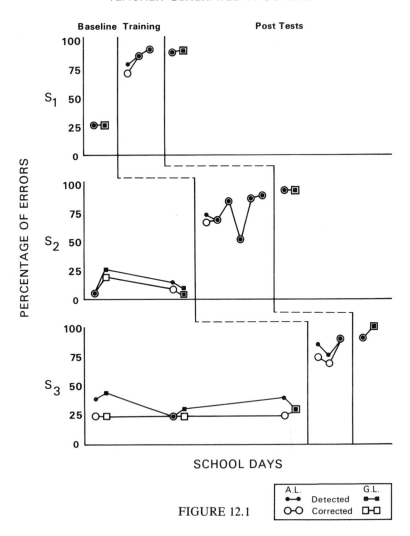

FIGURE 12.1

shown in the open symbols. The ability level (A.L.) test results are depicted with circles and the grade level (G.L.) test results are depicted with squares.

Before training, none of the students was correcting more than 25 percent of the errors in either ability level or grade level materials. Detection of errors was slightly higher than correction for $S_2$ and $S_3$. During training, $S_1$ required three practice passages, $S_2$ required 6 practice passages, and $S_3$ required three practice passages to reach the criterion of detecting and correcting 90 percent of the errors. Posttest results showed the students readily and immediately generalized their monitoring skills to the more difficult grade level passages. All three students scored at or above criterion level for both ability and grade level post tests.

Figure 12.2 shows the results for the student-generated passages for the same three students. The dots show the number of errors per word the student made before monitoring his/her work. The circles show the number of errors per word remaining after the student checked his/her work. During baseline, $S_1$ was making and failing to correct one error for every three words in his paragraph, $S_2$ was making and failing to correct one error for every four words, and $S_3$ was making and failing to correct as many as one error for every two words. $S_1$ and $S_2$ required two practice paragraphs and $S_3$ required only one practice paragraph before reaching criterion. On the final post-test, $S_1$ and $S_2$ had no errors in their final drafts and $S_3$ had fewer than one error for every twenty words.

The results for the other six students are very similar to these results.* None of the nine students required instruction in the grade level materials. Most of the students required only three practices in teacher-generated passages; six practices was the highest number required. Five of the students had one practice and four had two practices in student-generated paragraphs before reaching criterion.

The teacher time involved in the instruction was four hours of group instruction for the Describe and Model steps (Steps 2 & 3). Each practice on a teacher-generated passage took a student about 20 minutes with 5 to 10 minutes for scoring and feedback by the teacher. The individual analysis required about 20 minutes of teacher and student time. Each paragraph took about 30 to 35 minutes for the students to

---

*To obtain figures of these data, write to the authors at the Kansas Institute for Research in Learning Disabilities, 313 Carruth-O'Leary Hall, University of Kansas, Lawrence, Kansas 66045.

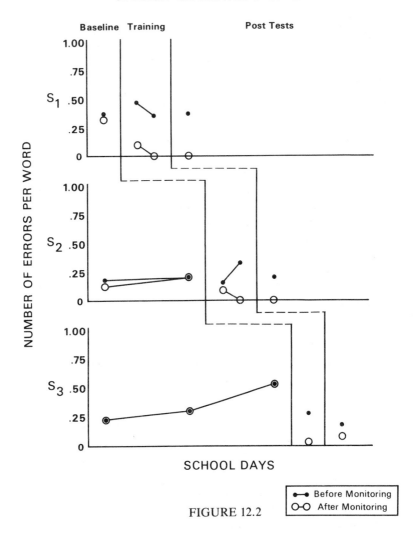

MONITORING OF
STUDENT GENERATED PARAGRAPHS

FIGURE 12.2

write and monitor and an additional 10 minutes for the teacher to score and give feedback. Thus, the average total amount of instructional time for a given student was about 7½ hours.

## DISCUSSION

The instructional procedures appear to be effective in teaching a learning strategy, specifically error monitoring, to learning disabled adolescents. Three replications of a multiple baseline design across students demonstrated that improved performance did not occur until after each student received instruction in the strategy. All of the students showed marked improvement immediately following instruction in their first practice lessons. Only one student ($S_2$) had what was termed "difficulty" by the teacher in reaching criterion on the Teacher-generated passages. When the lesson was couched as a "detection game" for this student, whereby the student could earn up to five points for the errors found and corrected in each of the COPS categories, the student improved quickly.

This study, unlike others reported in the literature on error monitoring, measured the effects of teaching a specific detection strategy to LD adolescents. While most previous research on error monitoring has focused on it as a learner characteristic, this study has demonstrated the efficacy of a monitoring procedure to successfully improve the performance of LD adolescents in both teacher-generated and self-generated materials.

The instructional procedures involved in teaching this strategy appear to be practical in that instruction can be imparted in relatively few hours while insuring criterion level gains in a majority of LD students. This is especially true since the initial instruction can be accomplished in a group format. It is unclear, however, whether all of the instructional steps are necessary in teaching this strategy. Indeed, it may not be necessary to teach the strategy using teacher-generated passages first. The reasoning behind this tactic was: (1) to eliminate any emotional attachment to the material being monitored while the student was initially learning the strategy, and (2) to give the student experience monitoring a wide variety of errors. Most of the students were making idiosyncratic errors and there were not opportunities to make some errors given the structure of our test situation. For example, there were few opportunities for a paper to be torn or crumpled since each paper was given to the teacher immediately after it had been written. The teacher-generated passages allowed the student to be confronted with a torn paper and necessitated a discrimination of when a given tear constituted an error necessitating remediation.

One limitation of the procedures is that they have not been tested with students reading below the 3.9 grade level. The student in this study who had the widest discrepancy between actual grade level and current reading level was in the 10th grade and was reading at the 3.9 grade level. Thus, the procedures have not been tested with students exhibiting wider discrepancies. Nevertheless, the wide discrepancy did not seem to hinder the student in our study. In fact, when compared to the other students, she was one of the quickest learners of the strategy, requiring only four practices in all to learn the whole strategy.

Another limitation of the procedures is that the COPS categories are somewhat restricted. Only the most frequent kinds of errors committed by students doing relatively simple writing were included in the categories. The strategy is not intended to be a means of teaching the many subtleties and complexities of grammar and syntax. The use of the individual analysis step (Step 8) allows the teacher to identify idiosyncratic errors for each student which may not be specified in the COPS questions. Thus, the procedure does not preclude the identification and discussion of errors not included in the COPS categories.

A final consideration regards the problem of generalization. From the results of this study, it remains unclear how the procedures will impact the students' performances in the regular class. This study took place in the summer. Thus, there were no opportunities to collect products the students completed in other classes; our class was the only one in session. Current and future research is focusing on the students' use of the new strategies they have learned outside of the resource room environment.

In summary, this study has exemplified some of the intervention research on learning strategies currently being conducted by the Kansas Institute for Research in Learning Disabilities. Single-subject designs are being utilized to validate the effectiveness of a general teaching methodology across a wide variety of learning strategies. The strategy featured here, error monitoring, appears to be effectively used by learning disabled secondary students after training such that they can eliminate most if not all of the errors in their own writing. This skill, if properly used, should enable the learning disabled student to better respond to the demands of the secondary setting in light of the many instances of written work required in that setting.

## REFERENCES

Adams, J. A. "A Closed-loop Theory of Motor Learning." *Journal of Motor Behavior* 3 (1971): 111–49.

Alley, G. R., and D. D. Deshler. *Teaching the Learning Disabled Adolescent: Strategies and Methods*. Denver: Love Publishing, 1979.

Alley, G. R., D. D. Deshler, and M. M. Warner. "Identification of Learning Disabled Adolescents: A Bayesian Approach." *Learning Disability Quarterly* 2(2) (1979): 76–83.

Baer, D. M., M. M. Wolf, and T. R. Risley. "Some Current Dimensions of Applied Behavior Analysis." *Journal of Applied Behavior Analysis* 1 (1968): 91–7.

Bilodeau, I. A. "Information Feedback." In *Principles of Skill Acquisition,* edited by E. A. Bilodeau and I. A. Bilodeau. New York: Academic Press, 1969, pp. 255–85.

Cutherbertson, E. B. "An Analysis of Secondary Testing and Grading Practices." Masters thesis. Lawrence, Kansas: The University of Kansas, 1979.

Deshler, D. D., G. R. Alley, and S. C. Carlson. "Learning Strategies: An Approach to Mainstreaming Secondary Students with Learning Disabilities." *Education Unlimited* 2(4) (1980): 6–11.

Deshler, D. D., G. R. Alley, M. M. Warner, and J. B. Schumaker. "Promoting the Acquisition and Generalization of Learning Strategies by Learning Disabled Adolescents." In *Learning Disabilities: Perspectives and Practices,* edited by D. G. Bachor. In press.

Deshler, D. D., W. R. Ferrell, and C. E. Kass. "Monitoring of Schoolwork Errors by LD Adolescents." *Journal of Learning Disabilities* 11(7) (1978): 10–23.

Deshler, D. D., N. Lowery, and G. R. Alley. "Programming Alternatives for Learning Disabled Adolescents: A Nationwide Survey." *Academic Therapy* 14 (1979): 54–63.

Hamacheck, D. E. "Teaching Techniques to Enhance Motivation and Learning." *Journal for Special Educators* 10 (1968): 71–77.

Laurita, R. E. "Rehearsal: A Technique for Improving Reading Comprehension." *Academic Therapy* 8 (1972): 103–11.

Moran, M. R. *An Investigation of the Demands on Oral Language Skills of Learning Disabled Students in Secondary Classrooms.* Research Report No. 1. Lawrence, Kansas: The University of Kansas Institute for Research in Learning Disabilities, 1980.

Powers, W. T. *Behavior: The Control of Perception.* Chicago: Aldine Publishing, 1973.

Schumaker, J. B., D. D. Deshler, G. R. Alley, M. M. Warner, and F. Clark, *Multipass: A Learning Strategy for Improving Reading Comprehension.* Research Report No. 32. Lawrence, Kansas: The University of Kansas Institute for Research in Learning Disabilities, 1981.

Siegel, E. *The Exceptional Child Grows Up.* New York: Dutton, 1974.

Welford, A. T. *Fundamentals of Skill.* London: Methuen, 1968.

# 13

## Improving Reading Skills Through
## Auricular Reading Techniques

*Joseph A. Bukovec*

W ITHIN RECENT YEARS, two little-known and largely neglected approaches to the improvement of reading skills have begun to emerge in remedial instruction. Only recently has information regarding the effectiveness of these approaches been reported in the professional literature. In a survey of new developments in remedial reading, Albert J. Harris mentions, among others, two innovative approaches: (a) simultaneous listening/reading and (b) repeated readings. He refers to these innovations as "small scale explorations that have not yet been followed up by controlled research," and further states that "it is important for remedial teachers to know about them and be prepared to try them with pupils who seem unable to learn from conventional remedial procedures" (Harris 1981).

The purpose of this article is to examine these innovative approaches and to explore their applicability as classroom instructional techniques for the learning disabled child. In the absence of standardized terminology, which is still evolving in this area, we will refer to these approaches as *auricular reading* (aural reading, simultaneous listening/reading) and as *multiple readings* (repeated readings).

### AURICULAR READING

In this instructional activity, the student reads a text silently while he simultaneously listens to it being read, usually on tape or phonograph. For children who have severe reading problems and after years of remedial instruction still remain at the decoding level, the auricular approach provides an opportunity to participate directly in the reading process, to experience firsthand the act of fluent reading. It involves them directly in an experience with the management of printed symbols, in particular, how those symbols are manipulated in the production of spoken language. The process literally bathes and saturates their senses with visual and phonological symbols in the most meaningful manner possible — as spoken language, heard in its natural melody of stress, pitch, and pause. In effect, the student experiences the written word as naturally expressed language rather than as a mechanical deciphering or decoding task with little or no attendant comprehension.

While this interaction with the printed text may not be considered as a totally independent act of reading since it does not necessarily entail the initiation or independent generation of the reading act, it does involve the student in a process of visually tracking printed symbols to the accompaniment of their associated sounds and the concomitant generation of a natural, effortless flow of meaning. It is, again, an experience of fluent reading, a genuine participation in the reading act.

The auricular approach bears a strong similarity to the neurological impress method developed by Heckleman (1969). Using this approach, the teacher is positioned behind the student as they read the text together orally. The teacher reads directly into the ear of the student in a voice slightly louder and ahead of the student's, setting an appropriate pace for the reading act, and at the same time, the teacher runs a finger below the text. According to Heckleman, "This reading technique should be considered a part of an audio-neural-conditioning process whereby the incorrect reading habits of the child are suppressed and then replaced with correct, fluid reading habits" (Heckleman 1966).

It may be noted that while the neurological impress method involves oral reading (the child reads aloud as he listens), the auricular approach, which we are considering in this discussion, involves a silent reading approach (the child reads silently as he listens). While it is not our purpose here to explore the implications that may possibly flow from this difference between the approaches, it may nonetheless be mentioned that a series of experiments conducted by Peter Mosenthal support the following hypotheses: "(1) that a common linguistic competence underlies both silent reading and oral-language processing; (2) that this linguistic competence is not shared by reading aloud." In effect, when reading orally, "the reader is faced with the problem of focusing simultaneously upon two different tasks—one, establishing meaning; the other, verbalizing the written surface structure" (Mosenthal 1976–77).

Should these conclusions hold up under further study, they suggest that, in relation to the attentional demands made upon the student, reading aloud while listening is a more complicated task for students to perform than reading silently while listening.

## MULTIPLE READINGS

The second innovative approach to remedial reading instruction, namely multiple readings, is a technique that is particularly helpful with students who have learning problems. Patricia Dahl (1974) and S. Jay Samuels (1979) have researched this method and have reported improvement in both fluency and comprehension.

The instructional procedure is relatively simple. The student is given a short reading selection of fifty to two hundred words. This selection may be a segment of a continuous story or may be a separate, self-contained narrative. The student reads the selection to the teacher, who records the reading speed and the number of word recognition errors. The student then practices reading the selection independently until he or she feels capable of reading it fluently at a predetermined reading rate. The student then reads the selection for the teacher a second time, and both the reading rate and number of word recognition errors are again recorded. This procedure is repeated until the criterion rate has been achieved, at which time the student proceeds to the next selection. Graphically charting the student's improvement in both rate and number of oral reading errors provides a strong stimulus to continued motivation since the student is encouraged by each successive improvement.

It should be noted that this approach may also be used with auditory assistance, in which case the student first listens to the text while reading along silently. The student may listen to the tape as often as necessary to enable him or her to read the selection without assistance and to practice it silently until he or she reaches the established criterion reading rate. Samuels describes the results achieved through use of this approach: "As reading speed increased, word recognition errors decreased. As the student continued to use this technique, the initial speed of reading each new selection was faster than initial speed on the previous selection. Also, the number of rereadings required to reach the criterion reading speed decreased as the student continued the technique, . . . fact(s) that indicate transfer of training and a general improvement in reading fluency" (Samuels 1979).

In using this technique, Samuels stressed speed rather than accuracy. An undue emphasis upon correct pronunciation may actually be counterproductive insofar as it tends to encourage the fear of making errors and results in a reduced rate of reading. Consequently, fluency is impeded rather than improved.

## COMPREHENSION IMPROVED

Not only was fluency improved through use of the repeated readings method, but comprehension was also enhanced as the student was required to expend less attention in the decoding act. The theoretical base for using this approach as a means of improving comprehension is founded in the theory of automatic information processing (La Berge and Samuels 1974).

The amount of attentional capacity available to a person during the reading act has clearly defined limitations; it is not unlimited. If, while reading, attention must be expended in phonological analysis, proportionately less attentional capacity is available for the comprehension act. This frequently occurs with children who are at the decoding stage of reading. As they proceed through a sentence, for instance, they encounter unfamiliar words that require them to pause and apply word attack skills. In doing so, they begin to focus attention on specific phonic elements within the unfamiliar words. As a result, their short term memory becomes overloaded and the information already gathered in the first part of the sentence quickly disintegrates. This loss of information removes all ability to anticipate what is coming in the balance of the sentence and, as a result, the student becomes enmeshed in slow, laborious, word-by-word reading and cannot comprehend the passage. In effect, too much attentional capacity is being expended in the decoding task and an insufficient amount remains available for comprehension.

The multiple reading instructional technique is designed to counter this phenomenon by raising the decoding act to the automatic level, thereby requiring the expenditure of little or no attentional energy for word recognition, and leaving the bulk of attentional capacity available for comprehension. Meaning is thereby achieved more easily and more rapidly. As Stanovich describes it, "the rapid word recognition of fluent readers simply short-circuits the conscious attention mechanism" (Stanovitch 1980).

### APPLICABILITY

These instructional techniques are useful at all levels because they permit the teacher to explore students' interests and to provide reading instruction within the context of materials that are personally satisfying and enjoyable to the students. In addition, these approaches may readily be combined with most traditional skill development techniques, while at the same time, they are particularly well suited to holistic approaches to reading development. Let us consider some examples.

Carol Chomsky, of the Harvard Graduate School of Education, was faced with the frustrating problem of developing fluency in third grade students who had acquired many phonic skills, but who could decode only slowly in a painful word-by-word manner, and whose progress in learning to read was at a standstill in spite of all instructional efforts (Chomsky 1978). She reflected on how her own children had practically taught themselves to read before entering school, and that her role in this learning process was simply to supply those words which the children wanted to know.

Chomsky decided to combine both the listening and multiple reading approaches and to follow them up with analytical phonetic drills and writing activities. Each student selected a book and engaged in read-along activities until they had memorized the story and could read it independently. Subsequent phonetic activities were carried out using the already familiar text as an instructional base. Finally, writing and art projects were completed, again using the familiar stories as a springboard.

As a result of these approaches, students "had a feeling of success right from the start, and a sense of progress, . . . willingness to undertake reading new material and original writing; . . . passivity about reading declined dramatically, confidence increased, and they began to pick up new books of their own choosing" (Chomsky 1978).

To illustrate an unusual situation in which both the auricular and the multiple reading techniques were used almost as a total instructional approach, let me briefly recount the story of Roger, a student at The Communications Workshop, and how he learned to read by reading. It should first be noted, however, that these approaches are normally not recommended as a total reading program or for use as an exclusive remediation technique, but are customarily used within a broader program of instructional activities.

Roger came to our program as an alienated eighth grader who exhibited classic symptoms of dyslexia. He had failed to respond to many years of remedial and supplemental instruction, and remained a virtual nonreader. When given a third grade level of the Gates-MacGinitie Reading Test, Roger scored off the low end of the scale, reading somewhere below second grade level. His phonic skills were extremely poor; he had recurring directionality problems; he was dysgraphic, his written work virtually indecipherable; his response to phonics and word attack instruction was very poor; finally, Roger either could not or would not tolerate workbooks or any other traditional skills development materials. There was one thing, however, that Roger did like. He was intensely interested in and knowledgeable about World War II. Unfortunately, there were no materials written at the second grade level that could satisfy Roger's informational level in the subject. However, there was a wealth of adult level material available in the public library. These books became Roger's reading program. Initially, the teacher recorded a few chapters at a time, and Roger read the text as he listened to it on tape. Later, materials requested from the Commission for the Blind and Handicapped were used. At the end of each reading session, Roger selected one paragraph which he listened to repeatedly until he could recognize all of the words. He then practiced reading the selection silently until he was able to read it fluently for the teacher.

Gradually, Roger was able to read without auditory assistance. He was in the CWS program for four and a half years, became successful as an actor and set designer for numerous high school dramatic productions, and graduated a half-year ahead of his class. Just before graduating, Roger, an avid reader, finished reading Tolkien's *Trilogy* without assistance. When he left the program in mid-year, Roger was tested using the twelfth grade level of the Gates-MacGinitie Reading Test. In comprehension, he achieved a grade equivalent score of 12.2, and in vocabulary knowledge, he scored off the high end of the scale (12.8). Roger, a classic dyslexic, literally taught himself to read by reading.

## ADVANTAGES

Both the auricular and the multiple reading approaches offer numerous advantages when they are appropriately and systematically incorporated in the reading instructional program. Among them are the following:

1. Provides students with a model of fluent reading.
2. Exposes students to a variety of grammatical styles and structures that are the link between meaning and its visual and auditory expression.
3. Permits students to read more difficult materials. In effect, enables them to read at their language comprehension level rather than at their sight vocabulary level.
4. Reduces the need for vocabulary control.
5. Eliminates complicated readability formulas.
6. Increases the quantity of student reading, and efficiently provides the large amounts of exposure to language that are required in order to learn to read.

7. Provides a failure-free activity in which students are able to overcome their difficulties in private and at their own pace.
8. Permits students with severe reading deficits to read the literature being read by their peers, and facilitates their active participation in relevant school or socially related discussions evolving from such readings.
9. Tends to offset the negative effects of using highly analytical strategies in reading instruction.
10. Provides an enjoyable individualized activity in which students experience efficient reading and enjoy achieving success where previously they had experienced frustration.

## OLD OR NEW METHODS?

While Albert J. Harris refers to these innovative approaches as "new" developments in remedial instruction (Harris 1981), there is ample evidence that the principles upon which they are based are, in reality, quite old.

Edmund Burke Huey, writing at the turn of the century, recounts a number of methods that were commonly used to teach reading. He states:

> Perhaps we should catalogue still another, the imitative method. In the Orient, children bawl in concert over a book, imitating their fellows or their teacher until they come to know what the page says and to read it for themselves. Many an American child cannot remember when reading began, having by a similar method pored over the books and pictures of nursery jingles and fairy tales that were told to him, until he could read them for himself.

We can only imagine how deeply into the shadows of the Oriental past these practices reach.

## REFERENCES

Chomsky, C. "When You Still Can't Read in Third Grade: After Decoding, What? In *What Research Has to Say About Reading Instruction,* edited by S. Jay Samuel. Newark. Delaware: International Reading Association, 1978.

Dahl, P. *An Experimental Program for Teaching High Speed Word Recognition and Comprehension Skills*. Final Report. Project #3–1154. National Institute of Education, 1974.

Harris, A. J. "What Is New in Remedial Reading?" *The Reading Teacher* 34 (January 1981): 405–10.

Heckleman, R. G. "Using the Neurological Impress Remedial Technique." *Academic Therapy Quarterly* 1 (October 1966): 235–9.

———. "A Neurological Impress Method of Reading Instruction." *Academic Therapy* 44 (1969): 277–82.

Huey, E. B. *The Psychology and Pedagogy of Reading*. New York: Macmillan, 1908, p. 274.

La Berge, D. and S. J. Samuels. "Toward a Theory of Automatic Information Processing in Reading." *Cognitive Psychology* 6 (1974): 293–323.

Mosenthal, P. "Psycholinguistic Properties of Aural and Visual Comprehension as Determined by Children's Abilities to Comprehend Syllogisms." *Reading Research Quarterly* 12(1) 1976–7): 87.

Samuels, S. J. "The Method of Repeated Readings." *The Reading Teacher* 32 (January 1979): 403–8.

Stanovich, K. E. "Toward an Interactive-compensatory Model of Individual Differences in the Development of Reading Fluency." *Reading Research Quarterly* 16(1) (1980): 32–71.

# 14

# Teaching and Assessing Disabled Readers

## A Strategies Approach

*N. Dworkin, Y. Dworkin, R. Huhn*

### PROBLEM-SOLVING STRATEGIES
### IN THE ASSESSMENT OF ADOLESCENTS AND ADULTS

T HE ASSESSMENT of adolescents and adults carries with it two con-straints which make the thrust of the analysis critically different from that of younger, elementary-grade children. First, there is considerably less remedial time before the students will leave school or go to voca-tional and/or professional careers. Second, inappropriate or inefficient learning behaviors have become habitual.

In terms of the remedial future, not only teaching approaches but diagnostic procedures as well, must start with the assumption that teaching time-frames will be compressed. It is necessary to find the general learning keys of the individual, rather than attacking specific sub-skills. The manipulation of language and mathematical structures provide exceptionally powerful comprehensive frameworks for such investigation. Each of the two is necessary to many intellectually related areas, and both, in concert, cover most contemporary subject matter.

From a diagnostic point of view, both these characteristics demand a reformulation of test procedures away from traditional assumptions and instrumentation. This is especially true where the learners have been previously identified as learning disabled and may, therefore, be processing or out-putting information in highly unique and individual-istic ways.

The issue of ingrained learning habits is critical. Most learners who have passed through seven or eight years of schooling have developed, or extended, generalized learning behaviors which mark their "natural" approaches to the absorption of information. While many of these learn-ing strategies may have been acquired through formal schooling, the fundamental learning behaviors are organic or systemic in nature. They grow out of genetic, neurological and physiological patterns which are not easily subject to change, if at all. Procedures which may be of little academic value may nevertheless grow out of internal structures which mark the strengths of the individual.

Many school failures are occasioned as much by the individual's poor match with teacher expectation as they are with an inability to handle standardized content. By the time students are in high school or beyond, they have either learned to adjust to the disparate demands of teachers (whose styles may be as different as those of the students), or they have come to view their own learning behaviors as inadequate or failing.

The diagnostician, as a result, must decide, sometimes on the basis of incomplete evidence, whether to undo prior behaviors and replace them with new ones, train the student to "cope" despite some inadequate strategies, or redirect the course of the students' future learning.

Such decisions often seem god-like, and are carried out in the face of learning styles which may be reasonably immutable. The problem may not be in the learning, but in the way we expect human organisms to perceive information. People, in the process of learning, are full of surprises. Teachers and diagnosticians are not always willing to be surprised.

In the assessment theory under consideration, there are a number of main themes which relate to the organic way in which humans receive information. From our perspective, the function of the diagnostician is to identify these internal learning systems, and adjust teaching procedures accordingly, rather than insist that the learning be changed to fit the teaching. Learning is an internal function, subject to all the natural laws that rule on human systems. Teaching is an external process, subject to the myriad of techniques we humans have developed to deliver information.

Although learning sub-skills constitute the major elements in the elementary curriculum, they are rarely the major areas of concern on the part of disabled learners or their families. Teachers and educational practitioners are, of necessity, focused on curriculum-oriented issues. But adolescents and adults experiencing learning difficulties, and the families of learning-disabled children, ask more fundamental questions. "What's wrong with my child?"; "Why do other people always finish their work before I do?"; "How come I get such poor grades if I'm so smart?"; "Why can't she remember what she just read?"; "I know my work, so why do I freeze up when I'm taking a test?"; "How come I have so much trouble taking notes?"

These, and other questions like them, have one common theme. They are all comparative statements. And therein lies the real issue. From the earliest school years on, learners have been placed in comparative systems. The measurements are never abstract, but are related to what other students are doing. We have taught students to count by minuses. As a result, they, their families and their teachers have lost sight of the learning strengths that make it possible for them to function.

Unfortunately, the thrust of traditional diagnosis has supported the negative view. Despite commitments to identifying strengths, the essential objective of most testing is to find the symptoms, and discover the causes of weakness. Regardless of how important such an investigation may be, it provides inadequate clues for the teaching process. Teaching models must be based on the power of an individual, and that power is best demonstrated through a problem-solving process.

## THE DOMINANT/FLEXIBLE CONTINUUM

There is a form of learning which is perhaps the most all-encompassing identifier of a learner's internal system, ranging from dominant to flexible. It should be made clear that these terms are neither political nor intellectual in import. Rather, they characterize the habitual manner in which varying organisms respond to problem conditions.

At the one extreme are the individuals who always tend to repeat a learned procedure in the same way—the way it was first received. They are frequently the youngsters about whom it is said, "He's so stubborn! I just taught him a better way to do the problem, but he keeps on going back to his own way."

Specifically, dominant learners have a tendency to return to those strategies which were originally associated with a given learning situation. If they are taught to circle words they will always circle words. If they are taught a slanted line in division, they will always use a slanted line. If they are taught any x in y manner, they will always return to y if they think they are dealing with x.

No! These are not stubborn or recalcitrant organisms — but they certainly are dominant in their style. They don't stick only to single strategies, and they are not limited in intellect. But, they are returners — they can use a new strategy *if* they see the problem as new or different. Thus, the burden is on the teacher at the earliest period of learning. For the truly dominant learner, *early teaching* and *immediate feedback* are absolutely essential. Such students find it difficult, if not impossible, to deal with alternatives until they have learned a few systems thoroughly. Thus, the teaching and assignments for such students must be carefully structured, with a maximum of immediate practice.

The great virtues of the dominant learner are certainty and self-motivation. Once something is learned, its techniques are not forgotten. More critically, the dominant learner knows what to do every time the same class of problems emerge. Indeed, there is almost a moral commitment to the method of execution. Other learners, trying to solve the problem in other ways, are often seen as cheaters. Lest we think that only learners are subject to a dominant style, there is nothing more disturbing to the student than to hear a teacher say (about a correct answer), "That's not the way I wanted you to do it."

What are the drawbacks to the dominant style? Well, mostly time. The more time that passes between the learning of a new technique and its practice, the more chance there is for something to go awry. Unfortunately, pieces of a strategy are not easily corrected because dominant learners see strategies as totalities, each part is equally relevant and equally sacrosanct. Remember, "The way I learned it is the way to do it."

There is a second problem dominant learners confront. In almost all of our school systems, positive feedback and reinforcement are offered primarily to flexible children — those who will try anything. Teachers and specialists respond to students who are willing to try new (that is, the teachers') techniques. Dominant learners require the maximum of teacher attention at the beginning of the learning process, need to practice what they have learned before errors creep into the formula, need to feel a sense of commitment to a strategy because they will use it over and over.

But how about those lucky, experimental, flexible learners? They, too, can have profound learning difficulties, and in adolescents the difficulties can lead to intense anxieties and failure. It's true that flexible learners don't become locked into single systems. It's also true that they are ready to start exploring new problems with a minimum of information from teachers. And their exploration in marvelously exciting. They don't require all that initial teacher energy, so difficult to give when teachers have large classes. But, wait a minute! Aren't they the learners who are called "lazy" and "underachievers?" They are the ones who are accused (even by themselves) of "never finishing anything." The fact that a learning system is open to nuance and change has very little relationship to efficiency. They're ready to try anything—but which of those anythings is the best way? The dominant learner doesn't have that problem. When there is only one way it is, by definition, the most efficient way. So, flexible learners become immobilized. They are angry at themselves. "Everything was going well. Why didn't I just stick with it?" Eventually, especially if there has been a history of negative results, the flexible learner stops taking risks. Dominant vs. Flexible is a systemic definition. Unfortunately it is frequently converted to teaching perceptions such as "Stubborn" vs. "Lazy," or "Non-perceptive" vs. "Perfectionist."

In truth, most learners occupy a wide territory in the middle of the continuum, but learners-in-difficulty tend to gravitate towards the extremes. They are neither stubborn nor lazy, rebellious nor underachievers. On the contrary, they are caught in a vise of their own learning style. They don't perform the way we expect them to, so we try to cure their condition—which is incurable because it is not sick—just unique.

## PRE-SHORT TERM MEMORY ORGANIZATION

For most clinicians, one of the primary referral complaints is poor memory. There is, however, too much theoretical and experimental work in the field to justify such a superficial definition of learning problems. Unless a massive physical or emotional trauma can be identified, it is likely that human memory will fall within the organically healthy range.

What often distinguishes good from poor students is their ability to organize information before it is committed to short, and ultimately to long-term memory. Part of the assessment function, therefore, is to discover the ability of the student to identify auditory and visual clues which make such organization possible.

Indeed, many of the young adults with a history of learning difficulty complain of poor organization. They do not know how to listen to a lecture, they cannot take notes on their reading or classwork, they do not know how to prepare for exams, and *oh*! How they suffer under timed tests! How often we've heard parents of high school students say to us, "Why don't you tell him or her—that an extra hour of homework every night could make the difference?" No, we can't just tell a learner that an hour would make the difference—not if their systems are truly collecting rather than synthesizing information. Besides, there is no work that is harder than staring at a history assignment for three hours and deriving little or no benefit from it. Yet, most learners in difficulty cannot "juggle" the variables necessary in organizing the input of information.

Ultimately, almost all adults experiencing difficulty are convinced that their problems are outgrowths of "poor memory." In truth, however, learners in difficulty rarely get a chance to use their memory. Rather, they lose track of information because they see data in random, rather than organized terms. They don't recognize most of the clues which have become second nature to efficient students. But those clues are the building blocks of memory without which chunking cannot take place. And recognition of clues cannot exist unless there is a conscious identification of the sturcture of the problem. Yet, for many adults putting things down on paper or taking short cuts through the organization of information violates their ethics. Dominant learners can't take short cuts, and flexible ones have been told that they shouldn't. What a tangled web we weave when first we practice to retrieve!

There are at least three parallel systems which must operate before the organization of information can take place. The first is an awareness of time; the second is an awareness of score or measure; and, the third, is an awareness of the inherent structure surrounding the data. It is a rare learner in difficulty, indeed, who can command two, let alone all three, systems.

The time element is important because most learning tension is at least in part related to a sense of non-completion. When the learner's internal clock is not in harmony with the time parameters of a problem, it is usually a sign that part of the feedback system has broken down. The effects on the human organism are visible. They are exemplified by bunched neck muscles, tightening of tendons, and a fully panoply of nervous behaviors. Learners who are aware that they are close to completion are usually also able to parcel out their work. Learners who are unaware, tend to intensify their work as they feel the time slipping by. From a strategic point of view, however, the most familiar and/or most comfortable strategies are normally the first to be selected. Thus, the learner who is unaware of time is trying to pack what may be the waning moments of a problem with as much output as possible while utilizing strategies which are no longer preferred or fresh since the initial ones have already been used up. In short, loss of time control is most frequently accompanied by an increase in desperation.

Compounding the problem, distance from the initial source of information creates an additional strain on memory. "Have I tried this before?" "Did I write this already?" and other similar questions are symptoms of the loss of time control. All that the learner senses is time passing. There is no task pulse-rate which allows for appropriate distribution of energy or concentration.

Lack of control over the second system, measure or score, creates as much havoc as lack of time control. All learning related tasks have short- and long-term objectives. Many involve scores of one kind or another, and all involve some form of measurement. Learners under tension are extremely poor counters. They cannot juggle the objectives and the intellectual content of the task at the same time. In effect, they are forced to make a choice, and for most learners, the choice is content. It is content because we have been taught to measure our worth against our ability to handle intellectual or academic tasks. What is most fascinating is how many learners will work well beyond the time and score boundaries of a task because they are concentrating on content and do not recognize that they've actually completed the task. Ironically, these are frequently the students who are accused of being lazy because they do not seem to complete their work.

That doesn't seem to make sense. How can people who overwork be accused of underwork? The logic of the accusation is related to the large number of learning disabled adolescents and adults for whom seemingly poor memory is related to extreme flexibility in learning style. Flexible learners may try anything, but there is no guarantee they will be efficient. And it is efficiency which is the issue in pre-memory organization. On the one hand, flexible learners will *re*start a problem if they believe they have found a better strategy. On the other hand, they will concentrate on the manipulation of content to the exclusion of other feedback systems. To the observer, they are wasteful of time and energy and unaware that they've completed the task. At least that's the view for time-bound tasks. But, for open-ended tasks, they tend either to double back when they come across another problem-solving strategy, or persevere because they are inefficient organizers.

The final system, and for most people the most critical, relates to the inherent structure of the problem. The operative word is "structure," as distinguished from "content." Throughout, we've been discussing learners who may be perfectly able to deal with the content of problems. But they are operationally short-circuited either through misperception of their unique systems or disorganization. Learners in difficulty are extremely likely to overlook or mismanage patterns, sequences and structures which constitute the core of a problem. They do not automatically seek out the visual and auditory clues which can serve to focus the learner's attention on the structural elements of the task. Even when some of the clues are made explicit, they will not be transferred to the next similar problem. Often, the difficulties are related to developmental issues: poor auditory development, inefficient visual systems, and the like. But the problem goes far beyond hearing aids and eyeglasses. There is an internal disorganization or disassociation which prevents learners from segmenting problems. Many are gestalt problem-solvers. They are very likely to give correct answers to total tasks, but they cannot articulate, and frequently don't even know, how they arrived at the answers. In high school and college, such behavior is often greeted with great suspicion. "How is it possible for you to get the answer if you don't know how you did it?" Clinicians hear such complaints from students and their parents. It is usually connected with a plea to explain to the teachers that the work is honest. And indeed it is! The difficulty lies in the non-recognition of the visual and auditory clues which make the problem hang together.

In addition to the common complaint about poor memory, there is an accompanying concern about organizing notes. Adolescent and adult learners find it necessary to summarize classroom lectures, extended reading, library research, etc. Where organization is lacking, it is unlikely that the learner can deal with either the format of note-taking or determine the critical elements in an auditory or visual presentation. Reviewing the notes of learners in difficulty is often tantamount to reading full verbatims.

Organizing notes is not the same as writing verbatims. Learners do the first; tape recorders do the second. So learners in trouble become tape recorders because they are so sure that they are not learners. They are sent to basic skills courses where they are taught to take notes. The trouble is that you have to take notes in order to learn how to take notes.

The process of note-taking is the same as the process of organization. One requires the ability to categorize auditory input, and the other the ability to categorize visual input. More importantly, both are necessary elements in the expansion of memory.

Students who do not know how close they are to completion, who have lost track of score and objective, or who cannot organize incoming data, either give up or live with nervous tension. Their internal operation is a well-kept secret. Are they brilliant problem-solvers? Maybe, but we rarely get to see their work—only their answers. And those answers can be partially, or totally, incorrect. They don't know how good they are. We don't know how good they are, and we are forced to evaluate the smallest part of their thinking process, namely, output, because we and they are locked out of the greater part of that process, namely, inference and logic.

## CLOSURE

Another necessary issue for students is the ability to work with negative, or missing information. Many learners have inordinate difficulty organizing data unless all the pieces of the "intellectual puzzle" are directly present. Since many of our earliest teaching techniques involve the manipulation of incomplete data frames, such assessment is particularly important. Students who have difficulty dealing with a void in language or information have usually become identified as "slow learners," "poor readers," "careless arithmeticians," etc. For many of these students, the difficulty does not lie in the content but, rather, in the method of production. Although they are capable of dealing with complex ideas and relationships, they require linguistic and visual closure. As in the other two assessment issues, the implications for teaching systems are quite powerful, as they are for assumptions about the learner's intelligence and development of self-image.

It is all too easy to assume that because content is simple, the learner should know how to solve a problem. Where the learner's system requires closure, the content doesn't even come into play until the format of the problem-statement is perceived. Consequently, the assessment procedures should focus on the techniques for recognizing the need for system closure.

The issue of closure is particularly poignant where logical or inferential systems are involved. All too often we correlate the ability to deal with negative information with a high level of intelligence. SATs, Miller Analogies, Number Lines, and many other procedures require the learner to infer a pattern. When that pattern is mathematical, or linguistic in nature, it is necessary to manipulate an entire set of data internally. Where the learner requires closure before a problem-solving process can be triggered, such internal manipulation is almost impossible.

For such learners, many school-related and job-related tasks become horror stories. Before the learner can attempt a solution to the problem, the data base must be completed. As a result, the learners add pieces of data which, from their perspective, serve to "fill up the holes" in the material. Unfortunately, that very process changes the nature of the problem. Thus, their answers seem incorrect, bizarre, or inconsequential. If, for example, a learner is asked to work out a pattern of geometric numbers (1 2 4 __ __) the expected answers are 8 and 16. The learner requiring closure, however, is likely to respond with a 3 and a 5. Both answers are essentially correct from the point of view of solving the problem of the data because the moment the number 3 has been placed between numbers 2 and 4, the objective of the problem has been shifted.

But the difficulty is that teachers and supervisors place a high value on the type of analytic thinking that leads to a response of "8 and 16." They give a concomitantly low value to the response of "3 and 5" since, from their perspective, it makes the entire problem overly simple. Such learners, however, have a high capacity for dealing with masses of information at the same time. Their drive for closure can be an exceptionally useful skill in areas that require servicing or repair, whether it be physical, social or mechanical. We like our surgeons to recognize when "something is missing." We like accountants to be responsive to total systems, and to fill in missing numbers. We just don't like it in the classroom. But it is in the classroom that closure-oriented students spend most of their time. If they don't get a reputation for being wrong, then they do get one for being dull or boring. But neither perception is accurate.

Systemic learning responses don't have any value — they just exist. It is we humans who impute a morality or ethic to what are truly organic ways of functioning. The learner who requires closure can do brilliant and exciting work if all of the materials are there. One would hardly accuse a Van Gogh or a Michelangelo of being dull or inconsequential. And yet, every muscle must be drawn or hacked out of stone, and every shade of color must be explored. Brilliance has nothing to do with how our systems function, but the ends to which we devote them.

Recently we presented a workshop to 350 teachers in a large district in one of our more romantic states, we on the stage, they in the audience. We asked them to track a series of triangles through a maze of randomly distributed symbols. They could see, hear, and communicate with each other. There were the circlers, and the checkers, and the dotters, and the counters. The dominant learners circled, checked, dotted or counted each triangle. They got faster and they got better—but they did not get different. The flexible learners sometimes circled, sometimes checked, sometimes dotted, sometimes counted, sometimes got better—but always got different.

The dominant learners looked at the flexible learners who were connecting groups, circling batches, checking pages, and said: You're cheating! The flexible learners watched the dominant learners, check, check, check, dot, dot, dot — and said, "You're not listening to the instructions."

They were both right. Dominant learners have systems whose receptors are different from flexible learners. They hear differently and produce differently, because they really learn differently. So why do we continue to teach them the same way?

## TWO STRATEGIES FOR TEACHING THE ADOLESCENT
## WITH READING/LEARNING PROBLEMS

The focus in this section will be on two teaching strategies. The first is for a very specific type of learner and, therefore, is a very specific strategy. The second is more comprehensive and intended for use by content area teachers, at the secondary level, to facilitate learning by students with reading/learning problems who have been mainstreamed.

Our first concern, then, is with the "impulsive responder." This is the student who gives an answer when asked either orally or by way of ditto sheet or workbook. In most cases, the answer is not close to the one desired, but it is usually immediate. Any elementary teacher, secondary resource teacher, or reading lab teacher is familiar with this student. He or she is the one who frustrates us when we attempt to determine a pattern of responses in order to prescribe an appropriate educational program. Our response is usually that there is no pattern — that the learner does not appear to be using any strategy other than *guessing*.

However, our work indicates that the student is, in fact, using a strategy to solve a problem—at least in the beginning—but, his or her perception of the problem is not the same as that of the teacher. For example, the standard approach used in reading instruction in the elementary school is read a passage — answer questions. If the child answers incorrectly, the teacher usually says something (or does something) to reinforce him or her for participating, then moves on to another student for the correct response or provides the correct response. In other words, the student is learning that responding is important, not the response or how the response was derived. Therefore, the "impulsive responder" perceives the problem as one of providing an answer before "all eyes" are focused on him or her and without delaying the "flow of the lesson." Thus, the strategy is to answer quickly. By junior high school, though, the occasional laughter and teasing from peers has shaped the response to "I don't know." "I don't know" and the earlier "guessing" responses do provide us with information for prescribing an educational program. The learner is saying something more than "I don't know" the answer; the learner is saying "I don't know" how to go about finding the answer.

We have found that by teaching these learners some very specific steps for thinking through a problem, they can be successful in solving the problem as perceived by the teacher. However, we have also found that the teacher must follow a fairly structured procedure when teaching a strategy to insure maximum benefits of the strategy to the student. To illustrate this, the following discussion will outline the procedure to be used when teaching a strategy for finding main idea to a student.

1. The first step is to motivate the student. With adolescents and adults, this is done by providing them with the rationale for learning the strategy. They need to know that what they are being asked to learn is not something else to confuse them, but rather something to help them clear up some of the confusion they are already facing. This was done at a community college, with a class of nursing students (Huhn 1977) as follows:

When I analyzed your test results and found that many of you were having difficulty with main idea, I wondered why. Then I recalled that your instruction in main idea consisted of the following. First, you were told that the main idea was the most important thing in the passage, or what the passage was all about. Then, later, when your teachers knew that you were learning how to write paragraphs in English class, you were told that the main idea is the topic sentence. At the same time, to teach topic sentences, the English teacher was saying that the topic sentence is the main idea. However, to get one you needed the other—and it seems that no one was providing much direction for that task. Therefore, I am going to teach you some very specific steps for finding the main idea of a passage. After you have been successful in applying these steps, then, you may develop a different strategy or modify this strategy, but at least you will know one strategy for finding the main idea.

2. The second step is to provide the students with the steps to the strategy. This is done most effectively by both giving them a handout with the steps on them and by going over them orally as follows:

The strategy for finding main idea, which I am going to share with you, is called hypothesis testing and has the following steps.
1. Read the first sentence and say, "This is the main idea."
2. Read the second sentence and ask, "Is there anything new or different stated here?"
3. If there is, add it to the first sentence; if there is not, hold on to your original statement.
4. Continue this process with each sentence.
5. You will complete the task when you have either found the statement that summarizes all that is in the paragraph or you will have developed that statement from parts of other sentences.

3. The third step is to model the strategy. The student(s) need to see how the process actually works. This is accomplished by the teacher taking a passage and talking through the steps in order that the student(s) can hear the process while they look at the passage.

4. The fourth step is guided practice. Both the teacher and the student(s) do a passage. The teacher's role here is to reinforce good decisions about "new and different" and to correct poor decisions through discussion.

5. The final step is for the student to apply the strategy independently. This step should utilize content area textbooks. Since the student is working silently, the teacher obviously cannot determine if all of the steps are being used. However, that is not important now. The only thing that is important at this point is success. If the student is being successful

(finding the main idea), the objective has been accomplished; if not, then more modeling and guided practice is required.

To reiterate, we have found that many students simply do not know how to begin when given a task. With these learners, teaching a strategy for thinking through a task provides them with a map for traversing the learning maze. We have developed strategies for such tasks as: identifying cause-effect relationships, recognizing order, making comparisons or contrasts, etc. Teachers can develop their own strategies by following a few simple steps:

1. Stop and think, "How do I do it?"
2. Write down how you do it.
3. Convert that narrative to simply stated steps that meet two criteria:
   a. as few steps as possible.
   b. enough steps to insure a high probability of success.

Our second concern is with the reading/learning disabled youth who is mainstreamed into regular education content area classes. Not only does that student have problems reading and learning from textbooks, but there are other students in the class who are having difficulty with that task. Even the teacher has become frustrated, because he or she, not having been trained to accommodate the various reading abilities and disabilities found in a normal secondary subject area class, has given up on using the textbook as a source of information for the student and settled into the unexciting and unrewarding routine of telling the students what they are supposed to know and testing them over what they have been told.

Through assistance from state grants, we have developed and researched an instructional model that:

1. Allows for the various abilities and disabilities of the students.
2. Uses the textbook as a source of information to be used by the student.
3. Recognizes that content area teachers are not reading teachers, but can be facilitators of reading comprehension.

The model is called Reading To Learn (RTL) and the lessons developed to implement the model are Reading To Learn Lessons (RTLL). Due to a shortage of time and space, it is not possible to discuss the model in great detail; however, it will be outlined here and further inquiries should be addressed to the author.

The RTL (Huhn 1979, 1980) has two major components: Informal Screening Test (IST) and the Reading To Learn Lesson (RTLL). The IST is for the purpose of identifying which students are independent readers, instructional readers, and frustrational readers relative to the textbook to be used.

The traditional approach has been to identify at what grade level a student is independent, instructional and frustrational; however, we felt that that kind of information was of little value to a content area teacher since he or she usually does not have a wide range of textbooks to use. Also, we chose to differentiate between learning to read, the responsibility of a reading teacher, and reading to learn, the responsibility of the content area teacher. For the first, the traditional approach provides valuable information; for the latter, the IST provides practical information.

The IST is developed by using five passages from the text of between 100 and 250 words and constructing five questions about each passage. An attempt is made to develop equal amounts of five types of questions: fact, inference, cause-effect, sequence and vocabulary from context. However, if the book being used does not accommodate certain types of questions, others are increased so that there are five questions for each passage for a total of 25 questions. The IST, then, assists the teacher in grouping the students for implementation of the RTLL.

The RTLL has six components: Objectives, Readiness, Reading Guides, Follow-Up, and Evaluation. The RTLL is developed before teaching a chapter or unit and functions as a teacher's guide—developed by the teacher for facilitating comprehension.

### Objectives

Objectives are written by the teacher after he or she has surveyed the chapter (unit) to be taught. The teacher simply determines what the students should know and be able to do at the completion of the RTLL. The function of the objectives is quite simple—to serve as a self-check to insure that what the students are being held responsible for they did, in fact, have an opportunity to learn.

Objectives should be developed at the literal, inferential, and generalization levels. In other words, students should be expected to know some facts, do something with those facts, and finally to generalize or apply what they have learned to a context other than the chapter.

### Readiness

We have found that at the secondary level, readiness is as important as it is at the elementary level, but often ignored. Huhn (1980) discusses the effect of readiness as a variable in subject area reading. To summarize, it is fairly widely stated that two factors which seem to influence comprehension significantly are what the reader already knows about the subject to be read and the purpose for reading. Readiness addresses the first.

Secondary students have had experience—personal out of school experiences and previous school learning experiences. But, all too often, they approach each reading/learning experience as a separate, distinct, isolated learning experience. Thus, instead of using what they already know to help them learn, they process the new information rotely, minimizing the probability of retention and recall.

Thus, the role of the teacher is to develop a readiness activity that will cause the student to recall what he or she already knows (relevant to what is to be learned) and thus, utilize that conceptual structure to internalize the new information. Also, the activity should not only be conceptually relevant, but it should be interesting. There is no reason why learning at the secondary level cannot be fun and interesting as it is in lower elementary school.

## Reading Guides

The Reading Guide component is used to establish purpose for reading and to adjust that purpose according to the needs of the students. Many times in a secondary content area classroom the following directions can be heard. "Read Chapter 2 tonight; we will discuss it in class tomorrow." While conducting teacher workshops on the RTLL, we suggest to teachers that those instructions are similar to, "You all study the local telephone directory this morning; this afternoon we are going to ask you for some phone numbers." In other words, only teacher knows what is going to be discussed. The students know only that it is probably somewhere in Chapter 2.

What do the students do? The independent readers read Chapter 2 and may answer some to most of the questions. The instructional readers may read Chapter 2 and remember things that they already knew or that they thought were funny, strange, interesting, or unusual. The frustrational students, overwhelmed by the task, gave up and did something else more rewarding (he never does his homework!).

What does the teacher do? The teacher comes to class with a well developed, inspired outline for the purpose of directing the discussion towards high levels of cognitive thinking only to find out that only a few students can participate at only the lowest levels. So, in frustration, he or she bemoans the fact the elementary teachers never taught the students to read, and the parents don't make students do homework, then proceeds to review what was in the chapter so that the students can copy it in their notebooks to study for Friday's test.

Instead of the above scenario, we suggest that when the chapter is assigned, the students be given reading guides to complete, which will prepare them for the discussion. The reading guides are developed at three levels: (1) literal, (2) inferential, and (3) generalization. They consist of questions which the students answer while reading. Independent readers use level 3, instructional readers use levels 2 and 3, and frustrational readers use levels 1, 2, and 3. This does not mean that the more problems you have—the more work you have; but rather, the more problems you have—the more guidance you receive.

## Discussion

The Discussion component consists of two parts. First, the teacher discusses the chapter using the Reading Guides. Secondly, the teacher can now teach—doing whatever he or she does effectively (modeling, lecture, demonstrations, movies, etc.). Too often, teachers attempt to teach before students are "ready" to learn. After Readiness and Reading Guides, the teacher can teach.

## Follow-Up

Follow-Up is another component that deviates somewhat from the traditional approach. For example, traditionally if a teacher has two weeks to cover a chapter, the teacher and the class do things together until the end of the two weeks. Then the students take a test, and everyone finds out how much they learned. However, in the RTLL, the teacher would pause after discussion and classify the students as "on task" or "not on task" and assign the appropriate follow-up activities.

The determination of "on task" or "not on task" is made by daily quizzes, class discussion, informal evaluation, or any combination of these. "On task" simply means the student seems to be understanding at this point, while "not on task" means the student is having some difficulties.

Follow-up activities then, are assigned to allow the "on task" students to extend comprehension; while providing the "not on task" additional opportunity and alternative approaches to get "on task." We have used "on task" to represent minimum competency or a "C" grade. Thus, follow-up would provide those who have achieved minimums the opportunity to go beyond, and those who have not the opportunity to do so.

### Evaluation

The final component is Evaluation. It is simply a plan that the teacher develops before beginning the unit which outlines what components will be assessed and how much weight each carries in determining the unit grade.

In conclusion, then, we have discussed two strategies. The first was a very specific strategy for a very specific type of learner. The second was a much more comprehensive model to be used by content area teachers, for facilitating comprehension in textbook reading, not only for the learning/reading disabled student, but for the entire class. Thus, the content teacher is not being required to do something "special" for the learning disabled adolescent (making him or her even more obvious and the teacher's task more complex), but rather something that should be of benefit to the entire class — making both learning and teaching more exciting.

### REFERENCES

Huhn, R. H. "A Study of the Effect of Reading-Learning Skills Instruction on Failure in Nursing." Doctoral dissertation, University of Missouri–Kansas City, Kansas City, Mo., 1977.

——. "Final Report: In-Service Training for Regular Teachers to Meet the Needs of Students with Language/Learning Disabilities." McNeese State University, Lake Charles, La., 1979.

——. "Training Manual: Reading to Learn (An Individualized Content Area Reading Model)." McNeese State University, Lake Charles, La., 1980.

——. "Readiness as a Variable Influencing Comprehension in Content-Area Reading at the Secondary Level: A Cognitive View." *Learning Disabilities Quarterly* 3 (1980): 29–33.

# WRITTEN LANGUAGE PROBLEMS

# 15

## Written Language Disorders in Learning Disabled College Students

### A Preliminary Report

*Susan A. Vogel and Mary Ross Moran*

T HE NUMBER of learning disabled (LD) adults with written language disorders has been estimated to be between 80 and 90 percent (Blalock 1981). Written language disorders in LD adults include limited productivity, deficits in punctuation and capitalization, in spelling, in sentence structure, in diction, in organization and development, and, of course, in legibility. Although limited research has been done in the area of written language disorders in LD adults, some research has been done on written language deficits in children.

The major research in the development of written language in normal and handicapped children was done by Myklebust (1965, 1973). Among the groups of handicapped children he studied were reading disabled, dyslexic, and moderately and severely learning disabled between the ages of seven and 17. Myklebust compared the written language samples of nondisabled and disabled children using the Picture Story Language Test (Myklebust 1965). The reading disability group was more severely deficient in written language than the dyslexic and LD groups (p < .001 on total words, total sentences, words per sentence, syntax, and abstract-concrete scales). The dyslexic group was significantly deficient on total words and sentences at most age levels and on syntax at ages nine and eleven. For both groups of LD children, performance on the syntax scale was the most seriously deficient, with performance on the abstract-concrete scale a close second. No significant difference was found in either subgroup of LD children on total sentences.

Poteet (1979) also used the Picture Story Language Test with a group of LD and non-LD children. He found, among other results, that the children made many more punctuation errors than their peers, but they did not differ significantly on the syntax scale. Hermreck (1979) found similar deficits in LD children using Poteet's Inventory of Written Expression (1980). Though differences were not statistically significant,

211

Hermreck also reported that the LD children seemed to write syntactically less complex structures than their nondisabled peers.

Poplin, Gray, Larsen, Banikowski, and Mehring (1980) compared groups of LD and achieving children in grades 3–8 on the Test of Written Language (Hammill and Larsen 1978). This measure yields five subscores and a total score, called the Written Language Quotient (WLQ). The WLQ plus three subscores using contrived sentences — Spelling, Word Usage, and Style—were significantly lower for the LD group at all grade levels. Vocabulary and Thematic Maturity, analyzed from an elicited story, were also significantly lower for the LD group in grades 7 and 8.

Moran (1981) compared the written language characteristics of 26 LD students with 26 low-achieving (LA) and 26 achieving (ACH) students in grades 7–10, using an elicited paragraph and analytic scoring. Spelling was the only feature significantly higher in the LA group. The ACH group earned significantly higher scores on Conventions, Spelling, Mechanics, and Mean Morphemes per T-unit (MMTU). However, LD and ACH students did not differ in variety of sentence types or word types, nor in percentage of complex T-units.

Similar deficits and strengths were reported by McGill-Franzen (1979). Her seventeen-year-old LD subject demonstrated serious problems with spelling and mechanics, but also produced mature syntactic structures.

No empirical data are available on the written language of LD adults, but several clinical observations have pinpointed some of the same problems found by Hermreck, Myklebust, Poplin et al., and Poteet; i.e., some of these problems seem to persist into adulthood. In the area of mechanics, punctuation is described as particularly problematic for LD adults (Herbert and Czerniejewski 1976). According to Blalock (1981), knowledge of the rules of punctuation and capitalization was severely limited for some LD adults, while others experienced problems at the level of monitoring errors. Critchley (1973) suggested that one way they circumvent these difficulties is by using punctuation marks sparingly to hide their incomplete grasp of the rules of punctuation. Cordoni (1979) reported that the lowest subscore on the Peabody Individual Achievement Test (Dunn and Markwardt, 1970) was on the Spelling subtest. Critchley (1973) observed that the ex-dyslexic is an inaccurate speller in spontaneous writing as well as on standardized spelling tests. LD adults themselves list spelling difficulties more frequently than any other deficit (Blalock 1981).

In addition to deficits in mechanics and spelling, Blalock (1981), Critchley (1973), and Herbert and Czerniejewski (1976) noted that LD adults also have difficulty writing complete sentences and varying sentence construction. Critchley (1973) observed that ex-dyslexics wrote sentences of approximately the same length, and their writing was stylistically unsatisfying and monotonous. Problems between sentences as well as within sentences were also observed. Herbert and Czerniejewski (1976) described problems of coherence between sentences and attributed this problem to insufficient use of transitional words and phrases. Cohesion between paragraphs and the lack of an overall organizational structure characterized their larger pieces of writing (Herbert and Czerniejewski, 1976).

Lastly, Critchley (1973) observed that ex-dyslexics use fewer multisyllabic words than their non-dyslexic peers. He attributed this difference to a limitation in the dyslexics' word knowledge. Related to this aspect of word choice is his hypothesis that the ratio of adjectives to verbs will differ in the writing of the ex-dyslexic as compared to the non-dyslexic. Herbert and Czerniejewski (1976) also found limitations in variety and agreement of adjectives and adverbs in the written language of the LD college students who comprised their sample.

The purpose of this pilot study was to provide preliminary empirical data to determine whether the observations of Blalock, Cordoni, Critchley, and Herbert and Czerniejewski could be confirmed when both holistic and analytic scoring were applied to elicited writing samples. The following questions were addressed:

1. Do LD college students differ significantly from entering freshmen in their overall writing ability and in their organization?
2. Do LD students differ significantly from their non-disabled peers in number and correctness of punctuation marks and capitalization, in correctness of spelling, sentence structure and usage, in syntactic complexity, and in word selection?

## METHOD

### Subjects

The eight LD subjects who participated in the pilot study were enrolled in a college program for LD women at Barat College, a small, four-year, liberal arts college. Most had been identified as LD prior to their entering this special program. Their Verbal or Performance IQ based on the Wechsler Adult Intelligence Scale fell within the average or above-average range. Their essays were compared holistically with essays written by 226 first-year students who met the admission criteria of the college and analytically with a random sample drawn from the 226. All of the LD subjects in this study were Caucasian native English speakers, and all were from middle-class and upper-middle class backgrounds. Writing ability of comparison groups represented the full range of ability.

## Procedures

All new degree-candidates participate in the college-wide assessment program which includes writing an expository essay on an assigned topic. The essays were scored in two ways.

### Holistic scoring

Holistic scoring was originally developed by the Educational Testing Service (who coined the term) as a method of rating a piece of writing impressionistically, quickly, and reliably. An essential ingredient of holistic scoring is that each essay is read by at least two trained readers. Barat College developed its own scoring procedures in which the total score is a sum of four subscores in the areas of mechanics, organization, development, and style (Vogel 1980). A four-point scale was selected, and verbal descriptions of each score within each area were used by the readers. Each essay is scored by four English faculty who are unaware of the author's group membership. The subscores range from one to four and the total scores from 4 to 16 (the lower the score, the better the writing). Means on the four subscores and total scores were calculated for each essay based on four reachers' scores. Reliability for total scores, estimated using Cronbach's alpha and the scores assigned by the four readers, fluctuated between .73 and .86 (Vogel 1980). Consensuality among readers was determined by correlating the essay scores of each reader with an estimate of the true mean score computed by taking the mean of the four scores. All four readers' correlations were very high (p < .001 in all but one instance), indicative of a very high degree of consensuality as well as reliability. Essays written by LD students were compared to those written by first-year students using the t test. Alpha level was set at .05.

*Analytic Scoring*

Selected scoring procedures of an experimental version of the Diagnostic Evaluation of Expository Paragraphs (DEEP), developed by Moran (1981) were employed. This scoring procedure provides an in-depth analysis of writing skills by assessing mechanics, spelling, conventions, complexity and variety of sentence structure, complexity of T-units, and word selection. Moran reported temporal and alternate-form reliabilities for the DEEP scoring system based upon scores from two samples for 27 students in grades 7 through 10. Reliabilities ranged from 88 percent to 100 percent on three of four subscores. The fourth subscore, Mechanics, yielded low frequencies on scorable items so that a difference of only one item between samples results in placement of subjects into different performance ranges. Though the reliabilities were 38 percent and 42 percent for temporal and alternate-form tests respectively, the measure may not be as unstable as it appears. MMTU, which does not yield a percentage figure for placement into performance categories, was tested by correlation (r = .56).

The DEEP scoring procedure was applied to the eight essays written by the LD college students and ten essays drawn randomly from those written by students who met the college admissions criteria. A maximum of 25 T-units was scored by a research assistant, unaware of group membership of authors, and trained in the DEEP scoring procedure at the Kansas Institute. Group mean scores were compared statistically using the t test and separate variance estimate for unequal groups (df = 16). Alpha level was set at .05.

## RESULTS

### Holistic Scoring

The LD students' essays were significantly poorer in overall quality than the essays written by the 226 entering students, (t = 3.32, p < .002). Not only were the total mean scores significantly different, but Table 15.1 shows that the essay that received the best score in the LD group was poorer than the average essay written by first-year students.

On all four subscores there was a significant difference favoring the first-year students. The LD students differed on the style subscore at the p < .002 level, on organization at the p < .01 level, and on the development and the mechanics subscores at the p < .05 level.

## TABLE 15.1
### Holistic* Scores on Written Language Samples for LD Students and Entering Freshmen

| Group | N | Mechanics | | | | Organization | | | | Development | | | | Style | | | | Total | | | |
|---|---|---|---|---|---|---|---|---|---|---|---|---|---|---|---|---|---|---|---|---|---|
| | | Mean | Range | SD | t-Values | Mean | Range | SD | t-Values | Mean | Range | SD | t-Values | Mean | Range | SD | t-Values | Mean | Range | SD | t-Values |
| LD | 7 | 2.75 | 2.25 to 3.00 | .29 | 2.58 | 2.64 | 2.00 to 3.00 | .35 | 2.87 | 2.61 | 2.00 to 3.25 | .45 | 2.30 | 2.75 | 2.25 to 3.00 | .29 | 3.30 | 10.75 | 9.25 to 12.00 | .87 | 3.32 |
| Entering Freshmen | 226 | 2.21† | 1.25 to 4.00 | .55 | | 2.06‡ | 1.25 to 4.00 | .53 | | 2.17† | 1.50 to 4.00 | .50 | | 2.16‖ | 1.00 to 4.00 | .47 | | 8.59‖ | 5.20 to 16.00 | 1.71 | |

*The lower the score, the better the writing.
†Significant at p < .05
‡Significant at p < .01
‖Significant at p < .002

TABLE 15.2

**Mean Scores on Written Language Samples for Two Groups**

| Measure | Group | N | Mean | Standard Deviation | t | Level of Significance |
|---|---|---|---|---|---|---|
| Total Points Punctuation | Controls | 10 | 153.50 | 55.98 | 2.37 | .031 |
| | LD | 8 | 102.50 | 34.43 | | |
| % Correct Punctuation | Controls | 10 | 85.30 | 9.95 | 2.70 | .019 |
| | LD | 8 | 68.63 | 15.04 | | |
| Total Points Capitalization | Controls | 10 | 138.00 | 50.51 | 2.76 | .015 |
| | LD | 8 | 85.63 | 28.96 | | |
| % Correct Capitalization | Controls | 10 | 93.20 | 6.37 | 2.26 | .050 |
| | LD | 8 | 80.50 | 14.80 | | |
| Spelling | Controls | 10 | 98.90 | .57 | 3.67 | .008 |
| | LD | 8 | 95.25 | 2.77 | | |
| Run-on's | Controls | 10 | 7.70 | 9.01 | −1.41 | .184 |
| | LD | 8 | 15.13 | 12.52 | | |
| Total Points Word Selection | Controls | 10 | 641.00 | 203.80 | .91 | .379 |
| | LD | 8 | 576.88 | 78.60 | | |
| Subject/Predicate Agreement | Controls | 10 | 32.60 | 9.48 | 2.22 | .042 |
| | LD | 8 | 24.50 | 5.86 | | |
| Total Points Sentences | Controls | 10 | 327.00 | 103.02 | 2.49 | .050 |
| | LD | 8 | 212.50 | .88.28 | | |
| % of Complex Sentences | Controls | 10 | 42.90 | 16.52 | 2.23 | .040 |
| | LD | 8 | 27.50 | 12.75 | | |
| % of Compound and Compound/Complex Sentences | Controls | 10 | 53.10 | 17.58 | 2.21 | .042 |
| | LD | 8 | 35.50 | 16.06 | | |
| Total Points T-Units | Controls | 10 | 409.00 | 104.37 | 1.73 | .200 |
| | LD | 8 | 330.50 | 82.39 | | |
| % of Complex T-Units | Controls | 10 | 49.10 | 16.82 | 1.65 | .124 |
| | LD | 8 | 34.13 | 20.89 | | |

## Analytic Scoring

The LD students scored significantly lower than the randomly selected students on mechanics, spelling, subject/predicate number agreement, total sentence points, percentage of complex sentences, and percentage of compound and compound/complex sentences. Although the LD group means were lower on Word Selection, total T-unit points, and the percent of complex T-units, the differences were not significant.

### Mechanics

LD adults used significantly fewer punctuation marks ($X = 102.50$ vs. $X = 153.50$, $p < .031$) than did the random sample of college students, confirming Critchley's (1973) observation. Not only did they use fewer periods, apostrophes, hyphens, and commas, but they more frequently used them incorrectly than did their peers. The LD students used 69 percent of the punctuation marks correctly as compared to 85 percent for their peers ($p < .019$). A similar discrepancy was found in the number of times the rules for capitalization of the first word in the sentence and for proper names were employed and for the percent of times they were employed correctly. In both cases, the performance of the LD students was significantly poorer (80 percent accuracy as compared to 93 percent, $p < .050$).

### Spelling

The number of correctly spelled words was divided by the total number of words in the essay to determine what percent of the words was correctly spelled. Although the percentages do not seem highly discrepant, 95.25 percent correct for LD students and 98.60 percent for their peers, the difference is significant at $p < .008$ level. It is interesting to note that seven out of the ten randomly selected students scored either 99 or 100 percent accuracy in spelling. (The remaining scores were 96 percent and 98 percent correct.) In contrast, in the LD group only one out of eight received a 99 percent and one a 98 percent correct; all the rest scored lower. Clearly, spelling ability remains a serious deficiency in LD adults, even in spontaneous writing in which they are free to avoid writing words that they cannot spell.

*Sentence Structure and Usage*

Difficulty writing correctly punctuated sentences is clearly indicated by the finding that, on the average, 15 percent of the sentences written by LD students were run-ons, as compared to 8 percent for the randomly selected group. Moreover, in the LD group, six out of the eight students, or 75 percent, wrote some run-on sentences, and the percent of run-on sentences in the sample ranged from nine to 38. In the randomly selected group, only 50 percent wrote run-on sentences, and for those that did, the range was from 7 percent to 23 percent. Though the difference in mean percent of run-on sentences was not statistically significant, difficulty in writing correctly punctuated sentences is a problem that does persist in three-fourths of the college-age LD students who comprised this sample and to a lesser degree in half of the contrast group.

Accuracy of usage is reflected in subject/predicate agreement. Students were given positive points for correct subject/predicate agreement and negative points for errors. The mean number of positive points in subject/predicate agreement in the contrast group exceeded the mean number in the LD group ($X = 32.60$ vs. $X = 24.50$, $p < .042$).

Another indication of correct usage that goes beyond the sentence level was the writer's consistent use of person throughout the essay. Two out of eight LD students remained consistent, while seven out of ten randomly selected students did so. Problems of coherence between sentences described by Herbert and Czerniejewski (1976) could perhaps be related to this inconsistency.

*Syntactic complexity*

Sentence structure complexity was reflected in five subscores: total sentence points, total T-unit points, the percent of correct complex sentences, compound and compound/complex sentences, and complex T-units. Significantly greater syntactic complexity was indicated by the subscores on three out of the five categories, favoring the contrast group. On the two subscores that were based on T-unit analysis, the differences favored the random sample but were not significant. While 25 percent (two out of eight) of the LD students wrote complex T-units more than 50 percent of the time, in the random sample more than half of the students (six out of ten) wrote complex T-units more than 50 percent of the time. When complexity of T-units is considered, i.e., without sentence-boundary markers of capitalization and punctuation, the discrepancy between the groups diminishes considerably.

Examination of Table 15.3 shows that both groups used all sentence constructions, but for the LD group the highest frequency occurred for simple sentences, while for the contrast group more complex sentences than simple sentences occurred. Approximately 50 percent of LD students' sentences were simple, as compared to 34 percent for the contrast group, and for each of the more complex sentence types, the mean percentages for the random sample were higher. These findings thus confirm the observation that LD adults have less variety and complexity in sentence construction.

Table 15.4 shows that the median scores for the mean morphemes per T-unit for the two groups were practically identical. This finding in conjunction with that reported above regarding the lack of significant difference on subscores for total T-unit points and the percentage of complex T-units indicates that when sentence-boundary markers were disregarded , the LD group's written language was not significantly different in syntactic complexity from their peers.

TABLE 15.3

**Percentage of Five Sentence Types,
Run-on's, and Fragments for Two Groups**

|  | LD Mean | Controls Mean | LD Median | Controls Median |
|---|---|---|---|---|
| Simple | 49.3 | 33.6 | 54.5 | 24 5 |
| Compound | 1.4 | 4.0 | .2 | .5 |
| Complex | 27.5 | 42.9 | 25.5 | 39.0 |
| Compound/Complex | 8.0 | 10.4 | .5 | 6.5 |
| Complex and Compound/Complex | 35.5 | 53.1 | 35.5 | 58.0 |
| Run-on's | 15.1 | 7.7 | 16.5 | .5 |
| Fragments | 1.1 | .8 | .6 | .4 |

TABLE 15.4

**Comparison of Median Scores on Mean
Morphemes per T-Unit for Two Groups**

| Groups | N | Median | Range | U Value | Level of Significance |
|---|---|---|---|---|---|
| LD | 8 | 16.51 | 12.64–23.45 | 37.0 | .8286 |
| Non-LD | 10 | 17.05 | 11.73–21.91 | | |

*Word selection*

Although Table 15.1 shows that the difference on Total Points for Word Selection favoring the random sample was not significant, mean frequencies for the eight categories within Word Selection reveal that the randomly selected students used more adjectives, adverbs, participles, modals, and have/be auxiliaries than did the LD students, as shown in Table 15.5. This finding confirms the observations of Herbert and Czerniejewski (1976) regarding the presence of fewer descriptive words in the writings of LD adults as compared to their peers. However, two secondary verbs (infinitives and gerunds) were used more frequently by the LD students.

## DISCUSSION

This study confirms many of the observations made by clinicians in the past regarding the written language of LD adults. Clearly, LD adults are significantly deficient in overall writing ability and in mechanics, organization, development, and style as measured by holistic scoring procedures. In contrast to the expected outcome, the difference between the two groups on the mechanical aspects of writing was not as discrepant

TABLE 15.5

**Frequency of Word Classes for Two Groups**

|  | LD Mean | LD Median | Controls Mean | Controls Median |
|---|---|---|---|---|
| Adjectives | 24.5 | 24.5 | 31.6 | 26.5 |
| Adverbs | 18.5 | 13.5 | 21.5 | 22.0 |
| Secondary Verbs: Participles | 2.5 | 2.8 | 3.7 | 4.5 |
| Secondary Verbs: Gerunds | 2.3 | 1.5 | 1.5 | 1.1 |
| Secondary Verbs: Infinitives | 6.1 | 4.5 | 4.6 | 3.5 |
| Modal Auxiliaries | 5.0 | 4.0 | 5.3 | 5.0 |
| Have/Be Auxiliaries | 4.6 | 4.5 | 7.6 | 5.5 |
| Prepositions | 25.5 | 23.2 | 26.3 | 26.5 |
| Conjunctions | 7.9 | 7.5 | 10.1 | 9.5 |
| Determiners | 18.1 | 18.5 | 16.0 | 15.5 |

as on style and organization, perhaps because entering freshmen also experience difficulties in punctuation and capitalization. Style, which included varied sentence structure and word selection, differentiated between the groups at a higher level of significance than any other subscore. The holistic scoring thus confirms the results of analytic scoring. However, analytic scoring revealed strengths that had been masked by the abundance of spelling and mechanical errors.

The lack of significant differences in mean morphemes per T-unit is an unexpected finding of this preliminary study. Closer inspection of the ranges reported in Table 15.4 reveals that there is both a higher minimum and maximum MMTU score in the LD group than in the contrast group. Moran's (1981) results provide comparative data. She found no significant differences between the LD students and LA students on median MMTU scores, (MMTU of approximately 12.0), but highly significant differences between the LD students and ACH students (median of 12.3 and 15.0, respectively). Assuming the randomly selected college students and achieving high school students were drawn from the same population, MMTU increased by only two points. Is it possible that MMTU reaches a plateau in normally achieving adolescents, while MMTU in LD students continues to increase? If so, why? Or would results differ if LD college students were compared with a group limited to achieving college students? Lastly, are the LD college students who comprised this sample perhaps less disabled than Moran's sample?

The second unexpected finding was that the LD students did not differ significantly from the contrast group in percentage of complex T-units. This finding confirms Moran's (1981) results and indicates that when visual markers are disregarded the LD college students' writing is not significantly different in syntactic complexity from the randomly selected writers. In light of the questions raised above, this finding must be considered with cautious optimism. However, teachers should be on the alert for the presence of complex T-units so that they can recognize this "hidden" strength in LD students' written language and utilize this information in program planning. Teaching students how to punctuate complex T-units that they already know how to write in a task very different from sentence construction.

Lastly, the increased use of infinitives and gerunds by the LD writers would be easy to dismiss as an insignificant occurrence, especially because it contradicts expectations. Gerunds and infinitives are particularly complex structures and rarely used, even by average 12th-graders (Hunt 1977). However, our findings provide corroboration for those of McGill-Franzen (1979) who found that not only did the LD adolescent whom she studied write approximately the same number of mean words per T-unit, mean clauses per T-unit, and mean words per clause as his non-disabled peers, but he also used two gerund phrases. The syntactic maturity demonstrated by that LD adolescent, the LD students in Moran's study, and the LD college students in this study warrants further investigation. Because T-unit analysis can transcend the punctuation and capitalization constraints imposed by sentence scoring, it could be a sensitive tool in future studies.

## LIMITATIONS

These findings must be considered in light of the selectivity and screening that are part of the admission procedures to both Barat and to this special program for LD women. The sample may not be representative of the general population of LD adults, and these findings must be considered as applying only to this small, select, female sample. Moreover, the number of LD individuals which comprised the group was very small and may not be representative of college-bound LD women. This study and the findings reported must, therefore, be considered as explorative.

## IMPLICATIONS

This preliminary study has perhaps raised more questions than it has answered. However, we have found that LD college students have many writing problems as well as strengths. There is a need for careful and complete assessment of writing ability, including T-unit analysis in order to determine each student's strengths as well as deficits. Holistic scoring, coupled with the DEEP procedures, should be useful in addressing some of the critical questions raised by this study.

We can assume that some, if not many, LD college students know how ho write complete and complex T-units, but they do not know how to punctuate them, nor to recognize when a sentence is a run-on. Remediation for 75 percent of LD college students may have to begin at the level of sentence sense and punctuation.

Lastly, organization of longer pieces of writing will not just "happen." Formal instruction and practice in paragraph writing in a variety of modes and organizational models should be provided. Attention to the pre-writing stage with emphasis on thinking, planning, discussion, and outlining is a prerequisite to improving organization and development in written language. Through an intensive, one-to-one, individually designed program of instruction based on in-depth assessment such as is provided by DEEP, it is hoped that the LD college student can move from dependence to independence in accomplishing this last hurdle in the hierarchy of language learning.

## REFERENCES

Blalock, Jane. "Persistent Problems and Concerns of Young Adults with Learning Disabilities." In *Bridges to Tomorrow, Volume 2, The Best of ACLD*, edited by William Cruickshank and Archie Silver, Syracuse: Syracuse University Press, 1981.

Cordoni, Barbara. "Assisting Dyslexic College Students: An Experimental Program Design at a University." *Bulletin of the Orton Society* 29 (1979): 263–68.

Critchley, MacDonald. "Some Problems of the Ex-Dyslexic." *Bulletin of the Orton Society* 23 (1973): 7–14.

Dunn, Lloyd, and Frederick Markwardt. *Peabody Individual Achievement Test.* Circle Pines, Minn.: American Guidance Service, 1970.

Herbert, Mary A., and Carol Czerniejewski. "Language and Learning Therapy in a Community College." *Bulletin of the Orton Society* 26 (1976): 96–106.

Hermreck, L. "A Comparison of the Written Language of Learning Disabled and Non-learning Disabled Elementary Children Using the Inventory of Written Expression and Spelling." Manuscript, University of Kansas, 1979.

Moran, Mary Ross. "The Diagnostic Evaluation of Expository Paragraphs." Kansas Institute for Research in Learning Disabilities. Research Report No. 34.

Myklebust, Helmer. *Development and Disorders of Written Language, Volume One: Picture Story Language Test.* New York: Grune and Stratton, 1965.

———. *Development and Disorders of Written Language, Volume Two: Studies of Normal and Exceptional Children.* New York: Grune and Stratton, 1973.

Poplin, Mary, Richard Gray, Stephen Larsen, Alison Banikowski, and Tes Mehring. "A Comparison of Components of Written Expression Abilities in Learning Disabled and Non-learning Disabled Students at Three Grade Levels." *Learning Disability Quarterly* 3 (1980): 46–53.

Poteet, James. "Characteristics of Written Expression of Learning Disabled and Non-learning Disabled Elementary School Students." *Diagnostique* 4 (1979): 60–74.

———. "Informal Assessment of Learning Disabilities," *Learning Disability Quarterly* 3 (1980): 88–98.

Vogel, Susan. "Measurement of Growth in Writing Ability in College Freshmen Using Paired Essays and Analytic Scale Scoring," Lake Forest, Ill.: Barat College, 1980.

# 16

# Write Right– or Left

## A Practical Approach to Handwriting

*Rosa A. Hagin and Archie A. Silver*

T HIS CHAPTER will propose a simplified handwriting method for children who have difficulty learning conventional handwriting patterns and who, after years of penmanship practice, continue to write illegibly, uncomfortably, and as infrequently as possible. This essential skill is not taken very seriously. Youngsters with poor handwriting are jokingly advised to become doctors. Only slightly more realistic is the suggestion that they learn to type immediately. Most of the time, however, we merely try to persuade these youngsters to mend the ways of their poor penmanship. Over and over again, we see written at the top of the child's schoolwork paper, a teacher's comment: "Write neater!" This entreaty is repeated frequently, but there is little constructive help given in just how to go about accomplishing this objective.

Handwriting may represent a gap in the current training of teachers. Enstrom (1966) has suggested that handwriting is one of the most poorly taught components in the elementary school curriculum. King (1961) found that only one in ten schools requires its teachers to have some kind of handwriting training. For the teacher seeking information on the subject, the education literature, with a few exceptions, is not very helpful. For example, the prestigious *Second Handbook of Research on Teaching* (Travers 1973) surveys the educational process from ability grouping to zeitgeist, yet denotes only a few lines to the subject of handwriting: "Researching the teaching of handwriting and devising scales to measure achievement were common activities from 1910 to 1920. Before mid-century the subject withered in time and prominence and specialist teachers became rare" (p. 7). There are no other references to handwriting in this 1400-page volume.

### NEUROLOGICAL ORGANIZATION IN WRITING

The process of writing is a uniquely human and exceedingly complex process. It involves interrelated neurological functions of perception,

226

association, memory, and motor execution. Copying even a symmetrical circle, for example, requires the ability to recognize the form of the circle (perception), transfer that pattern to the part of the brain (association), which controls the muscles of the hand and fingers in a coordinated way to reproduce the image of the circle (motor expression).

If we now introduce a verbal stimulus, as for example, asking the child to write a specific word, an even more complex activity arises from the reception of sound in the temporal lobe, the temporal patterning of sounds, the association of sounds with their visual representation, and the transfer of sounds to the motor cortex and to the muscles which will write the word. Moreover, in our English language the words will be written from left to right. In most of us who use the right hand for writing, the perception of spatial stimuli finds its way into the right parietal-temporal lobe; the temporal sequence of auditory stimuli and the concept of verbalization are mediated by the left temporal cortex, and it is the left premotor and motor areas which control the movements of our right hand. These, of course, are the neurological functions of hemisphere specialization and handedness.

Thus writing is not a simple act. It is the integrated activity of a chain of many neuropsychological functions which may break down at any point in the chain. For any child with difficulty in handwriting, therefore, analysis of those part functions which make up writing is in order. Luria (1973) describes this process:

> In the initial stages, writing depends on memorizing the graphic form of every letter. It takes place through a chain of isolated motor impulses, each of which is responsible for the performance of only one element of the graphic structure; with practice, this structure of the process is radically altered and writing is converted into a single "kinetic melody," no longer requiring the memorizing of the visual form of each isolated letter of individual motor impulses for making every stroke. The same situation applies to the process in which the change to a highly automatized engram (such as a signature) ceases to depend on analysis of the acoustic complex of the word or the visual form of its individual letters, but begins to be performed as a single "kinetic melody." (p. 32)

It is helpful to trace the problems of children with handwriting difficulties back through Lucia's developmental continuum. Is it that they find writing so distasteful and uncomfortable that they do not have the opportunity to develop the "kinetic melody" essential to writing as a tool? Is it that they fail to memorize the graphic form of the letter? Does the problem reside still earlier in building the chain of motor impulses responsible for performance of the elements in the graphic structure of that letter? Or is it even more fundamentally a failure of the capacity to initiate and complete the voluntary movements required to form the elements of the letter?

Practically, they may be studied within the framework of sensory acuity, perception, association, and motor performance. For most children with writing difficulty, the peripheral sensory apparatus of vision and hearing are not sufficiently impaired to be reflected in writing. On the other hand, the way the brain receives stimuli and interprets stimuli is frequently much impaired. If the child, for example, cannot perceive the correct orientation of an asymmetric visual stimulus, his ability to reproduce that stimulus must also be impaired. Perception is the process by which stimuli are transferred to the associational and then to the motor areas of the cortex, to emerge eventually in writing.

As a result of our interest in the central processes involved in reading, we have been able to study normative groups through individual examinations of every child in the first grade in schools in New York City. These studies have focused our attention on properties of receiving and processing information from visual, auditory, tactile, and body-image modalities. In the visual area, we have been concerned with the discrimination and recall of asymmetric stimuli, with visual-figure ground perception. In the auditory area, we have tested the phenomenon of extinction; in the body-image area, we have been concerned with orientation of the body in space as in finger-gnosis, praxis, and right-left discrimination. In each of these functions, a developmental sequence is found. Immaturity in the maturation of any of the perceptual functions mentioned above may be the basis for impaired handwriting. It is essential, therefore, that the correction of handwriting must start with an analysis of the child's perceptual maturity.

In addition to the more usual study of visual and auditory perception, we have stressed body-image perception. Until the child is aware of right and left orientation, can identify his fingers in space, and can imitate fine motor movements relative to his fingers in space (praxis), he will have difficulty not only in the correct orientation of letters, but also in the ability of his fingers to reproduce these letters.

So important is body-image development in the process of reading and writing that we have come to recognize a triad — immaturity on right-left discrimination, in praxis, and in finger-gnosis—which is almost pathognomonic of the child with developmental language disability.

Writing, however, demands another skill: fine motor coordination. All the perceptual skills described above may be adequate, yet the child may not reproduce legible letters. This, of course, is the emissive component in the chain of functions necessary for writing. The developmental sequence of fine motor coordination has been studied by Gessell and

Amatruda (1943). At seven months the child can use only his whole hand in raking at a pellet. By one year he can now pick up the pellet in a neat pincer grasp. Holding a crayon or pencil, however, progresses from a crude palmar grasp at eighteen months to a thumb and forefinger grasp at age three. His block tower progresses from a two-block tower at one year, six-blocks at two years, and finally a ten-block tower at three years. These landmarks can be identified in young children. At school age, however, fine motor coordination is easily tested using finger-to-finger touching as the clinical condition. While norms for this test have not been statistically identified and age levels are not obtained, the experienced clinician can easily identify fine motor coordination difficulty with the finger-to-finger touching test.

The identification of these various levels of perception, integration, and motor performance offers clues to the remedial methods most effective for a particular child.

The synthesis of all the neuropsychological processes involved in writing may, of course, be seen in deceptively simple visual-motor tests, such as those of the Gesell sequence or the Bender Visual-Motor Gestalt Test. These are deceptively simple because they are so easy to administer. They reveal developmental levels and developmental sequences: (1) the primitive vertical nature of the visual-motor function characterizing the eighteen month stage, (2) the progression of the vertical to the horizontal line as we go from age three to age five, (3) the ability to deal with angles by age seven. Verticalization of diagonal lines and distortion of the angles of geometric figures may continue far beyond those ages in children with learning disabilities (Silver and Hagin). When one considers the difficulties these children have in drawing simple designs, it is not surprising that conventional cursive writing, with its diagonal slant, reciprocal movements, and complex letter forms, presents problems for them.

To identify these developmental signposts, important as they are, does not give clear indication of the neuropsychological process which may be impaired. For that we must break the visual-motor and auditory-motor task into its component aspects of perception, association and memory, and motor execution.

## PRACTICAL IMPLICATIONS

What are the practical implications of the neuropsychological formulations for the teaching of handwriting? They suggest some necessary conditions for a handwriting approach:

1. The style of writing should be appropriate to the child's level of motor control so that the initial chain of isolated motor impulses that produce the graphic form of the letter can gradually be mastered and transformed with a reasonable amount of training to the "kinetic melody" that is mature handwriting.

2. Handwriting should be taught not just as a visual task, nor just as a motor task, but as a process that involves body image, spatial orientation, awareness of kinesthetic feedback, and temporal sequencing; a handwriting program must take the full process into account.

3. The approach must give the child practice with visualizing and re-visualizing the graphic form of the letters being taught.

4. The use of verbal cues, shared with the adult teacher at first, and then gradually faded out until they become sub-vocal in the child, would help to establish control over voluntary movements.

5. Teaching should be direct, not casual; individual, not group. There should be adjustment to individual rates of mastery. There should be specific training with elements of the process, and provision for transfer to spontaneous writing.

6. Children should be taught to monitor their work and to make corrections on the basis of this feedback.

7. There should be opportunity for overlearning through spaced practice.

8. Finally, handwriting should not be dismissed as a simple task for these children.


There is, at present, no standard accepted handwriting form for teaching beginners. Many people advocate a manuscript alphabet; others just as strongly recommend cursive, connected writing from the start. In 1913, when Edward Johnson first proposed a simple manuscript alphabet for beginners, it was accepted by primary teachers somewhat more rapidly than most new ideas in the slowly adapting field of education. By the 1920's and 1930's, manuscript writing was generally accepted as a beginning approach for use in first and second grades, with cursive writing introduced some time during the third grade for most children. This is the modal practice to the present time. Manuscript is advocated for beginners for a number of reasons:

1. It is regarded as being easier to learn because the letter forms are simpler.

2. It resembles the print in books, so that the child does not have to accommodate to two graphic styles.

3. Beginning writing in manuscript is more legible than cursive.

4. It is required throughout life in applications and documents.

5. It promotes the independence of letters within words in teaching spelling.

A strong case has also been made for cursive writing in recent years, particularly as a beginning approach for teaching learning disabled children: (1) The connected cursive style permits the learner to deal with words as units; (2) the individual letters are difficult to reverse, in contrast to the manuscript letters; (3) cursive writing is faster than manuscript because its flow does not require the separate movements of the pencil for each letter.

Not all of these claims have been supported by educational research. Indeed, a thorough synopsis of research by Graham and Miller (1980) indicates that the superiority of either method has not been proven. Ease of learning and legibility criterial appear to favor manuscript; parent sentiment seems to favor cursive. However, with regard to facilitation of beginning reading, transitions to reading and writing cursive, and fluency, investigations can be found to support each style of writing. Since there is no clear advantage of one style over the other, it appears to be advisable to select the advantages of both styles and integrate them in a system for use with children who find it difficult to learn handwriting.

*Write Right or Left* is the approach to handwriting by which one of us (RAH), in many years of teaching learning disabled people, has tried to meet these conditions. It is a simplified handwriting method designed for people who have difficulty learning conventional handwriting patterns. It is based on the vertical downstroke, rather than the diagonal slant necessary to cursive writing. It builds on the motor patterns of manuscript letters taught in the early years, but adds connecting strokes that permit faster writing than is possible with the separated letters of print.

*Write Right or Left* is based on the principle that handwriting is a complex visual-motor-body, image-kinesthetic-verbal skill that must be automatic to be effective. Handwriting skill is acquired through repetition of a series of motor patterns until they become easily accessible to the writer—i.e., they are mastered. If the visual form of these patterns is overemphasized, or if the letters are too difficult for the writer to accomplish easily, writing becomes a drawing task which is not only too slow for efficient communication, but also interfering with the processing of meaningful messages. As with any motor task, there are more efficient ways of executing it. Effective handwriting involves consideration of posture, position of the paper, the way the pencil is grasped, arm movements across the paper, visual matching of the letter patterns with the graphic model, and timing of feedback. Provision for these aspects of handwriting is made in the lessons of *Write Right or Left*.

The chalkboard is used as a medium for introducing new letter forms for a number of reasons. Work in the vertical plane (at the chalkboard) is easier than in the horizontal plane (at a desk) because it comes closer to gross motor activity. The vertical plane also provides firmer cues for correct left-to-right orientation. Finally, writing on the chalkboard permits the writer to observe the results as the various elements of the letter patterns are joined.

*Write Right or Left* uses manuscript letters as a bridge to a simplified writing style with connections between letters made by the natural movement to the next vertical downstroke. The vertical line is emphasized because it is easier than the diagonal line necessary for conventional cursive writing. The importance of this distinction is documented by the persistence of printing with many youngsters, long after cursive writing has been taught in their schools. Maybe these children have been trying to tell us something! They may continue to print because they have not mastered the complex forms of conventional cursive letters. However, print becomes less serviceable as more and more written work is required at school. The need to lift the pencil after each letter makes printing too slow for work beyond the primary grades, and few people can produce rapid print that is not untidy or illegible.

In emphasizing the vertical downstroke and the natural connections between manuscript letters, the writing style of *Write Right or Left* combines the simplicity of manuscript with the speed of cursive writing. The program is designed to develop clear, comfortable handwriting through a series of lessons. Handwriting position is taught in the first lesson through four checkpoints:

1. Writing hand — the writing hand holds the pencil in an oppositional (pincers) grip.
2. Helping hand—the helping hand rests at the top of the page to keep the page from slipping away as the writing hand moves across it. It is also ready to move the page up as work proceeds.
3. Page—the page is placed with the longer side parallel to the writing arm, slanting diagonally on the desk. This means that left-handed writers are helped to avoid the hooked arm position which places so much stress upon the wrist of the writer.
4. Elbow—the elbow is anchored on the desk so that the arm, as it pivots, can reach across the page without repositioning.

These guides for position—writing hand, helping hand, page, and elbow —are reviewed throughout the lessons as is a reminder for oppositional pencil grip. They are relatively straight forward for right-handers, but may need more explanation for children who write with the left hand.

Left-handed children should be encouraged to position the paper with the longer side parallel to the writing arm whenever possible, so that they can learn to sweep the arm across the page as they write, without repositioning it after every few words. This will relieve the stress placed on the wrist when the hooked arm posture is used. This change in handwriting position may be difficult for youngsters who have become accustomed to writing in the hooked arm position for a number of years. Thus, patience and tact must accompany instructions for changing the habitual position, no matter how inconvenient it is. We should also remember that our left-to-right direction in handwriting is disadvantageous for left-handed people. The natural directions for movement is from the center of the body outward. Thus, for right-handers, the left-to-right direction is appropriate; for left-handers, it is contrary to the natural flow of movement. While the right-hander can pull the pencil along in a natural direction, the left-hander must push it in a direction contrary to his or her natural orientation. The left-hander is further handicapped by the difficulty in seeing what he or she has written if he or she uses the hooked arm position. Furthermore, left-handers seldom have appropriately left-handed models to teach them. Time and effort spent helping left-handers to adjust their writing positions is time well spent.

In the *Write Right or Left* approach, letter forms are taught through some simple motifs on the chalkboard, using methods first learned from Newell C. Kephart at Glen Haven Camp in Colorado. These motifs include ferryboats, which are used to teach smooth pivoting movements across the page, and four motifs that serve as foundations for lower case letters: waves, the foundation motif for a, c, d, g, q, pearls, the foundation motif for e, i, h, j, m, n, u, y, z, boxcars, the foundation motif for o, v, b, w, x, arrows, the foundation motif for k, l, t, r, f.

A motif and its associated letters are first practiced on the chalkboard, and then transition is made to the desk. The following steps comprise the lesson at the desk:

*Trace*
This step provides unlimited guided practice with the motif and associated letters, by tracing with crayon on an acetate sheet placed over the printed model. Verbal cues related to the direction of movement (e.g. "over and back") are shared by the teacher and the child. As the letters are learned, the directional cues are replaced by the name of the letter, said aloud at first, and later, subvocally, as greater speed of movement is achieved.

*Try*
The next step provides opportunity for the child to write the letters without a model on the acetate, which is now placed over blank printed lines.

*Match*

The third step provides feedback to the students for letters written during the Try step, by having them place the acetate over the printed model. Together the student and the teacher judge whether the writing on the acetate matches the model, and whether more practice is needed on the acetate or whether the student is ready to go on to the next step.

*Mastery*

This step provides closure by asking the student to write a permanent record of the motifs and letters he has worked on in that lesson.

*Sample*

The final step in the lesson permits the student to assess progress in transferring patterns and skills learned in the lessons to copying and spontaneous writing. These dated samples provide a concrete record of handwriting progress for the student by a comparison of the initial sample with those written during succeeding lessons.

Connections of letters are taught through a chalkboard technique we call "the flat chalk alphabet." Lower case manuscript letters are printed on the chalkboard with the student using the side of the chalk. The student then retraces the letters with the tip of the chalk, making natural connections between the letters. As each successive group of lower case letters is mastered, they are reviewed with connecting lines as a group and in relevant words. Game-type exercise and speed drills are provided to promote fluency as the letters are mastered.

After the lower case letters of the four motif groups and the special letters *s* and *p* are taught, the upper case letters are taught through a condensed version of the steps described above. Seventeen of the upper case letters are duplicates of the lower case, only of larger size. Other upper case letters are taught individually or in groups, depending upon the visual-motor components required by their forms. The numerals are taught using similar methods: chalkboard to desk; Trace, Try, Match, Mastery sequences.

Self-evaluation, rather than grading or criticism by the teacher, is encouraged through written review of the position guides and through comparisons of the dated writing samples.

## SUMMARY

On the basis of research in the fields of education and neuropsychology, an approach to penmanship is proposed to combine the simplicity of manuscript with the speed of cursive writing. This simplified style of handwriting is proposed because it is appropriate to the lags in visual-motor control which frequently characterize children with learning disabilities. This teaching approach conceptualizes handwriting as a process involving elements of visual-spatial, body-image, awareness of kinesthetic feedback, and timing of correction—all guided by the use of verbal cues. From this formulation, a teaching approach is recommended which provides mastery experiences through tracing, trying, matching, and self–evaluation.

## REFERENCES

Andersen, D. "What Makes Writing Legible?" *Elementary School Journal* 69 (1969): 365–68.

Bender, L. *A Visual Motor Gestalt Test and Its Clinical Use.* New York: American Orthopsychiatric Association, 1938.

Briggs, D. "Influence of Handwriting on Assessment." *Educational Research* 13 (1970): 50–5.

Chase, C. "The Impact of Some Obvious Variables on Essay Test Scores." *Journal of Educational Measurement* 5 (1968): 315–8.

Enstron, A. "Improving Handwriting." *Improving College and University Teaching* 15 (1967): 168–9.

Frank, L. K. "Projective Methods for the Study of Personality." In *Handbook of Projective Techniques,* edited by B. I. Murstein. New York: Basic Books, 1965.

Freeman, F. "Teaching Handwriting." *What Research Says to Teachers* 4 (1954): 1–33.

Graham, S., and L. Miller. "Handwriting Research and Practice: A Unified Approach." *Focus on Exceptional Children* 13(2) (1980).

Groff, P. "New Speeds in Handwriting." *Elementary English* 38 (1961): 564–5.

Hécaen, H., and J. de Ajuriagerra. *Lefthandedness.* New York: Grune and Stratton, 1964.

Kephart, N. C. *The Slow Learner in the Classroom.* Columbus, Ohio: Merrill, 1960.

King, R. "Handwriting Practices in Our Schools Today." *Elementary English* 38 (1961): 483–6.

Lewis, E. "An Analysis of Children's Manuscript Handwriting." Doctoral dissertation. Berkeley: University of California, 1964.

Luria, A. R. *The Working Brain.* London: Penguin Books, 1973.

Newland, E. "An Analytic Study of the Development of Illegibilities in Handwriting from the Lower Grades to Adulthood." *Journal of Educational Research* 26 (1932): 249–58.

Silver, A. A., and R. A. Hagin. "Fascinating Journey: Paths to Prediction and Prevention of Reading Disability." *Bulletin of the Orton Society* 25 (1975): 24–36.

Travers, R. M. W. *Second Handbook of Research on Teaching*. Chicago, Ill.: Rand McNally, 1973.

**COMING OF AGE**

was composed in 10-point VIP Times Roman and leaded two points,
with Times Roman display type by Partners Composition;
printed sheet-fed offset on 50-pound, acid-free Glatfelter Antique Cream,
adhesive bound, with Corvon 220-13 covers printed by Frank A. West Co.,
by Maple-Vail Book Manufacturing Group, Inc.;
and published by

SYRACUSE UNIVERSITY PRESS

SYRACUSE, NEW YORK 13210